behind enemy lines

Laurie Matthew

A 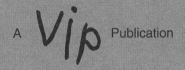 Publication

Author © Laurie Matthew
First Published 2005
by
Young Women's Centre (Trading) Ltd
1 Victoria Road
Dundee
DD1 1EL

ISBN 0-9543464-1-6

Designed by DM Graphics
Printed and Bound in Scotland by
Woods of Perth Ltd

CONTENTS

ACKNOWLEDGEMENTS

Thanks to the many survivors who contributed in so many different ways to this book. Some of you must have begun to regard me as such a pain in the neck for constantly harassing you to send in your contributions. Sorry, but I would have hated to have missed you out.

Thank you Anne for not only holding the fort at the office while I locked myself away determined to finish this, but also for lifting my spirits when I was ready to quit. Thanks also for the proofreading.

Thanks to my children for their usual patience and understanding. Good job they are all relatively grown up and able to fend for themselves or they could have starved to death.

Special thanks are due here to my youngest daughter Jerricah. During the work on this book, she was totally deprived of the computer for many weeks and her Internet Deprivation could so easily have led to a deeper depression. Jerri, I promise to save for a new computer before I write another book.

I need to mention my daughter Nicole here too for reminding me of all the right reasons that it was right to write this book. Every time I gave up you reminded me that I must not quit. Thanks also for your positive comments and the perfect proofreading.

Marley, yet another daughter, has to be thanked for giving me a reason, in the shape of a too large Golden Retriever called Sithe, for walking daily in the hills. Without these walks, this book would still be festering in the back of my mind. Also, it is notable that the book was finished just days before Sithe's first birthday.

My sons Keiran and Matthew are great too okay! They just put up with me.

Newt, thanks for the use of your personal space when I needed a quiet place to work on this book. The budgies were a bit noisy but it was quieter than my office or home. Thanks for feeding me when I could not stop typing long enough to cook a meal. Thanks for your support, encouragement and understanding while I was being pig ignorant and anti-social.

Last word is for Lily, my writing companion. We were both on a long hard trek with Martin the Monk as inspiration. Though we shared Martin, you owe him a pair of sandals as he had to walk further with you. Though my book has more words, yours was a newer and more ground breaking journey.

PREAMBLE

This book is written entirely from the perspectives of a number of survivors of ritual abuse.

The experiences shared and the opinions given are entirely those of the survivors who contributed to this book. These experiences and opinions do not necessarily reflect all survivors' views and experiences. Attempts were made to include as many survivors as could be reached in order to give as balanced and wide a view as possible and attempts were made to be as inclusive as possible.

Some of the views and experiences outlined in this book give a very negative view of many agencies, but in particular, statutory agencies. Please be clear when reading this book that, if you work for one of these agencies, you may not like or appreciate the survivors' perspectives. Please also be clear that whether you like it or not, these are the real experiences of these particular survivors. This is not a personal attack on you, please do not regard it as such!

Agencies which have been criticised by the survivors can react in several ways. They can just not listen to the survivors' perspectives and disregard them as unimportant. They can simply not believe the survivors. They can get defensive about what has been said and deny survivors their own reality. Or they can listen, believe and be part of making the improvements that are so badly needed for survivors.

My hope is that most people in all agencies will react by attempting to do the last and most challenging of these. The fact that you are reading this book indicates to me a willingness to at least listen to survivors of ritual abuse.

behind
enemy**lines**

FOREWORD

I was a long-term serving Police Officer who worked in Great Britain. I purposefully do not reveal my identity here not because of my fear of the exposure, but I do this in order that I can write in a more honest and truthful way, about the current climate, surrounding ritual abuse and survivors of it in this country. I have experience of this in my past work.

I had always, well nearly always, enjoyed being a Police Officer. It was one of the many professions I wished for as a young child. The basic reason for this was plain and simple. I wanted to make a real difference to people who had difficulties in their lives.

As time went by and my 'career' began to unfold, I realised that I was able to be a good, kind and fair Officer who was extremely open minded. I was good at my job and in fact it was more than just a job to me.

I did come across many sorry sights during my work, but none more so than young children who were being abused, physically, sexually, emotionally and on top of all that, were being downright neglected. I guess this was the part of my job that caused me to feel an uncanny tugging on the old heart strings. This was an area of my work where I always knew that I would like to specialise. At that time, this was a scary prospect for a young enthusiastic copper who knew nothing of child protection. I filled in the application forms though and decided at that point to give it a try.

I had a successful 'interview' and was appointed to a position in a specialised abuse unit. The training I was afforded, was adequate, and I was taught *'how to'* speak to youngsters in such a way that they would hopefully open up and tell all their deepest, darkest secrets.

I had an uncanny knack in obtaining information from young people, but I also found that more and more, older survivors were coming forward and reporting incidents of historical child sexual abuse. I increasingly found I was not doing this job from just a police perspective. It was, for me becoming more than a matter of gathering just enough evidence to substantiate an arrest and eventually get a prosecution.

This was beginning to get personal as more and more survivors came forward. It appeared to me at that time that statutory agencies, including the one that I worked for, were not entirely open to listening to adult survivors of

abuse. The 'time' of the agencies was deemed far too precious, and these 'historic' inquiries, we were told, should be dealt with in a quick but professional manner. The emphasis was on the word quick.

Inevitably, I did not listen to this and chose the alternative route, which I have done on so many occasions. Repeatedly I afforded the adult abuse survivors all the time *they* needed to disclose information at *their* own pace. Who am I to put a time limit on these survivors?

As survivors began to trust me more, my confidence grew, and the confidence within voluntary agencies which worked with abuse survivors grew in relation to me. They began to realise that there was a Police Officer who was, what has been described as, 'unbiased and very approachable'.

In the end, I devoted several years full-time of my professional life in training, and consulting in the field of sexual abuse of children. The issues of child sexual abuse, child prostitution and pornography, were all a big part of my professional life's work. These issues are ones which I continue to hold a great interest in, and continue to work with and research.

I have no reason at all to deny the existence or serious nature of child sexual abuse, child pornography or child prostitution. In fact I have spent much of my energy in trying to raise people's awareness about all of it and highlight the issues as a serious and ongoing problem in our society. Some agencies would prefer to deny that these things are happening with children and young people today. The blinkered approach works well for many agencies and it means that they do not have to tackle the problem. So too it is with ritual and organised abuse.

It almost seems like a lifetime ago, but back in the 1990's, I first began to hear *'strange stories'* of what I construed to be something akin to satanic or ritual 'goings-on'. I began to ask myself the questions**, *"Could this be really happening in this day and age?" "Am I the only person in my profession that has ever heard of this?"***

The stories I was beginning to hear were of Satanic abuse, ritual abuse and organised abuse which were also being said in connection with allegations of the sexual abuse of children, young people and adult survivors. It took me a while to let what I was actually hearing sink in, but I continued to listen with an open mind, and gathered as much literature and information as I could find to help me understand. There was not a lot of information available out there, but whatever there was I found it.

I then read and digested information about a whole belief system and culture, which was the world of many of the Satanic, ritual and organised abuse survivors. Unbeknown to me, I had in fact been dealing with survivors of this type of bizarre and deviant behaviour for many years, throughout my term in the highly specialised unit. But only upon reading and learning more about this type of abuse was I able to realise it.

I would like to take this opportunity to apologise to any survivor of Satanic abuse, ritual abuse or organised abuse, who ever attempted to tell me or drop hints in my direction, with regards to their experiences. If there were any hints dropped, at the time, they had obviously gone right over my head. It's not that I hadn't listened or at least tried to listen. It's the fact that I hadn't been aware enough of the issues to properly hear what was being said. Now I am ready though in my current job it is unlikely that many survivors will be able to get help from me.

Through time I had listened to the *'normal'* perversions of individuals or heard of 'groups' of people acting together in the abuse of survivors. I have also listened to survivors of Satanic abuse, ritualised abuse and organised abuse. It took a while but I finally began to realise and believe that almost anything was possible.

I then got to know a small voluntary agency, which has a vast knowledge base and many years of practical experience. As I got to know them they began to put their trust in me and started to give my name to ritual abuse survivors as an "okay police person" to approach for help. I began to work with many of these survivors and at one time I was working with up to a dozen at the same time. Hard work when you feel you are alone and no one else seems to have opened their minds to the existence of such abuse or the survivors of it. In fact, certain people in statutory agencies just did *not believe* that this whole Satanic abuse or ritualised abuse thing existed at all. I slowly deduced and began to accept that in my own agency I was to be very alone in the fight against these perpetrators of Satanic, ritualised abuse and organised abuse.

I was very isolated and thought that I was the one being betrayed as my enthusiasm grew to put a stop to, or expose certain people's involvement, in ritual or organised abuse. Yet, I was constantly being pushed away by my bosses and told to wrap all this *'nonsense'* up. As far as the agencies were concerned I was just dealing with some highly 'mentally disturbed' individuals. I now know and think I can understand *'the brick wall'* survivors crash into every time they attempt to say anything to the authorities. It is hard enough for survivors to go and talk to the police in the first place. It is a feat of great courage.

What other workers in the unit could not accept at all was that in many ways this type of abuse is no different from any other historical child sexual abuse case, whichever way you look at it. The only real difference is that some people involved in the abuse would dress up in ceremonial gowns and add in complex rules and beliefs and hold ceremonial events. Having established and accepted this, disclosures made to me were all very similar. For that reason the survivors were treated no differently to anyone else.

From my perspective, I can't see the horns coming out the side of someone's head when they try to talk about difficult or different things. What I always tried to see were the survivors who were desperate but determined to try and tell about the abuse, for which every single one of them should be commended.

A certain person who identified to me as a survivor of Satanic abuse once challenged me, on *MY* beliefs. My knowledge about ritual abuse was deemed by this person to be unacceptably high for an *'outsider'*. This same survivor accused me of being a baddie who had successfully infiltrated the police to facilitate a whole cover up operation in relation to the subject matter. That would be why I was working so hard to get it on the agenda then?

At this point though I knew I was actually getting somewhere. At last I was making an impression on someone. The baddies knew that they were being identified by a young cop who they would have thought was naive and unaware. Can I just say to those perpetrators who have actually bought this book, and I know you will….***YOU ARE SO WRONG. YOUR TIME IS COMING!***

This person who accused me was not a survivor. This person was on the other side. This person was carefully placed to destroy working relations between the statutory and voluntary sectors. It nearly worked, and had we been weaker people, and not worked through this together as professional workers, it would have worked.

I first met the Author of this book some years back during my involvement with a survivor of abuse. A friendship, based on mutual respect was struck up and we would speak regularly on the phone, meet up when she came down to my part of the world for conferences or training and sometimes she was a life-line of support for me. I used her as a useful source of information and would pick her brains unashamedly whenever I could get the chance.

I have now read the trilogy of books on the subject of ritual abuse by the Author. "Who Dares Wins" (Matthew, 2001) was the first masterpiece written

and aimed at the workers who would come into contact with survivors. It is a basic step by step guide to helping survivors of Satanic ritual abuse and organised abuse.

The second book "Where Angels Fear" (Matthew, 2002) is a more explanatory book aimed at the professionals who care to read it. The belief systems, hierarchy, symbolisms, cults and the generalisation of the abuse have been described in this book in layman's terms which makes for very easy and informative reading.

"Behind Enemy Lines" is the latest in this trilogy and appears somewhat different from any other book I have ever read. Behind Enemy Lines is a book which has been written by survivors, for survivors of Satanic abuse, ritual and organised abuse, which in itself is very unique. It gives true accounts of events which have actually happened in real survivors lives. These events have been brought together in this book under different headings and subjects. This is no mean feat.

As individuals, having received therapy or through psychiatry, some survivors have been told that they are mad or suffering from some form of mental illness. They are not. In this book the courage and sanity of the survivors shines through.

As you read on, you will begin to realise that the authors of individual pieces are from different parts of the country and from different backgrounds. The common thing that they share is of being the survivors of Satanic, ritual and organised abuse, and it is the same for all. Not identical in the experiences they have lived, but very similar stories and themes indeed. Is all this just a coincidence? Have these survivors got together and constructed a number of similar stories? Or could it be the case that these survivors are actually beginning to break the silence at last? Perhaps what they say is true. Why would it not be?

Breaking this silence is a cardinal sin for many survivors, and life threatening to some others. However, they are prepared to risk everything to write their thoughts and have their say in this unique publication. Many people can write on subjects through academic studies, but there are no truer words spoken than those of the survivors.

Now correct me if I am wrong in thinking and saying this, but if this type of abuse doesn't exist, then why are there common themes throughout what the survivors are saying? The common themes and

issues recur despite the survivors being from different places and completely unknown to each other. These survivors have, I believe, never met or even spoken to each other.

"Behind Enemy Lines" compliments the previous two books, and carries on with the perspective and awareness raising coming from the survivors' point of view.

This is a book written by many *'nameless'* survivors, but they know who they are, and that's what matters. Had they not 'sacrificed', excuse the pun, their time and effort to write accounts of their experiences, then this book could never have existed.

If you are looking for graphic detail and blow by blow accounts of what actually happens during a ritual ceremony....then forget it. Put the book down and don't waste any more of your time. You won't find much in the way of explicit details in this book. That's not what is being exposed here.

I worked with survivors of all kinds of abuse for some years, and continue at every opportunity to raise awareness about abuse though it is no longer my main job. Abuse is however everybody's business and paid job or not, I do continue to try and do my part wherever I can. Awareness is shifting. If, in the next ten years, this type of abuse is still not fully recognised in this society then I will eat my hat!!! (This is only a figure of speech so please don't anyone hold me to this as it may be quite tough and chewy.)

My last word on the subject....We talk of the so called 'experts', I need you to ask yourselves, who are the real experts in this subject? I know who I think they are and think that if you read this book you are in fact being informed by a team of experts.

INTRODUCTION

The writing of this book has been an incredible experience for me and indeed for most of the people around me. For the past two years this book has lived and grown with me to the point that although I am relieved to have finished it at last, I am also going to be completely lost without it. I have carried this book in my lap top computer and in my memory key everywhere I have gone. I have never let it leave my side. I am a very busy person with a full-time job, five grown up children, a part-time five year old boy and two lively dogs. On top of all that I do voluntary work. I have had to try and snatch any spare moment I could get to write and edit this book hence the reason for carrying it everywhere with me.

This is a very well travelled book. I have written bits of this book while travelling in the car (not with me driving of course), while on the bus, and on trains and planes. I have written bits while in Scotland, in England, in America and even while on the Canary Islands. On one very memorable occasion I was a passenger in a car which was travelling to Glasgow. For my birthday we were all going to see my hero, Meat Loaf. I was typing away as usual when we were suddenly involved in a car crash. Everyone leapt out of the car to check the damage, check for injuries and call for help. I glanced up to see if everyone was okay then kept right on typing as I did not want to lose my train of thought. I typed till the battery ran out on my computer.

My dedication to this book was talked about for a long time afterwards in the office by my fellow travellers. No one could believe that anyone would keep writing during and after a crash and even through the breakdown services attending to the vehicle. From my perspective, no way was I letting a car crash and the whiplash it caused stop me from writing this book. The thing was that the car crash actually gave me a window of opportunity in the shape of more time than I would otherwise have had. Not of course that I am glad we crashed, but, given that we did, I simply utilised the extra time it afforded to my own advantage. Oh, and we made it to see Meat Loaf though it was touch and go for a while.

This book intends to take a brief glimpse at the world through the eyes of some people who have lived with, or been affected by a particular kind of abuse. It is hoped that through reading this book more people will begin to have some awareness, gain a little insight and perhaps find a way to better understand some of the issues and problems, from the perspective of the actual survivors of this type of abuse. Ultimately I hope that this will mean that more people will become more able to offer appropriate assistance

and support to the survivors they come into contact with. Or, even if after reading this book people feel that they cannot do that much, at least I would hope that they can try to keep an open mind and be more prepared to believe the survivors. The type of abuse I am talking about in this book is most commonly called ritual abuse or organised abuse.

There are now many books available on the subject of ritual abuse but as far as I am aware there has never been a book quite like this one. This book has set out to be very different from most books about ritual abuse. It is definitely not, and deliberately not, an academic work though academics might be well advised to read it and perhaps learn a little from it. Neither is it a book written by professionals, excepting of course for those survivors who are professionals themselves. Professionals from all disciplines would be well advised to read it and learn from it. This book is totally unique in that it is a co-operative effort by some very real people with a variety of expertise and experience in the field of ritual abuse.

The expertise contained in these pages may not ever be publicly acknowledged by most professionals as expertise, and the writers in this book may never want to be recognised in any way either. None the less they are the experts and the people who really do know what they are talking about in regard to this particular subject. Only the survivors can ever really know all that there is to know as they are the ones who have actually lived through and survived the experiences. Intelligent people would do well to listen to them and learn all that they can from them.

The idea for this book came to me after writing and publishing two books on the subject of ritual abuse. My first book, 'Who Dares Wins' (Matthew, 2001) was rapidly followed by 'Where Angels Fear' (Matthew, 2002). Then the book of short stories about ritual abuse, "Fight! Rabbit! Fight!" (Matthew, 2004) was printed. This was the fourth book in the trilogy but was printed before the third was even finished so as to totally confuse everyone. Anyway, as I sat back to think about the last book in my trilogy, many things began to happen around me.

Calls began to come into my work from workers in many different agencies asking for advice and information about ritual abuse and wanting to run their 'cases' by me. Professionals from all disciplines wanted to pick my brain and ask me a variety of questions about the subject. I was totally bemused by this. As I sat back to ponder the mystery of why on Earth all these people would ask me this stuff, people who in the past had remained silent on the subject began to talk about

ritual abuse in my presence in a way that I had never heard before. Clearly something strange was beginning to happen in the universe.

However the most important thing that happened, at least in terms of the conception of this book, was that I began to be approached by a lot of survivors of ritual abuse who were seeking to pass comment on my books or just have a chat with me. I am happy to say that the comments, up until now at least, have been positive and very constructive. Many of these survivors are now in regular contact with me and one day, on talking to one of them about the need to get the viewpoint of survivors over to the world at large, it suddenly came to me how we could do it. We could simply all write a book, together!

I said this to the young woman I was talking to and she and I began to discuss how we would do this and what it would involve. We both got a bit excited and totally carried away with the notion of getting survivors to each write bits that would all be put together under different chapter headings. At the time we were so enthusiastic every time we spoke on the phone that we could see no problems at all with the idea. The problems were to come later and we would get round them. As it turned out, my young friend was not around for long enough to continue this journey with me but her spark and enthusiasm for the idea has kept me slogging on with the book. This is it!

To get it moving, I, with the help of a small group of survivors, drew up lists of things we wanted to tell the world about. Though we all never met together, frequent phone conversations kept the ideas flowing. In time we wrote chapter headings and a list of open questions and distributed them amongst as many survivors of ritual abuse as we could find. The idea became that survivors could write as much or as little as they wanted to under each chapter heading and question.

My job became to write the framework of each chapter to outline and summarise what we were talking about and, while doing so, present the views of lots of survivors in each chapter. Initially the idea seemed simple and certainly as an idea it was simple. Turning simple ideas into action proved much more difficult though especially for someone like myself who works full time, has too many children and dogs and only writes in my spare time. 'What spare time?' became the most major problem to overcome in the end. Still though, here it is. Nothing worth doing is ever very easy to do.

This book is completely written by survivors of ritual abuse and gives survivors perspectives in a way that is seldom attempted and rarely achieved. In this book we do not enter into the argument about whether or not such

abuse can happen here in Britain. Survivors of ritual abuse already know that ritual abuse happens here because they lived it here and survived it here. Let us not insult survivors with any more of these stupid debates that serve only to confuse, frustrate and further silence individuals. So if you are looking for discussion on whether or not ritual abuse happens, you are quite simply reading the wrong book.

This book would not be possible without the courage shown by those survivors who have provided input to it and who have been prepared to share some of their lives on paper. This is not an easy thing for anyone to do, let alone a survivor of such abuse, and I doubt if many people could ever fully appreciate or comprehend the gift that survivors who have contributed to this book are giving you. It costs survivors of ritual abuse dearly to reveal things about the groups and about their lives. All have been taught to not talk about such things. It hurts survivors to break the silence and expose even a small part of the truth and it hurts even more to be ridiculed and not believed by an ignorant public and judged by media. The reason that survivors have fought through fear and been prepared to tell a little here in this book is simply to try and help other survivors of this abuse. As long as the world remains in ignorance, children will continue to endure what adult survivors are now revealing.

Although there are many types of cults and groups, some operating under the name of different religions and using widely different trappings, it becomes clear from reading the writings and listening to the words of survivors that many share very similar experiences. Though the religion, the cult, the group, the trappings and the symbolism may vary considerably, there are distinct similarities in the methods of manipulation, brainwashing and training that makes possible total control over the individual and sustains the abuse of the survivor over a very long period of time. The enforced silence of survivors often maintained well into adulthood, the absolute terror that survivors live with and the myriad of problems that many survivors encounter in trying to live a normal life are all similarities shared by many survivors of ritual abuse.

This book is not any one person's story, though it could be. Rather it is the cumulated experience of the type of life that is led and has been led by many survivors of this abuse. Though the specific details vary amongst individuals, the base line reality is often similar for many survivors and the outcome sometimes almost inevitable and predictable. Survivors, even as adults, do not readily trust anyone and seldom do

they ever completely break the silence. The full story is seldom told by anyone. Many have learned through bitter experience that sometimes not sharing the whole truth is better that being judged.

Survivors of any abuse are individuals and therefore differ in how they react to their experiences both during the abuse and at different stages in their lives afterwards. This book cannot begin to show or explain the reality of what it really feels like to grow up with and survive ritual abuse. No one book could ever do that. It is instead merely an attempt to help readers step into the well-worn shoes of a ritual abuse survivor for a short time and become more deeply aware of the complexities and difficulties that are faced daily by most survivors even long after they have escaped from an abusive group. Escaping the group is for many only the beginning of a long, hard and lonely journey through a foreign land.

While I cannot cover absolutely everything in one small book and there will be many important issues left untouched, I am at least making an attempt at covering the most important aspects, as identified by the survivors themselves, that many survivors eventually manage to talk about and may need help with. There are many aspects of this kind of abuse that survivors never ever disclose to anyone. At least, not yet!

In writing and editing this book, I am not breaching the confidentiality of any survivors. Any stories or parts of stories in this book are written with the full consent of the survivors consulted and all have been made fully anonymous. I am certain that any survivor who reads this will be more than able to identify, in part, with many of the issues covered. I do hope that anyone identifying with any part of this book will take strength from the fact that other survivors have now broken some of the silence and are stronger for doing so. Many of the survivors who wrote for this book said that writing the stuff down actually helped them address some things they never had looked at before.

I also hope that those who read this book will remember, on some level, the tremendous gift that those who have broken the silence of the abusers have bestowed upon you. This gift is intended to help anyone reading this book be more aware and more vigilant especially for the children who are currently suffering from abuse. If only one child is found and removed from this abuse then all this effort is worth it. Also, I hope readers will be more able to provide better-informed support to survivors of ritual abuse and generally become more able to seek out the truth and reveal that truth no matter how horrible, unbelievable and ugly the truth might be.

I have constantly found through my work with survivors of this type of abuse that few ever identify as survivors of sexual abuse at first. Many, though not all, survivors do not regard the sexual abuse part of ritual abuse as the worst part of it. Many who have survived do not see the same things that many workers would regard as truly horrendous in this light. Rather, many have their own relative perspectives on what was unbearable for them and often the sexual abuse is quite low down on their agenda. People working with survivors should also try to remember this.

I am also aware that there are people in this country and others who claim to practise such religions as Satanism and Paganism but claim that they do not act abusively towards other people and children. These non-abusive people are not included in anything I say about ritual abuse in this book. I am focusing on the abuse here, not on religion. I am not seeking to castigate anyone because of his or her particular religion or beliefs and I am aware that abuse can be carried out in the name of any religion or any deity.

I focus in this book on ritual abuse as it is dictated by the experiences of those survivors who have written for this book. There are many other survivors out there with similar and different stories to tell and I hope that this book will encourage many more survivors to tell their own stories in whatever way they possibly can. If the whole truth ever comes out it will not be the survivors who inevitably suffer but the abusers, even those in high places, who will be exposed and hopefully some day they will be brought to account. Hopefully someday there will be no position or profession too high for abusers to hide behind.

The last words here really have to be the powerful words of an angry survivor "look out abusers we are on to you. We fear you no longer and we will not quit until we have won. This we will do. We are exposing ourselves as survivors of a crime which is not yet even regarded as a crime in this country but in doing so we are also exposing you, the perpetrators of the invisible crime to eventually be judged by society. A growing army of survivors are now breaking silence in a myriad of different ways and there will soon be no where left for the abusers to hide. This book is part of the beginning of your end!"

THE BEGINNING

This book has taken me an extremely long time to write and edit for a number of reasons, which I feel I must share. From the start, I have been determined to get as many views and contributions from survivors of ritual abuse as possible for this book, and it has taken some time for some people to get back to me. I have waited for the contributions from some survivors who were going through difficult patches but had let me know that they still wanted to be involved in this. Others I have had to encourage and plead with to write a few words after they indicated they were going to write but repeatedly failed to produce the written goods for me.

Some survivors have found it relatively easy to put their thoughts and feelings down on paper, while others have found it a very difficult thing to do indeed and have needed a fair bit of support and encouragement to provide their views. Some survivors had actually written and submitted contributions for this book but then for one reason or another, taken cold feet and asked that I remove their contribution completely. This I have done though I have to say that it added greatly to my workload when the particular contribution was already written into the book. Each chapter had to be redone and every reference to the survivor removed.

Every time this happened, it delayed the book further and cast me deep into the pits of despair. Three times this happened and three times I fell back into the pit and had to struggle back out and find the enthusiasm again to get back to writing and editing the book. At one point I thought I might be writing and rewriting this book forever. I could see no end to it. At other points, I felt like binning it all forever. Sometimes, indeed quite frequently, I wondered what on Earth I was doing in putting myself through this. It began to feel like a strange form of self-harm. Yet, here the finished article finally is! If anyone now wants me to remove their contribution, too bad!

This book is a joint effort by many different people. It is an unusual book in that it is written entirely by survivors of ritual abuse all of whom are in different places in their lives and in their healing. Few of these survivors have ever met each other and even those who have met would not know of each other's involvement in or contribution to this book project. Only one person has any knowledge of all the individuals who contributed, and my lips are forever sealed. If any survivors themselves want to state to anyone else their own involvement in writing this book, that will be entirely their own decision. For now and for always as far as I am concerned, all contributors to this book are completely anonymous.

In the beginning there was such wild enthusiasm for the idea for the book that chapter headings and a list of questions rapidly evolved courtesy of the survivors. There were many long telephone conversations, e-mails, snail mail and texts about it. Thus was born the outline, chapters and questions for survivors that would assist survivors in contributing to this book. The next step was to send the book outline to as many survivors as possible and invite their responses under the various chapter headings. Out of the response to this, came 'Behind Enemy Lines'. This is, in my opinion a unique and innovative way to bring the experiences and views of ritual abuse survivors together in what is a readable and understandable format. It is also a safe way for survivors to give their perspectives to the world.

After the initial enthusiasm for this book though, it has to be said that many who had entered the race began to drop out for a variety of reasons. I slogged on and often felt completely isolated and alone with it. Sometimes I was criticised for a number of things. Things such as; not getting it finished fast enough, for approaching vulnerable people and inviting them to write, for not being available to support the survivors who were writing bits, for attempting such a project at all. I do not take criticism very well at all particularly as I work so hard at ending all abuse and trying to help the survivors. It is so easy to be negative, criticise and be destructive. It is not so easy to be positive and create.

This has not been an easy book to write or to edit. In fact, it was, for the many survivors who contributed to it, a huge step to take and it took a great leap of faith and trust for them to send me their personal contributions. The fact that it has been achieved so well is truly remarkable. Many survivors who took part in this project have reported that taking part in itself was very much a part of their journey of healing. Some said it was challenging and that they learned a great deal about themselves by taking part. Two survivors amazingly went on and wrote their own stories in their own books and used the 'Behind Enemy Lines' outline as the framework for what they did. All of this tells me that even if the book itself is a total flop, good things came out of the process of writing this book for survivors and for their supporters.

I did not use all of the contributions I was sent for the book. I make no apologies for this. Some I did not use because the views expressed in the contributions were completely outwith the philosophy of this particular book. Others I did not use quite simply because there would not be enough space in this book to put it all in. Some of the contributions very explicitly named abusers and places they lived and I felt it would not be appropriate to use these contributions here. A few contributions were rather explicit in terms of the abuse experienced and I have edited some of these very carefully so

as not to lose the context. In keeping with my previous books, I have tried to avoid graphic details and horror stories and have tried to keep the style simple, readable, factual and informative. I want this to be a book that anyone can read and it will not horrify anyone or trigger survivors into flashbacks or panic attacks. Hopefully this has been achieved.

I was given a lot of poetry along with the written contributions from many survivors but after a great deal of thought and much discussion with survivors, I decided not to include it in this particular book. There is so much of it and it is all so very good, but I felt that either it would all have to go into the book, or none of it. In the end, it really just got down to a financial decision. The bigger the book is the more costly the book becomes to get printed and therefore becomes more costly to buy. In the end, I left the poetry out to keep the costs down. Perhaps the poetry will follow in another book at some time in the future?

THE SURVIVORS

There were a total of twenty-seven survivors of ritual abuse who all contributed in some way to this book. Each of them brought something different to the project and each contributed in their own way. All of them gave something precious of themselves to it. All gave as much of themselves as they could give at the time. It also needs to be said here that this was not a cost free exercise for the survivors involved. It was a cost to them all in some way. Not one person who has contributed or written in this book will benefit personally in any way as a result of taking part in this. They contributed for the sole reason of trying to raise awareness in society about ritual abuse and in the hope of helping other survivors. Any profits made from the sale of this book are given to the charity Eighteen And Under to help abused children and young people.

Though I have not actually met all of those who took part in this book, I do feel as though I have come to know them all in some way and I find myself enriched by this experience. Some, a few only, I have met in person. Some I have spoken to on the telephone and some I have corresponded with either through e-mail, text or through snail mail. To my knowledge, none of the survivors involved have ever met each other and none of them, until this book is published has ever seen what any other survivor has written. All contributions came directly to me and have been edited by me alone. Some survivors helped with other aspects of the book but only I have had actual sight of the personal contributions. There is an incredible similarity about a lot of what the survivors say and there are quite clearly experiences and feelings which are remarkably common to many.

The ways that survivors have contributed to this book are as varied as the individuals are. Some survivors helped design the original chapter headings and the lists of questions. Some have acted as advisors to the writing of the book. Some have helped to proof the book and some have chosen to write their responses in some or all of the chapters. A few other survivors have lent encouragement for the idea of the book but not felt ready yet to contribute more at the present time. This encouragement helps too and has been a vital part of the process of producing this book.

I have tried to reproduce the words that the survivors wrote as accurately as I could and though I have to some degree corrected spelling and some obvious grammar mistakes, I have tried hard to keep as closely to the survivors written accounts as possible. Some of this has been quite difficult as many of the contributions were hand-written and some were not easy to read because

of this. I have done my best though to get it right and apologise in advance for any mistakes I have made. Some parts I have had to shorten, but I have tried to keep the sense of what the survivor was saying in context. I have removed as far as I possibly could anything which might possibly identify any survivors as this is not the purpose of this book.

The names that I have given to the survivors in each chapter are entirely fictional and I hope that the names I have chosen at random to represent each person cause no offence to any of the survivors concerned. I have only put a name in for each person in order to allow for some continuity throughout. This way, readers can begin to build up a picture of what an individual survivor has been saying chapter by chapter throughout the book.

The survivors involved in this book are all very different and though their stories are similar in many ways they are all clearly unique individuals. They range in ages from the late teens to very late fifties. They come originally from Scotland, England, Wales and South Africa and all now live in the United Kingdom. There is a higher degree of input from survivors in Scotland and I make no apology for this at all as it just happens to be where I live and work and it has been easier to encourage Scottish survivors to take part as they know me better and know of my work in this field. Though the majority of the survivors who took part in this project were female, three male survivors did get involved to some extent and one did write pieces for this book.

The survivors are also varied in where they are at in their lives. The younger ones, perhaps not surprisingly, were generally more concerned about the backlash and were closer to their families and thus the abusers though not always by choice. Some are still having serious problems with their abusers and are not yet physically safe. For me, this makes it all the more incredible that they were prepared to help out in any way with this book. The older survivors tended to be further away from it all and probably because they have had more time to heal, they tended to be a bit more forthcoming and less frightened of the abusers.

Some of the survivors work full time; some part time and some do not work because they are unemployed, a houseparent or disabled. Four are disabled as a direct result of the abuse they experienced. Half of the survivors who took part have children of their own and have managed to keep them safe. Three of the survivors work as professionals in various fields. Many of the survivors give their time as volunteers in their own area and on a variety of projects. Most of the survivors who helped in the production of this book have some experience of trying to talk to the police but none reported that this was a success though most stated that they hoped this would change in the future. This is not to say that there has never been a positive outcome in talking to

the police, only that those involved in this book have had negative experiences. I did start out with many more survivors contributions than actually appear in this book. This is due to several survivors sending me written contributions and then subsequently withdrawing them. Though there were slightly different reasons for each person asking to withdraw their contributions, the base line was fear and concern. No one can blame a survivor for thinking things over and then safeguarding themselves. I just hope that it helped these survivors to even think about and write the contributions in the first place and I also hope that having written a bit they will in time use what they have written as part of their own books.

Thanks are due to all who helped with the production of this book. The work behind the scenes is just as important as the written words produced and absolutely invaluable. Without all the help and contributions this would not ever have been written. Not everyone is yet at the stage of writing and not everyone would chose to write about abuse anyway. A particular word needs to be said about a young woman I used to talk to on the telephone. It was she who, several years ago sparked the initial idea of writing this book and of the things that ought to be in it. Without that initial spark this book would never have been. I miss that young women greatly and wish that she had been able to contribute to this more directly. I wish she could have contributed as she was a brilliant writer. It is amazing what can grow from a very small spark.

There are many other survivors out there and hopefully some of them will be able to read this book. I hope that what they read will inspire them to write their own stories. Perhaps this could happen in a similar way to the way this book was created or perhaps survivors will come up with other ways of getting their experiences out into the world in a safe way for themselves. If we could achieve this, so can other people.

Not everyone will agree with the opinions they read in this book and that is okay. It is okay for there to be different opinions, different ideals and different perspectives. People are different and survivors are people too. In this book I tried to involve as many survivors as I possibly could. Obviously I could not reach everyone. I tried to let survivors know about this project through word of mouth, a conference, a web site and a newsletter. It is amazing that so many got involved.

For those of you who wanted to contribute but never did get round to sending me anything, I am sorry that I could wait no longer for you. Already it is two years since this project started and I decided that I could not wait any longer. Hopefully there will be other opportunities for those survivors who either have cold feet at the moment, have difficulties of one kind or another or have not got round to it yet. All things are possible and great things can come out of a spark or a dream.

AGITATORS

AGITATORS

These are not to be confused with alligators but can be equally as deadly.

Anyone who works with survivors of ritual and organised abuse can all too easily become a target for those people who act as agitators and who might seek to disrupt support services and end up causing trouble for an agency or an individual within an agency. The reasons behind anyone wanting to disrupt services that are trying to support and help survivors of ritual or organised abuse are probably not all that difficult to work out. It would not normally be the survivors of abuse who would seek to cause any disruption of services. Survivors usually tend to have a need for the support services and a tendency to feel quite grateful that the services are there for them in the first place. The plain truth is that the only people who might actually benefit from disrupting a support service for survivors of abuse are the abusers or those who support abusers.

Then again, it could be argued that there are also some very disturbed people out there in the world who either crave attention of any kind or feel the need to cause trouble in order to satisfy some weird need that they may have within themselves. These people can perhaps sometimes be responsible for causing some of the disruption that support services often experience. At the end of the day, no matter what the reason is for any disruption which can be caused by a person or people being agitators, organisations ought to remain alert to the possibility of agitators getting involved with them. If organisations and individuals are aware of the potential for people to cause problems they may be able to limit the potential damage.

Since the publication and distribution of specific books focusing on ritual and organised abuse, there has been an increased general interest in the work of a certain very small voluntary organisation in Dundee called Eighteen And Under. This organisation does not work specifically with ritual abuse survivors though it does have contact with many. In actual fact, its sole remit is to work with children and young people who have been abused in any way.

However, by coincidence, the author of these particular books about ritual abuse is the co-ordinator of this small voluntary organisation and the publications are distributed from there. What the books indicate is a very high level of awareness about the subject of ritual abuse and there is an invitation in the books to telephone the author to clarify any issues raised in the books. The telephone number is printed in the books. As a result of this

Eighteen And Under has an increasingly high degree of contact with ritual abuse survivors and their supporters and with other people with views on the subject.

There have been a number of very interesting and unusual things that have happened in Dundee since these books went out into the public domain. There have been some very unusual phone calls and several interesting letters received by Eighteen And Under. There have been a number of strange and interesting discussions with a variety of individuals, contacts with interesting people and agencies and some very unusual requests for help. Perhaps the most interesting thing to have happened though has been the number of ritual abuse survivors and their supporters who have actually travelled to Dundee to meet with and talk to the author of 'Who Dares Wins' and 'Where Angels Fear'.

The vast majority of the people that I have met with and spoken to as a result of writing and publishing books on the subject of ritual abuse are totally genuine people and entirely truthful in what they do and say. Some of them do not talk much at first but most of them do ask many questions about what has been written and sometimes what hasn't been written. Some talk ceaselessly and with some relief that they have found a safe place and some safe people who have some understanding of the issues they are experiencing or have experienced. There is sometimes a huge relief that they do not have to explain everything in great detail or teach the listener about the subject matter. Rather they can just talk and ask any questions they want.

Some survivors have even relocated and come to live in Dundee where they feel there is a greater awareness of ritual abuse and more support available for them. Some feel that the agencies in Dundee are more able to accept them and more open to at the very least remaining open-minded about the issues involved. Whether this actually is the case or not is debatable, but the fact for the survivors is that if they feel that this is the case, then it is the case for them. I suppose it depends on what survivors are used to getting in the way of awareness and support from agencies, or not getting for that matter, in other parts of the country. Because awareness is quite high in Dundee, sometimes it is easy to forget that some people and some agencies still have no awareness at all about organised or ritualised abuse.

In Dundee, all agencies tend to have some basic awareness about abuse, many have received training and many have been involved with helping survivors. Ritual abuse is constantly placed on the agenda with all agencies by Eighteen And Under. Books, web sites, talks, seminars and conferences

all serve to keep the issues at the forefront both locally and nationally. More importantly, the needs of abuse survivors and the real experiences of the survivors are constantly raised at every opportunity. Because of this, perhaps the survivors are right and there is a higher degree of awareness in Dundee than is generally the case elsewhere.

With every person I meet through this work, I assume that they are genuine in all that they say and do until I have positive proof that they are not. Even then, I leave lots of room for understanding that some people may not be able to, or want to tell me the whole truth about some things. I do not really need it anyway. I have no problem at all in any survivor bending the truth, or hiding the truth from anyone in order to protect themselves or people they care about. There are things that I do not wish or need to know about an individual. The vast majority of the people I have met as a result of publishing my books have been survivors of ritual abuse and nearly all have been totally amazing and very genuine people. Nearly all have been genuine and truthful I have to say but, unfortunately not every single one of them.

It is not only survivors of ritual abuse who have shown an interest in the books I have written and the things that I have said in the books. People who work with survivors have also been very interested and many have called me for a chat and a discussion about ritual abuse and some have also even found their way to Dundee. While I expected that there would be some interest once the books went out into the world I certainly never expected the actual amount of interest that has resulted. There I was thinking that there was no real interest in ritual and organised abuse and it turns out that I was completely mistaken. It turns out that all over the United Kingdom there are workers based in many different agencies working away quietly with survivors. The most common theme shared by most of these workers is the isolation they have experienced in working with the subject.

Many workers in a variety of organisations have found themselves isolated simply because they have been prepared to believe a survivor and try and offer them a service. Some workers have been accused by their colleagues of being gullible and some have been told by their management committees not to work with the survivors. Some workers have found that their careers have been adversely affected by the judgements of those who are not prepared to stay open-minded about ritual abuse. Some workers have received threats from the abusers and from people unknown to them and some have become so stressed by trying to help the survivors in complete isolation that they have ended up unwell as a result of it. Many of these workers have made contact with Eighteen And Under and many are now in touch with one another so that they are no longer so isolated in their work.

The other people that have shown some interest, though in a less direct manner, are the abusers and those who insist that there is no such thing as ritual abuse in this country. I can understand that the former group of people might have a vested interest in silencing, ridiculing and discrediting any literature on the subject, while they themselves remain invisible. I can also understand their need to remain anonymous in their threats and their ridicule. After all, these people cannot allow the world to take on the belief that there just might possibly be some small element of truth in what is being said about ritual abuse. These people cannot directly stand up and discredit those who support survivors or share any information about the subject matter. As the abusers they rely upon silence and secrecy and must be discreet about any attacks or threats they make.

But then there are the ones who claim with great vehemence that ritual abuse is in the same category as alien abduction and mind control. By this they mean to state that it does not exist and that anyone who believes in any of these things is crazy. I find their intense desire to fervently persuade everyone that something does not exist very interesting. If I believed that something did not exist, I would expend no energy at all in trying to persuade others about it. After all, what does it matter if people believe something that I do not? It seems that it does not work like that for everyone though. An amazing number of people who talk to me want to try and persuade me that I have been conned, mistaken and misguided in what I write, say and believe. Some just want to argue with me and tell me that I am wrong. It seems that I am expected to shut my eyes and ears to the survivors that I meet, deny them their experiences and effectively also deny my own reality and experience.

In addition to all of this, in Dundee we have now had a great deal of experience in dealing with people claiming to be survivors of ritual abuse who for one reason or another end up causing absolute havoc, take up a lot of worker time and generally create huge additional problems for other survivors and for the agencies which support them. These people are very skilled at getting around a variety of agencies, accessing support and information and persuading people that they are genuine and very much in a state of perpetual crisis. They are very good at getting people in a variety of agencies to become over-reactive to the supposed (but not always real) situations that are being played out.

It could be the case that this type of trouble and disruption is carefully planned by abusers and then carried out by the agitator. It could be that the agitator is in the employ of the abusers and being directed by them to cause maximum chaos. Certainly it sometimes feels like that is the case. Or it

could be that the agitator's behaviour is the result of some bizarre form of undiagnosed mental illness. At the end of the day it is not actually all that important to know what is behind the actions of the agitator because no matter what the reason is for what the person is actually doing, the end result is usually the same. The particular agency involved suffers, working relationships with other agencies often suffer severely and survivors of ritual abuse suffer as a consequence of the disruption which has been directly caused by, or come out in the aftermath of the chaos that a disrupter brings along with them.

Though I have experienced this type of thing several times now I am still amazed at just how effective it is in causing problems for survivors and workers who are trying to help them. Part of the problem in dealing with this type of thing though, is that it is very hard to know what it is that is going on at first. By the time you work out that you are being manipulated, perhaps lied to and certainly led a merry dance, it is often too late and the damage has already been done. Only with hindsight can you look back and begin to work it all out. This has certainly been my experience.

Perhaps the best example of an agitator we have had to deal with in Dundee is a young woman whom we now call Blodwin in order to protect her true identity. Blodwin claimed at the time of first contact to be a survivor of satanic ritual abuse who was trying to get out of an abusive group. She was living at the time in England and talking quite desperately on the telephone to many different people in a variety of support agencies across the country. Some of these workers were finding it hard to know how to respond and were talking to me about her and asking for my advice on a number of the presenting issues. Some of the workers were finding her calls and the details that she was providing quite harrowing to listen to and some workers were in need of support themselves as a result of what they were hearing.

Although the woman was not being named by any worker that I spoke to, I guessed very early on that the person I was hearing about from all these different workers was the same person saying slightly different things. At the time, based only on those who I was talking to, I estimated that she was getting about ten hours of support daily from a huge number of agencies and individuals all of whom thought that she was completely isolated and alone. That was one of the things she was saying and everyone automatically believed her. The main thing that all the supporters had in common was that each thought that they were the only one she was talking to and they were becoming increasingly desperate to save her life. They all believed that she was in extreme mortal danger and many had provided her with their home telephone numbers for emergencies. There were many nightly emergencies.

The horror stories that I was being told, initially by workers and then over the next few weeks by the woman herself as she began to phone me, I found almost completely impossible to believe. I had to say to the support workers at the time that the things being said quite simply did not add up in any logical way. The workers supported the woman to the hilt and came up with all sorts of reasons for things not adding up. I was willing to believe at the time that the woman was indeed a survivor and that she was in desperate need of help, but I could not quite believe some of the details that I was being told. This was very unusual for me as I am well used to hearing and believing very strange stories. But there are some things, that when you hear them, you just know them to be inaccurate or even a lie. This stuff that I was hearing was not adding up in any way and did not ring true even in part as far as I was concerned.

One of the most memorable things that I was told about was that the young woman claimed the 'cult' members came to her home every day to drain pints of her blood for use in the 'ritual' ceremonies to be held later that evening. Being quite a practical person, I had to question the manner in which the blood was supposedly being taken and then stored until the evening. I could not quite imagine the abusive group members slicing and chewing through the congealed mess that must accompany the ceremonial use of six hours old blood. I was also informed that the reason the abusers must have this particular blood was that the woman was a 'high priestess' in this group and had been since the age of four. I found it hard to imagine how any self respecting group would continue to have a 'high priestess' who informed on the group at every opportunity even talking to strangers on the telephone. Then there was the age that she claimed to have been 'ordained', not to mention the fact that she was only nineteen years old now? I thought that it all sounded a bit young to have attained the status of 'high priestess'? Perhaps I was out of date and satanic groups were lowering their ages and their standards?

This young woman continued to talk about being abused in a variety of horrendous ways and each story she gave was more graphic and extreme than the previous. She spoke about being bled dry in her own home on a daily basis and being given blood transfusions to bring her back to life again! She spoke about regular child and baby murders which she witnessed and also took part in, reluctantly of course. When asked how she managed to get access to a phone while things were happening within the group ceremonies and rituals, she said that they, the group members, gave her six minutes talk time on her mobile every time they raped her. She claimed many rapes each day.

There was never any explanation of how she could spend so much time on the Internet each day while being bled dry, raped, tortured and involved in numerous child murders. There were so many things that did not add up at all. Then one day, Blodwin let me know that she was desperate and about to be murdered by the group and therefore needed to flee to a place of safety. She got on a train and came to Dundee, which was beginning to feel a bit like the RA Mecca city. I, being a helpful soul, went to meet her at the railway station.

I have to confess that I got quite a surprise that day when I went to meet Blodwin at the railway station. For a start, she was there. She really had left her home and come to Dundee. Not only did she show up but I was surprised to see that Blodwin was a very large and very healthy looking young woman. This was not at all what I had expected to see. She did not look at all like someone who had been losing pints of blood daily and did not seem to be in any way traumatised by her constant on-going abuse. Rather she seemed quite excited and gave the impression of someone who was having a great time. She was confident, chatty and self assured and was accompanied by an incredibly huge amount of personal luggage including a lap top computer. Not that I would hold any of this against her but it was surprising.

I have, over many years met a lot of desperate people fleeing from extreme abuse and violence but have to say I had never before met someone in such a position who had managed to pack and escape with, what appeared to be their whole household. She had about six large cases on wheels, several holdalls, 2 rucksacks and several substantial carrier bags. She had so much stuff with her that I had considerable difficulty getting it up the station stairs and then into my car.

The next thing that I noticed about Blodwin, as she squeezed into my over-stuffed car, was that she had extremely poor hygiene. She was not very clean. In fact, not to put too fine a point on it, she was very unclean with ingrained dirt on the parts of her skin that I could see and her glasses were so grubby that I thought her sight must be severely restricted. She smelled as though she had not bathed or even washed in a very long time. I had to open all the car windows in order to drive the car without throwing up. I have a strong stomach and am used to different standards of hygiene but that was a very difficult car journey for me and I do have to confess to breaking the speed limit in order to get it over with quicker.

I would not have thought anything much of her poor standards of hygiene as people do have different standards and a variety of reasons for not bathing; except for the small fact that she had said that she had been getting

used in satanic ritual settings and ceremonies over the past few days, weeks and months. This I confess totally confused me. I was staying open to believing the unbelievable but this was completely outside my experience. Perhaps the standards of the satanists had completely fallen to rock bottom?

In all of my experience, group members were normally quite fussy about hygiene. Their cleansing rituals before any event would have scrubbed up one of their 'victims' to a high degree of cleanliness and most certainly a high priestess would have to be clean. To not be clean would be sacrilegious to the faith in the extreme. Could anyone ever imagine going to church or some other place of worship dirty? Or even worse, could you imagine the vicar, minister, priest or any other religious leaders leading a church service whilst unclean? It is the same with the alternative 'religion' of satanistism. It would be completely unthinkable for anyone to consider attending any kind of worship, service or ceremony whilst unclean.

The other thing that I noticed about Blodwin was the lack of something that I would have expected from someone who had been abused in such a way, particularly from someone who had clearly not washed herself for a while. I noticed that there was no smell of any abuse from her, only the smell of stale sweat and dirt. I would have expected smells associated with all kinds of bodily fluids. I would have expected other strong smells to be hovering round her, perhaps smoke from candles or fire, incense, death, men or animal smells. There were none of these at all. I wondered how someone who had not washed could have been raped so many times without there being some lingering sensory evidence remaining.

Still, though the stories I had been hearing did not add up, I gave her the benefit of the doubt. She surely had not uprooted her whole life for no reason? I reasoned that there must be a reason for her claims of abuse and perhaps it was that she was remembering or reliving the abuse? I did not know what was going on and it was impossible to speculate. Perhaps in time things would become clearer? At the time, I could only act on what I knew for sure and that was that this young woman was in Dundee and now homeless. I now had to find some safe accommodation for her.

I duly deposited the woman in a local women's aid refuge and before the week was out, I was informed by the women's aid group that they were evicting her. This was not entirely unexpected. I was expecting this to happen as the women's aid workers had been liaising with me. I was informed that the woman was endlessly talking to other women and children in the refuge about satanic abuse, child murder, rape and other associated things. She was being very graphic in what she said, even in front of the children and

was going into great detail. She was asked by workers and the other women to stop talking about it but seemed unable to stop herself. The more frightened women and children got, the more the woman talked about it. In the end, she was simply asked to leave and was put in touch with other housing agencies. Such was the terrible experience of the women's aid group with this particular young woman that they afterwards refused to provide refuge accommodation for other survivors of ritual abuse.

Blodwin moved into a hostel. She had been in Dundee less than a week and was now claiming to be involved in satanic group abuse in Dundee. She claimed that local groups had contacted her because they knew she was a high priestess. She also claimed that members of her own abusive groups had come to Dundee and had introduced her to the cults in Dundee. She claimed she was still being raped, bled and abused on a daily basis. She also began to claim that she was being involved in child murders in the area. I suggested to her that if all this was going on then she should speak to the police about it and get some help. Much to my surprise she seemed very keen and jumped at the opportunity to make police statements. The police came to my office that day and she began to tell them her stories in great detail.

At that time, we had very good strong links with the local police. I did let the senior officer know when I made the referral of Blodwin that I did not consider her to be entirely truthful. Unfortunately, this information was not passed on to the police officer who was appointed to deal with Blodwin. This meant that the officer did not know about my doubts and therefore took everything very seriously. Perhaps this was not entirely a bad thing but in the end it did lead to a lot of police time and resources being wasted. This poor officer and others were sent to woods and farms to look for evidence of child murders and were frequently racing round the streets in search of the latest alleged child victim.

The police liaised closely with Eighteen And Under and very quickly there was a realisation that all might not be as Blodwin stated. Blodwin was by now involved with several churches, counsellors, drugs agencies, support agencies and a variety of voluntary agencies. Most of this we knew because distressed workers were contacting us from a variety of organisations raising concerns about child murders and the prevalence of satanic abuse in Dundee. Blodwin was also busily naming the names of everyone she had met in Dundee as members of the cult which was raping her. She was claiming that the workers in the hostel she was in were raping her nightly. She was claiming that the police officers and the members of the churches she was attending were satanists. It was all a bit much particularly as

everyone was trying so hard to believe her. No one knew how much truth there was in any of her statements. If we all believed her then all workers in all agencies were involved in organised abuse. It would have been easy to get paranoid and suspect everyone.

After a few weeks, I began to hear such inconsistencies in her stories that I had to begin to confront her about this. At this point she let me know that she was going that night to help murder two babies and a toddler. When I asked her to tell me more about it she told me that she knew the address it was going to happen at but she refused to tell me the address. This was for me the last straw and I immediately confronted her about her stories, the need to protect children and basically told her that I thought she was lying to me. It turned out that the police had also had strong and similar words with her earlier that day.

Blodwin went back to the hostel, packed her stuff and moved to another area. Over the course of the next few months, police, social services, health and some voluntary organisations began to contact us from the area she had moved to. It was the same story of talking graphically but inappropriately, child murder, rape and accusing all people she met of abuse and involvement in cults. Eventually, someone confronted her about it. She immediately packed and moved to another area. Again the whole thing was repeated. This was the fourth time to my knowledge. In each area she had been she left people believing that people lie about such abuse. She left people feeling bewildered, some workers went off sick through stress and many people in a variety of organisations refusing to work ever again with survivors of ritual abuse. Some people became very afraid while working with her as they began to believe that the abusers really were everywhere and especially in positions such as high up in the police and the legal profession.

To cut a very long story short, Blodwin eventually confessed to me, and subsequently to the police, that she had lied about everything she had ever said. She told me that she had made the whole thing up and that she had never been abused at all. She insisted that she had meant no harm to anyone by this but on being told of the harm that had been caused she was unconcerned and totally unrepentant. She continued to tell lies even at the time she was confessing all. The reason she said that she was confessing to all the lies was that she now wanted to get on with her life. She moved back to live near her family and said that she had now had her adventure and wanted to settle down with a clear conscience.

There is no way of knowing whether or not Blodwin did all this herself or whether she was put up to it by someone else. She seemed to have an

endless supply of money, seemed to be able to move very fast and accessed services with a rapidity that was amazing for someone who had just moved into an area. On one level it was impressive. What was not impressive was the damage that she did to many individuals, agencies and more importantly survivors of abuse. She seemed in every area she moved into to be able to find such survivors very quickly and befriend them. Regardless of whether the woman did all this by herself or not, the end result of her activities was a negative focus on ritual abuse which was very damaging to ritual abuse survivors and the agencies which are most likely to support them. Blodwin was a very skilled agitator.

Blodwin, despite her lack of personal hygiene was a likeable and intelligent personality. She presented with an open and honest attitude and was chatty and cheerful at all times. She was quite skilled at making friends, engaging in conversation and maintaining a conversation. Though she said that she had many different personalities, she did not seem to lose track of time or conversations. Effectively, she presented as extremely normal except for the things that she claimed. Blodwin was easy to like and easy to believe. I wish other survivors were as able to talk with such confidence and assurance as I suspect that was the main reason she was readily believed, even as she was talking complete nonsense.

SURVIVORS EXPERIENCES OF AGENCIES

SURVIVORS EXPERIENCES
OF AGENCIES

The responses that the majority of survivors receive from most agencies are surprisingly standard across the whole of the United Kingdom. Unfortunately, the responses of agencies though standard are not particularly supportive and in general are fairly unhelpful to the survivor. Most agencies seem to have little or no awareness of organised or ritual abuse and few have received any specific training on any of the issues. The overwhelming denial of the existence of such abuse and the many myths that accompany ritual and organised abuse and the survivors of it tends to prevail at every level of our society. For this reason it is not so very surprising that awareness of ritual abuse is low and responses of many agencies unhelpful.

Having said that, survivors have sometimes been very lucky and managed to find an individual worker, sometimes even within an unhelpful agency, who has listened to them and been more prepared to learn about the issues involved in offering a suitable service. On occasions this has led to the agency supporting its worker and even taking on awareness and some more specific training and thus in time becoming more open and responsive to survivors of ritual abuse. More frequently though, there is a negative outcome for both the worker and the survivor if the agency is not supportive of its staff member. It appears generally that the larger statutory agencies tend to be the ones least supportive of their individual staff members being innovative and open minded. These agencies are often extremely rigid and unaccommodating of change or risk-taking of any kind. They are also seldom very keen to tackle any unpopular or controversial issues.

Sometimes the individual worker who tries to help a survivor ends up being pushed out on a limb within his or her own agency and thereby becomes very isolated as a result of this. The worker is sometimes regarded as being too gullible for believing the survivor in the first place or can even be seen as possibly bringing disrepute or even danger to the organisation. In some cases, the worker is actually stopped from working with the survivors, either by having them moved to a different department in the organisation or by their managers simply forbidding them to work with that particular person or issue. This sometimes, but not always ends any assistance or support that the worker was providing to the survivor.

Some workers have become so determined not to be stopped from working with a survivor or the issues that they have dug their heels in and resisted

in a variety of ways. How effective or varied this resistance can be depends on the agency and the individual worker concerned. Some workers have simply ignored their bosses and continued the work they have been involved in. Others have hidden the work they are doing under the guise of working with different issues such as 'ordinary' abuse. Others yet have continued to do the work in their own time. All of these workers are amazing human beings but they do often end up struggling under enormous pressure and become extremely isolated. Workers who support survivors really ought to have some support for themselves.

The following accounts for each agency are based on what survivors of this type of abuse have reported about their own experiences with the different agencies. The opinions and comments have all been generalised and rendered anonymous to safeguard the identity of the individual survivors some of whom still depend on some of these agencies. It is hoped that by survivors giving their personal views and accounts, agencies might find ways to improve some of their practices with survivors rather than becoming defensive and hostile about their practice. Unfortunately, the latter reaction is the most usual outcome.

No matter how negative the views are of those survivors who have shared their experiences of different agencies, these are their real and personal experiences. If they are negative experiences, then that has been the reality for the survivors with these particular agencies and this cannot continue to be swept under the carpet. The agencies who offer a service to survivors in whatever capacity need to start to listen to these service users' opinions. There is little point in having a service which is not suitable to the needs of one particular group of people. Services, particularly public services, ought to be inclusive and accessible to all people.

I know that there are some agencies and some individual workers who will have a go at me for presenting any negative accounts of their agency. I also know that there are those who hold the view that it is not helpful to ever criticise any agencies. But, this is a book which is entirely presenting the views and experiences of survivors and this includes their views and experiences with the agencies. Censorship to safeguard the feelings of workers or agencies is simply not appropriate here. Agencies can either get defensive about what survivors are saying or they can listen to what survivors are saying and make some small improvements.

This book seeks only to allow survivors the space to say what they need to say. This is a very rare thing as these survivors are rarely heard or listened to by many. This book seeks only to reveal survivors' own truths. Comments

made about agencies are general and no disrespect is intended towards any particular agency or worker within any agency. Many of these agencies probably offer an excellent service for the majority of people most of the time. Hopefully this will expand as their awareness grows. There are also many good people working in all of these agencies who are already listening to survivors and doing their level best to raise awareness from the inside. Hopefully more people will continue to listen to survivors as time goes on.

POLICE

The main work of the police is to investigate crimes, which may have happened and to prevent other crimes from happening in the first case. In general there appears to be a standard approach to the services offered across the whole country, which one would certainly expect from such an important and large statutory agency. If your home has been burgled or your car has been stolen you can expect there to be very little difference in how things will be dealt with by any police force based anywhere in the United Kingdom.

With more serious crimes such as sexual assault and child abuse, there are now so-called 'specialised' units in most parts of the United Kingdom, which deal more specifically with these types of crimes. These are not standard across the country and what work they do can vary considerably from unit to unit and area to area. Some deal with all kinds of sexual crimes while others deal only with child abuse. Some have separate premises away from the main police station and others are contained within it. Some work as part of a multi-agency team and others regard the police as the only agency which should be involved in an investigation. There is quite a considerable variation in these units across the country.

The police officers who work in these specialised units receive extra training on such things as how to speak with children, child protection issues and interviewing skills. The idea of the units is that the officers are able to become more specialised and single focused than those out on the street dealing with more general crimes. They are trained to carry out joint investigations with social work in cases involving children or child protection and they can, if they choose to, spend more time networking with other agencies in the field.

Unfortunately this idea of specialisation, which is actually a very good idea, is completely spoiled by the fact that most of these specialised units turn round their staff every three or four years. This means that just as an officer is beginning to get some skill, experience and awareness of the complex

issues involved in abuse they are moved to another, often unassociated department! Just as an officer is beginning to forge close links with survivor organisations, they get moved out of the unit! It is a very strange thing for any 'specialised' department to do repeatedly. It is difficult when looking in from the outside to see the logic in repeatedly moving the most experienced workers from such a department and replacing them with totally inexperienced workers.

It can take many years to learn how to work effectively and sensitively with survivors of abuse and many years for trust to be built with an individual survivor. Some officers choose to never learn about abuse or be bothered building any trust with anyone outside their own agency. It takes only a few minutes to move a skilled and trusted officer and destroy the trust of a survivor. It takes only a few minutes to move a skilled worker and remove a wealth of experience from such a unit. A new officer goes into the unit, usually directly from the beat knowing nothing about abuse at all and the learning and mistakes happen all over again for the next few years until they are more skilled. Then they get moved out of the unit!

The police sometimes claim that they move the officers from the specialised units in order to avoid stress on these officers. Yet many thousands of workers in other agencies have worked for twenty and thirty odd years or more with abuse survivors and not succumbed to work-related stress. Police work of all kinds is surely quite stressful as a whole and officers are surely encouraged to seek support if they are stressed by any of their work. I suspect that the supposed stress which might be caused by working with abuse survivors is more likely to be an assumption rather than based on any concrete research.

The other claim we have heard is that moving skilled officers out of the specialised units every few years spreads the skills and awareness they have gained throughout the whole police force. This is an incredible claim given that only the officers in the specialised units work directly with the abuse survivors. This means that the previously 'skilled' officer who has left the unit is now completely deskilled and out on the street, dealing with petty crime. If they ever do come across any abuse survivors in the course of their police work, they will have to pass the survivor on to the officers in the specialised unit (now containing the brand new unskilled and inexperienced officers).

It seems an incredible way to claim to get specialisation and raised awareness in an agency. It is also very frustrating for any survivors who have built some trust to find the officer they trusted has been moved on. The survivor often loses the one person they trusted in the police and most will simply stop speaking to anyone in this agency. It is also incredibly frustrating for survivor

organisations to try and keep good working relationships with the police when the personnel in a department keep on changing and no one has the job of keeping any relationship alive.

Then, when we look more closely at ritual abuse survivors and their experience of the police, an interesting picture begins to form. Survivors from all over the United Kingdom have tried on occasions and in different ways to talk to the police about their experiences. Nearly all of them have been met with disbelief and very negative reactions. It is very rare to find a survivor of ritual abuse who has encountered any awareness of the issues or indeed of the subject itself on approaching the police in their own area. Occasionally, as with all agencies, an individual officer might be prepared to listen and be prepared to try and find out more about the subject, but this is a very rare reaction indeed.

The expectation of the police, including those in the specialised departments, is that, when survivors are ready, they will walk into the department and simply make a complaint. The expectation is also that they will talk, preferably quickly and clearly, and provide huge amounts of information in great detail. The expectation is that they will fit into the times that suit a particular officer and be able to switch off talking when the officer's hand 'gets a bit sore with all the writing', as one officer said after thirty minutes. The expectation also is that they will have consideration for the feelings of the poor officers who have to 'listen to such horrible things', to quote that same officer.

It is also better if the survivor does not get too emotional while talking or they will be judged as, "just not ready to talk" and the officer will walk out and refuse to deal with them. This has happened to two survivors that I know about. One survivor began to get angry at the abusers while talking and expressed this anger and frustration by punching the nearby chair. The officer who was noting the statement said that she did not have time for such nonsense and such displays of emotion and left the survivor to, "calm down and be prepared to talk more calmly in future". This survivor was trying to talk about the murder of a child, witnessed in early childhood. As something to talk about, it did not lend itself easily to calmness.

The other survivor began crying while talking and the officers simply went off and had a tea break until she had stopped. Every time the survivor broke down and cried, the officers walked out of the room, looking at their watches and mumbling about how busy they were. After the third time, the officers declared that it was clearly too hard for the survivor to talk and too hard for them to listen to also. One of the officers said that it was upsetting her. They then walked out.

Some officers from the specialised units openly state that they do not believe that ritual abuse happens anywhere in Britain. They are quite simply not prepared to take it on at any level. Many are at best dismissive of it and at worst openly aggressive and hostile with survivors of ritual abuse. Some survivors talk about the way they have been treated by the police and how often the very first questions asked are about the mental health of the survivor. The assumption here has to be that someone with mental health problems is probably not as believable or that they are perhaps making things up. Some survivors have been accused of wasting police time even as they are trying to talk.

It is very rare for the specialised units in the police to ask for training and awareness from survivor organisations despite the many years of experience and expertise these agencies have of working with abuse. Unlike the police, the workers in these agencies do not move on and as a result they continue to gain experience for many, many years. It is even rarer for training and awareness of organised and ritual abuse to be asked for or taken up, even when offered to other agencies such as the police free of charge.

For example, for many years now, a voluntary organisation, which works with young survivors of abuse and with ritual abuse survivors has offered free places to the police (and other agencies) on all trainings, seminars and conferences on a range of abuse issues, including ritual abuse. Over the past ten years, only two officers have ever chosen to take up this free offer. These two did work with survivors of ritual abuse. Only two officers have ever attended any of the trainings despite the fact that this organisation has won national acclaim and numerous national and even international awards for its work and its good practice in child protection and working with abuse survivors of all kinds.

The organisation, despite being small and unfunded, continues to offer awareness and training but sadly most police officers have absolutely no interest in learning anything at all from the voluntary sector. Some have that professional snobbery that lets them believe they are so much better than anyone in the voluntary sector. Some officers think that they know it all already. Others have no interest in survivors or their issues even though they work with it daily. They simply do not care whether they get it right for people or not or worse, do not think they have anything at all to learn from abuse survivors.

Interestingly these two very rare officers who did attend the free training courses ended up being approached by many ritual abuse survivors who

wanted advice or even to make statements to the police. Some survivors travelled from other parts of Scotland and indeed from as far away as England and Wales just so that they could talk with a police officer who they believed clearly had a great deal more understanding of ritual abuse than most.

Both of these officers were at least open to listening and learning about the issues of abuse. They also took on to learn more in their own time and kept open minds with the survivor. This is very rare to find in the police including in the specialised units. Both of these officers took the time to build relationships with the survivor support agencies and thus gained the trust of these agencies and the individuals involved. This meant that the agencies concerned could and did in good faith refer survivors of all kinds, including ritual abuse survivors, to these particular officers.

Another point of interest with the police specialised units seems to be the fact that as soon as an officer becomes aware enough of ritual abuse, and starts to do any quality work with the survivors of it, they seem to very rapidly move out of the specialised departments. Is this just a strange bit of bad timing perhaps? Clearly, from an outside perspective, the police do not want survivors of ritual abuse going forward to share information or make a complaint about it. Otherwise why would the only officers who are prepared to learn or be open to listening be moved out of the specialised units and the less able officers be kept on?

Recently, three survivors of ritual abuse who had been talking to a particular officer for several months and were beginning to build trust and even make written statements were told they could no longer talk to that particular officer. The reason for this was that the officer had been moved out of the department at short notice. One has to suppose and even wonder if perhaps this particular officer was maybe doing too good a job. These survivors were just left high and dry and are very unlikely to continue talking to the police. When one of them phoned the police to try and find out when she could continue with her statements, Officers who took her call were rude and dismissive of her.

One of the main functions of the police force in Scotland is supposed to be to protect life and property and the prevention of crime.

It is relatively easy to frighten and put a survivor of ritual abuse off talking and the police appear to do this regularly. The very few who are prepared to learn a bit more and listen to the survivors soon end up with countless survivors of ritual abuse willing to, and wanting to talk to them. But this is

not encouraged at all. Rather it is actively discouraged. Survivors will not talk to just any police officer. They will talk only to people who have shown themselves to be trustworthy and interested. If the police really were willing to protect life and prevent crime, they would at least try to listen to the survivors of abuse and the organisations which support them.

Often it seems as though the wrong type of officer ends up working in the specialised units. Some officers have openly admitted that they request to work there because they don't have to work long shifts or weekends. It would be interesting to see how many would still want to work there if they had to work the same shifts as regular officers. Some of them go shopping, gossip and generally seem to work hard at avoiding working with the survivors. The units are often regarded as a 'cushy number' by many. Many who work within it do not have the commitment or even the ability to work with vulnerable children, young people and survivors of abuse in general.

All of the support agencies for survivors quickly get to know who they would recommend a survivor speak to in the police and who to suggest the survivor actively avoid. This view is based on the experience of seeing particular officers interviewing or talking to abuse survivors. When survivor agencies are working closely with the police and have trust in a particular officer, many more survivors are encouraged to go forward and report the crimes against them. When there is a reshuffle in the units and there are only unskilled officers, or officers who are not regarded very highly left working there, fewer abuse survivors are encouraged to talk to the police by the survivor agencies.

Proper evaluations of the work police officers carry out in specialised units should include asking survivors and survivor organisations to comment on the performance of each individual officer. Perhaps this would help some officers develop their skills and personalities a bit more. Police officers are assessed on their work performance annually. This appears to be done internally only. It would perhaps be much more useful if agencies who have worked with the officer were asked to comment on individual performance during investigations where there had been some joint work. This would be a great opportunity to get some truth into the assessment. It would also make sure that officers were more likely to do a better job when working in a multi-agency capacity.

Another useful measurement would be to check out how many survivors want to talk to a particular named officer and how many say they do not want another particular officer. It would be quickly discovered that there is generally a very good reason for this preference.

Every time a really good officer is moved from the specialised departments, survivor organisations have to start again to raise awareness, build bridges and get to know the new totally unskilled and usually uninterested officers. These officers do not see why they should spend any time getting to know survivor organisations at first because they have no awareness at all of the needs of abuse survivors or of the issues involved. Some also see themselves as being above voluntary organisations. It often takes about another three years before an officer might have learned enough for support organisations to have faith enough in them to be able to suggest that any survivor go forward and talk to them. These officers will by then have made many mistakes with many abuse survivors.

When there is no one skilled enough in the so-called specialised departments, ritual abuse survivors in particular become totally silenced. They find it difficult to talk in the first place and usually need to take time to build trust. They need highly experienced officers who know about all kinds of abuse including ritual abuse. Often they need someone they trust to recommend a particular officer to them. They need officers who have had specific training and who are not dismissive or unable to keep an open mind. When the experienced officers move on, all experience is gone. Trust is lost and so also is awareness and experience within the police specialist units.

Time and again, either unwittingly or deliberately, survivors are short changed. The things that survivors most need such as time to build a relationship of trust, trained and experienced officers and continuity are denied as the specialised Officers tenure runs out, in far too short a time, or officers who listen are moved on. Effectively, when survivors are denied what they need to talk and make a complaint ritual abuse does not get heard about and can be quickly swept under the carpet. It is not visible and therefore not a problem. Those with the problems are the survivors who are left dealing with it by themselves once again.

It would be a good idea if the police would take the time to listen to the organisations with many years of real specialisation in issues of abuse. It would be really good if they would listen to the survivors of abuse, particularly those who have tried to tell the police already and failed. Perhaps something could be learned from the failures too. It would be good if the police, just for a small while even, allowed for a proper specialised unit to form and gain real experience and skill, informed by those who need to use the services rather than dictated by those with other axes to grind and internal politics.

SOCIAL WORK

The social work department is a huge seemingly unwieldy machine that must destroy several rain forests a year in its constant quest to write reports. They are very good at writing reports.

This is one of the main statutory organisations, which is meant to be in the front line of protecting children from all forms of abuse. Unfortunately they are not very good at protecting children from abuse. They are in fact much better at writing reports and blaming others when there is yet another inquiry into a child's untimely and totally, with hindsight, avoidable death. Most inquiries held after a child's death expose the fact that there was a great deal more that the social work department and other involved agencies could have done to prevent a child from dying or being killed. Most usually the child has been known to the social work department and other agencies for some time. Yet, again and again, something breaks down in the child protection system and there is a complete failure to protect some children. We can only hope that eventually some lessons will be learned from some of these inquiries.

One would think that because the social work department are a child protection agency that they might be quite aware of ritual abuse and organised abuse and indeed, according to some survivors, they often are quite well aware. They never seem to be prepared to admit this awareness to anyone else though. Rather, they seem to expend a huge amount of effort in trying to hide things to do with more serious organised child abuse cases. This sometimes includes not even informing the police about what is going on in some cases. It is as though they get too embarrassed or want to cover some things up. This more usually occurs when a child is well known to social services through being in care or on the 'at risk' register.

One of the biggest fears of the social work departments seems to be having to 'look after' (as they call it) a child who is at risk. They seem to hate removing a child from the family home even when the home is a place of fear and abuse for the child. The answer they most usually come up with in cases of abuse is to provide more 'support' for the parent. One does naively have to wonder why the negligent or abusive parent gets seemingly endless support and not the child who is the one actually at risk of harm. It has to be said though that under our current legislation there is a huge over-emphasis on keeping families together. It is often quite difficult for social workers to remove a child from its home and the huge amount of proof required of risk to a child or abuse can become a huge barrier to actually safeguarding the child.

Several survivors of ritual abuse who had been taken into care when younger for various reasons have reported that they were placed into foster homes of other people who were involved as group members in the abuse. This had the effect of continuing the abuse unabated. Some survivors talk about becoming involved in ritual abuse through growing up in foster care rather than because of their birth families. One survivor commented on the irony of being removed from the care of her mother, due to her mother's depression (no abuse) and being placed in a children's home where some of the staff were involved in organised abuse.

Some survivors talk about the fact that their social worker at the time was also involved in the abusive group. For the young survivor in this position, there can be no help available from social services unless the survivor can tell someone else. This is usually impossible. To be in this position also reinforces the belief that the abusers are absolutely everywhere and can indeed control everything as they often claim. They are in fact not everywhere but they most certainly can work anywhere. They sometimes have professions, which give them positions of power and authority, which they of course then make full use of to maintain their authority over the survivors.

There are many, many very good social workers out there trying to protect children as best they can. They are often unable to make any real impact though because their management is bogged down with protecting limited resources and covering their own backs. The individual social workers are seldom allowed to make the important decisions about safeguarding children and those who do most often make these decisions are the people who are usually most distant from the child. Many of the good social workers become so disillusioned and frustrated that they give up their jobs and go and work in settings where they consider they will be able to do more good for children. It is sad that many people are trying hard to help children but the child protection system itself becomes a barrier to being able to achieve this.

Social workers who stumble across ritual abuse are usually quickly rendered silent by their management. Such has been the backlash caused by the activities in places such as Cleveland, Nottingham, Ayrshire and Orkney that the social work departments across the country seem to live in a state of terror of coming across such a thing. When such abuse does come to light, no one will actually name it for what it is. Rather, if it is called anything, it is called child abuse, which of course it is also. There is a lot of potential backlash lurking in a simple little name like ritual or organised when it is attached to the word abuse.

Some social workers have stumbled across ritual abuse from time to time and when they have tried to take some action, they have simply been removed from the case. It is incredible how often this happens in many statutory agencies. Some others have actually come across it and not recognised it for what it really was. Some survivors talk about social workers being involved with their families due to a number of problems but not having the awareness to recognise what the real underlying problems were. This is not entirely their fault as social workers do not usually receive any training or awareness about ritual abuse. It is difficult to find and recognise something that you have no knowledge or awareness of and even more difficult to know how best to help any survivors that are somehow stumbled across. It has to be said here though that some social workers, even without awareness at the time, have stuck their necks out and helped some survivors tremendously.

Most social workers are in that line of work because they care about people and genuinely want to help them. They also work with people who have a variety of problems. This means that sometimes social workers are best placed to find out about abuse which is happening in the home. If social workers were more aware of all the issues involved in organised and ritualised abuse, and knew what to look out for in the younger children who are suffering from the abuse, perhaps more child survivors could be found sooner and helped. Also, if workers were to be encouraged to be open and honest about what they think they may have come across, rather than the complete opposite, ritual abuse might one day become fully exposed in this country.

There would be no harm in raising the awareness of social workers about ritual and organised abuse. There would be no harm either in offering some training to social workers who work in child protection. There might even end up being some good coming out of it. If anything, more training and awareness might just possibly mean that at some point a child might not have to endure years of abuse or abusers might even be stopped from continuing their activities. Unfortunately the biggest block to providing training is often the management who often prefer not to acknowledge that there is a problem.

HEALTH

In this country national health services are free to all and are relatively easy for most individuals to access. There are a wide range of health services and various specialised health professionals. Most people at some stage in their early lives and indeed throughout their whole lives

come into contact with health professionals of one kind or the other. Most babies are born in hospital these days and the majority of children are health screened at various ages through regular check ups. Many children attend nursery school and the vast majority of children go on to primary and then secondary school. Most schools have a health professional attached to the school. This affords ample opportunity for many professionals to have quite a high degree of regular contact with young children.

Within an abusive group, there are those individuals who are completely hidden away from all in society, and are never allowed into contact with any authorities at all. Most are born out with the more normal routes, either at home, in a group setting or somewhere else. These children are not known at all to any public authorities and are completely unaccounted for in society. There is little or nothing that can ever be done for these particular individuals unless they can be found and identified. This is an almost impossible task made even more impossible by the fact that no one believes this sort of thing happens in the first place therefore no one even looks for these children.

Health professionals have seen the majority of adult survivors of ritual abuse at some point in their lives according to the survivors. Those survivors who make it into adulthood and succeed in escaping from the group tend to be the luckier ones and also tend to be the ones who were registered at birth and were therefore, to some degree, accounted for in the world. The fact that health and other agencies have had some contact with them means that there have almost certainly been many missed opportunities to help the survivor, particularly in their childhood.

Health visitors are currently ideally placed to notice children who may be suffering from any kind of abuse. They are not able to insist on getting access to younger children for health check ups as they have no legal power. But, when they do get access to the children, they could, if they were adequately trained, spot potential problems for children very early on. Indeed, some do. So it is too with GP's and practise nurses at the health centres who could also benefit from training.

Younger children are less able to hide the effects of the abusive experiences they have suffered and are less capable of hiding the signs and symptoms than older children. If health workers only knew what to watch out for and what to do about it when they do notice something, younger 'victims' of all kinds of abuse might well be spotted sooner and helped. Though the abusers often try to keep the younger children away from health workers when there are injuries, there are other times that there might be contact. Even a child

getting their inoculations is an opportunity for a health worker to engage with the child and perhaps be able to notice something.

It is the same when a child for some reason or other is admitted to a hospital. Once again, if the professionals were only to look wider than the particular symptom they are currently treating then the young 'victim' could perhaps be recognised and helped. Many adult survivors of ritual abuse report various times in their lives when they were involved with health services yet nothing of relevance was asked about or apparently noticed. Even when the child had presented with injuries, the adult's more plausible account had been listened to ahead of the child's apparently 'strange story'. Often the child had been briefed by the adults on what to say but most adult survivors believe that a health professional digging a bit deeper or being a bit more perceptive might have made all the difference to them.

Adult survivors of ritual abuse do not talk favourably about health services and in particular psychiatric services and mental health professionals. Survivors talk of being labelled, judged and not listened to or believed. They talk about control being taken away from them at times when they most needed to be empowered and in control of their own lives. In general, adult survivors most often claim that there is little or no awareness about ritual abuse and the needs of survivors are not being met at all by psychiatric services. It is rare indeed to hear a positive comment about statutory psychiatric services from an abuse survivor of any kind.

With general health services, the issues of abuse are still rarely considered important. Survivors talk of a complete disregard of their dignity and many assumptions being made about abuse survivors. One example related by a survivor is of a male doctor telling a female survivor to calm down as he is not a male person at all but just a doctor. He could not accept that the woman could not cope with his presence.

The survivor was very afraid of men, for very good reason and this was stated in the medical notes as well as related to the doctor by the support person who accompanied the woman. The woman felt that on top of not being listened to that she was being mocked, intimidated and put down. There were female doctors on duty that day but this particular doctor was annoyed that the woman had stated any preference of a doctor's gender. He declared himself a doctor first and a man second. He did not see what bearing his gender had. He still looked like a man to that woman though, even though he was a doctor also!

Health services are beginning to wake up in some parts of the country though particularly in relation to domestic violence. There are some health projects

where some women survivors can access a broad range of support and information and there are several local examples of good practice and innovation, projects such as the Eva Project based in Coatbridge for example. Increasingly there is awareness that all health workers need to be trained in issues of abuse and in some parts of the country progress is being made in this area. Hopefully over time these health projects will be expanded and examples of good practice will be used to inform services elsewhere.

EDUCATION

Children and young people spend at least eleven years in full-time education in this country. They attend for five days full-time. They probably spend more time in school than they do at home or in any other place. One would think and hope that spending so much time in the education system would have some positive influence over them. One would also think and hope that during those eleven years, some teachers might get to know the pupils quite well and perhaps even notice if they were having any problems. One would hope that a teacher might be the person most likely to notice that something might be wrong and be able to ask the child. Then again, one would think and even hope that eleven years of full-time learning would teach a child to at least be able to read and write adequately! Unfortunately, what one might think and hope for does not always come true.

Teachers are the people who are probably best placed to notice if a child or young person is being abused. Yet according to research carried out with several thousand children and young people (Consultations with young people 1997 (Young Women's Project, 1997), 2000 (Dundee Young Women's Centre, 2000) and 2003 (Eighteen And Under, 2003), the person the child is **least** likely to tell about any abuse they may be experiencing is a teacher. Only 3% of young people in all these consultations say they would ever tell a teacher about abuse. This is quite sad and perhaps is something that should be addressed.

Many adult survivors of all kinds of abuse mention the fact that, with hindsight, they are surprised that their teachers did not notice what was going on for them. Many felt that the teachers should have, and could have noticed and helped them. Some survivors comment on their changes in behaviour and constant tiredness at school. Some survivors comment on the fact that some of their teachers most definitely did notice signs of the abuse, such as bruising but did nothing at all about it. Certainly most adult survivors have strong feelings that the teachers in their lives all had some responsibility

to notice the abuse that was happening and take some positive steps to protect them as children.

These days more and more teachers are receiving training in child protection. Most schools now have designated child protection workers and all have child protection policies and procedures in place. This is, according to many survivors, a definite step in the right direction but is still not enough to protect children from abuse. Not only does there need to be training for teachers but there also needs to be thought put into removing some of the barriers between the teachers and the young people so that the young people feel more able to approach the teachers for help.

In this country many education departments and teachers still regard the parents as having more rights than the child. In many cases, particularly those involving primary aged children, the parents are the first people informed if there is reason to believe the child is being abused. This is despite the known fact that the biggest risk to a child is usually from those people who are closest to the child. Children are still to a large extent regarded as belonging to their parents and parents are still more readily listened to and believed rather than the child.

There is not nearly enough work being done to prevent abuse from happening in the first place and in encouraging young people to disclose sooner if they are being abused. There are prevention programmes such as the VIP Project (Violence Is Preventable) which could be placed in every school in the country if there were only the willingness to prevent abuse. This programme is not costly and is inclusive of all children of all ages.

There needs to be work done in looking at why children find it almost impossible to tell about abuse. Even when they do tell, the way that the child protection system works causes many children to swiftly retract their allegations. The teachers who focus only on the academic achievements of pupils and expect them to 'leave their problems at the door' positively discourage disclosures. So too do the many teachers who tell the child 'not to tell tales.' Unfortunately, this is still all too common.

Some teachers would comment that their job is to teach young people and nothing else but this is a very narrow-minded view to hold. Child protection is the responsibility of absolutely everyone. A child cannot learn effectively if they are living with abuse. No one, especially a child, can ever be expected to leave personal problems such as abuse outside the school and learn in isolation from the abusive life they are living at home. Abuse impacts on all aspects of a child's life and development and this includes the school life.

Everyone has a moral responsibility to protect children from harm and those who turn a blind eye to any sort of abuse are to some degree to blame for the continuation of the abuse and are colluding with the abuser. This includes teachers.

There are many good teachers who become very frustrated at the child protection system. Sometimes such a teacher has an excellent relationship with a young person and is very aware of some of the difficulties they are experiencing. Teachers like this do sometimes get disclosures from young people which they then have to take action on. Sometimes this means that they might also have experience of the child protection system then failing the young person. The end result for the young person is often more suffering. If the system fails for whatever reason and the abuse cannot be proven, the young person may continue to be abused.

Some teachers who have experienced the failures of the system and seen young people badly let down become loathe to put another young person through this. Such a teacher might go on and actively discourage a young person from disclosing to them. The teacher may then suggest another person to talk to who is not bound by the same child protection policies on hearing a disclosure. Sometimes the reality is that a teacher may know about the abuse but nothing can be done about it as it cannot be proven.

Some survivors of ritual abuse who were in the education system as children express surprise that their teachers never noticed and never took any action. Survivors talk about such things as regularly being absent from school without good cause and sometimes for quite long periods of time. They talk about being totally unable to think or concentrate and incapable of doing any school work. They talk about extremes of behaviour and being unable to socialise in any way with other children or look anyone in the eye. Many survivors, though they may not have spoken out about the abuse at the time feel that there were many signs that something was going badly wrong in their lives.

Survivors who went on to further education also talk about a general lack of awareness about abuse issues. Even as young adults there were often signs that abuse was an issue, yet, essays still had to be in on time. Though some survivors report that some lecturers and support staff noticed there were problems, they seldom seemed to know what to do or say about it. It is always much easier to continue to talk about whatever the academic subject is than to ask about cuts and bruises seen on a person.

The general consensus from survivors is that teachers and educators ought to have increased training and awareness in issues of all kinds of abuse so

that they become more able to help today's children. Teachers, particularly nursery and primary teachers are in a very privileged position in relation to young children and if they had greater awareness of the issues involved they might be able to identify and help children and young people who are currently being abused. If the children were identified sooner, the abuse could be ended sooner and less damage be done to the child.

OTHER STATUTORY AGENCIES

In Scotland, the housing departments have a duty to accommodate people who are homeless as long as they are not intentionally homeless. There are homeless units and flats in most towns and cities and in most towns there is usually twenty four hour emergency help available. At the point of leaving abuse, many survivors fit the category of being homeless though few would care to try and explain to a housing official the true reason for leaving their home. Many survivors of abuse do not take the time to plan their escape but just take whatever opportunity presents and run away from home. These survivors should be able to qualify for homeless accommodation.

In Scotland people can legally leave home at the age of sixteen and are entitled at that age to get a home of their own. In reality though this is not always all that easy to achieve. Often the first thing that housing officers do if a sixteen or seventeen year old presents to them as a homeless person, is contact the young person's family and ask them if they will take the young person back home. Most families, but in particular those who abuse their own children will say that they will take the young person home again. If the young person is being abused but cannot tell the housing officer, obviously the housing official will remain unaware of the true situation.

The young person is then refused homeless accommodation as they are not regarded as homeless if the parents say they can go home. This is because parents are deemed to have a responsibility to provide accommodation for their children and it is assumed that the young person can safely go home. Few would stop and think about any possible reasons that the young person might have for not wanting to live with their own family. Housing officers would seldom think to ask the young person if there was any good reason for not going home. Housing officers are sometimes trained in issues of domestic abuse in relation to women, but would rarely know anything about any other forms of abuse.

Those survivors who are over eighteen years old are in a slightly better situation and can usually access homeless accommodation without too much trouble. The accommodation is usually offered in the area they are from and most people living in the area would know where it is. This can be a major problem for a survivor. This means that the abusers do not have to think too hard to know where to find the survivor who is trying to escape from them. It is common for the survivor in this position to receive harassment from the abusers and it is unlikely that the survivor will report any of this to anyone in authority. Survivors often accept being threatened and harassed as normal. For them it most usually is.

Some survivors who have run away and travelled to other parts of the country have been told to return to their own area. The reason given is that they are not entitled to housing services out with their own area. This can happen particularly in areas with limited resources for the homeless and to some degree makes some kind of sense. Unfortunately this also makes it harder for the survivor who flees to the bigger cities. If the survivor is unable to say and be clear what they are fleeing from, they may feel that they have to return to their own area. Few survivors are able to say anything about the abuse to housing officers and most just accept it when they are told to go back to their own area. Yet if they were only to stand firm and let the housing official know that there is a threat of violence, they would be accommodated.

If the survivor is female they can be advised to mention domestic violence as an issue. This way they may be better able to get help and support. Those who mention domestic abuse are more likely to be accommodated without question even if they have moved to another area. There is an increasing awareness about domestic violence in most agencies and usually these days, women are accommodated and treated fairly sensitively.

The other problem sometimes encountered by survivors who are trying to access homeless accommodation is paying the rent. Homeless accommodation is very expensive because it is both supported and furnished accommodation. People who are claiming benefits are usually entitled to claim housing benefit but not all survivors claim benefits. People who are in paid employment or are students are not entitled to claim any housing benefits. Few people can afford to stay in homeless accommodation unless they are in receipt of housing benefit. This allows for a catch 22 situation for some people who need the accommodation but whose wages are not enough to pay the rent. It is the same with students who could never afford to stay in homeless accommodation.

Some ritual abuse survivors talk about the problems they encountered when trying to get benefits of any kind for the first time. Very lengthy delays have been experienced, and documented, lasting in some cases up to a year. Some survivors have had no benefits at all over this period despite being entitled to them. This has in some instances forced some survivors to return to an abusive home. These survivors believe that the delays happened because of group members who work in the benefit agencies and who deliberately find ways to delay the claim.

Some survivors have found that their benefit claim forms have repeatedly gone missing and they have had to constantly reapply. Others have found their forms constantly appearing at the bottom of a pile. Survivors with backing from support agencies usually manage better but few survivors have a support service at the point when they first escape their abusive situation. Though most of the survivors are entitled to benefits of some kind, some have to try and find ways of managing to live without until they can find support to complain and cause embarrassment to the agency concerned. This usually does it in the end.

Survivors who have no means of personal identification have particular problems. Those who were not registered by their parents at birth have no birth certificate, no national health number and no national insurance number. People in this situation have to fight their way through the system to be provided with identification that is acceptable and understood by the system. Without the necessary identification, survivors cannot access the benefits system.

WOMEN'S AID

Thanks to the hard work of women activists and feminists over many years, Women's Aid groups now exist in many towns and cities throughout the United Kingdom. They offer an extensive range of support and practical services to women and their children who have experienced domestic abuse. Most are also able to offer refuge space for women and their children who are fleeing from violence.

Survivors of ritual abuse have also sought refuge from Women's Aid groups over the years and some have been met with an excellent response. Some Women's Aid groups have not hesitated to provide refuge accommodation for survivors of ritual abuse even on knowing the type of abuse involved. Some of these groups have not only provided refuge and support for the woman at the time but have gone on and raised their own awareness of many of the issues surrounding such abuse. Some have brought in training

for workers and assisted the survivors in accessing further, more specialised support agencies.

Unfortunately, excellent though some of those Women's Aid groups have been, this is not as yet a universal service across the whole country. Survivors who are fleeing violence and are in desperate need of refuge are sometimes best advised to stay silent about the type of survivor that they really are. Due to a lack of awareness, limited resources or even a bad experience, some Women's Aid groups will not accept a survivor of ritual abuse into their refuges. Some have even, on discovering more about the type of abuse suffered by the woman, asked a woman to leave the refuge.

In fairness to some of these Women's Aid groups; it has to be pointed out that they often have had an extremely bad experience with a particular ritual abuse survivor, which has then coloured their views about such survivors and the abusers. Some groups have offered refuge to a woman only to find the woman behaving in such a way as to be a danger to other women and children in the refuge. This would quite rightly lead to ejecting such a tenant. The really unfortunate part of this is that sometimes all other survivors of ritual abuse become judged in response to the behaviour of one person.

One has to wonder if a really good tactic of the abusers would be to send women round refuges claiming to be ritual abuse survivors and then causing havoc. The outcome of this would tend to be that some Women's Aid groups would then react by judging all ritual abuse survivors to be in some way a problem or a danger and they would not then provide a service to any such survivor. This would certainly have the effect of limiting the choices of some women who need refuge in order to escape from a group and would be a good tactic for the abusers to use. I certainly wonder if there is not a degree of this happening already. I can certainly think of at least one good example of such havoc caused by a woman who later confessed that she had been lying about being a survivor of ritual abuse.

No one can criticise any organisation for trying to protect other women particularly vulnerable women and their children. But it is sad to think that any feminist group would fall into the trap of thinking that all survivors are the same and that any survivor of a particular type of abuse is automatically a danger to others. Hopefully the continued good practice of the Women's Aid groups who are helping all abuse survivors will in time filter through to all the Women's Aid groups. Refuge space is a basic necessity for ritual abuse survivors as it is for anyone fleeing any kind of violence in the home.

Another difficult issue for any woman in need of refuge space or other homeless accommodation is the price of it. The rent costs for refuge accommodation are extremely high and are most commonly met for most women by Housing Benefits. There is an assumption that all women who need homeless or refuge accommodation must be in receipt of benefits. This is not always the case and does mean in reality that some women who are in paid employment or are students cannot afford to access refuge space simply because they cannot afford the high rent. Occasionally a Women's Aid group has found a way round this and taken a woman into refuge anyway. But this means that the group is then operating at a loss, something no voluntary organisation can afford to maintain for very long.

RAPE CRISIS

Rape crisis centres were originally set up in a similar way to women's aid groups as a collective of women and a grass roots movement for change. They were set up by feminist women who sought to address the issues of male violence against women and children by campaigning for change, raising awareness and offering support services to women who had experienced rape or sexual violence. One of the fundamental principles was that women, as women shared a common experience of the power of patriarchy and the woman offering support to a survivor of abuse today could as easily be the woman needing support tomorrow. Women worked together with the principal that all were equal and they tried to challenge at all levels, the inequalities in society that often led to the abuse of power.

Over the years, these groups have changed and evolved. In Scotland now, many have changed their names and throughout the UK there seems to have become more of a focus on offering direct support services to women than on campaigning. Perhaps in time and with better resources, this will swing back. Many rape crisis groups (or sexual assault centres as some of them have become now) no longer offer support services to survivors of ritual abuse. Though the reasons appear to be as rich and as varied as the different groups are themselves, it does all get down in the end to seeing this type of survivor as in some way different from other survivors of sexual violence. There is a growing tendency to judge ritual abuse survivors as being more needy and demanding, more in need of 'specialised' help (whatever that is) or even regarding such survivors as dangerous and manipulative.

In the past, most if not all rape crisis/sexual assault centres offered very limited services to survivors of sexual abuse. This was the very best they

could provide as they had such very limited finances and resources available to them. Yet all centres provided the same services to all abuse survivors and did not categorise those survivors that they supported. In the past, any woman survivor of any type of sexual violence could get access to the same limited support services. Unfortunately, this is now no longer the case.

Those centres which still provide an excellent service for survivors of ritual abuse are becoming increasingly rare in England and Wales. That some still do is excellent and hopefully, in time, they will prove to other centres that work with all survivors of abuse is valuable and part of the battle against men's violence against women and children. This battle has not yet been won. In Scotland though there are still few centres, some of them still provide good services for all female survivors of sexual abuse including ritual abuse.

It is difficult to know what exactly has brought about the changes in policies of some of these centres. Certainly there have, as with women's aid, been some challenging women who have accessed such centres for support and have subsequently caused problems for workers and the agency concerned. As with women's aid, the difficulties caused by one person claiming to be a survivor of ritual abuse and then causing problems seems to have led, with some of the centres to the conclusion that all survivors of ritual abuse will be the same and will present with the same complex issues. In some cases this has caused these centres to make the not quite logical decision not to work with any survivors of ritual abuse at all. Again, survivors of one particular type of abuse are judged all to be the same.

Another important change took place over the past few years in rape crisis/ sexual assault centres in that most of them have managed to secure some paid staff. This is great and not before time. But one has to wonder whether the move away from volunteers who were so committed to survivors that they were prepared to give their time freely, to workers who are paid to do a job, impacted on the type of work which was then carried out? Some of these centres do not even use volunteers any more. Many of these centres now do less face to face and telephone support than in the days when it was all done voluntary. Many of these centres see fewer women now than before. Few, if any, of these centres ever fully evaluate the work they do and check with the women that the service is to their satisfaction.

Many of these centres now offer counselling rather than support. For some it is no longer women supporting women supporting women with the ultimate equaliser of 'today it is her and tomorrow it might be me' attitude.

There has also been a move towards becoming more 'professional'. Perhaps along with the becoming more professional, some of the centres have also picked up some of the attitudes of the professionals towards ritual abuse survivors? Thankfully this has not happened to all centres and some of them are centres of excellence in terms of the support services they offer to all survivors of sexual abuse. Unfortunately, the number of these appears to be declining year by year.

SURVIVOR ORGANISATIONS

There are a variety of organisations set up specifically for survivors of sexual abuse. Many of them have been set up by abuse survivors themselves and most of them offer support and information to abuse survivors. Some of these organisations are to some degree also campaigning groups and seek to raise awareness of the issues and campaign for improvements in all services for survivors.

Some of these survivor organisations are very small and completely unfunded grass roots groups. They tend to be created by the coming together of like-minded people who have encountered a gap in service provision or seen the need to campaign for changes in legislation or services. Some offer group support, some a help line for support, some offer face to face support and others do not offer a direct service but signpost survivors to agencies and offer them information. Some offer advocacy services and some offer awareness training. They are all different and not generally affiliated to any one organisation. Some do go on to raise some funding and end up employing a few staff. This is rare though and most continue because of the level of commitment of a handful of volunteers.

The one thing that most of these survivor organisations seem to do extremely well is offer the same services to all abuse survivors in their remit. Survivors of ritual abuse who have come across these smaller organisations tend to be of the same opinion. These organisations do not discriminate against ritual abuse survivors in any way. This is quite similar to the way that rape crisis groups behaved in the past when they were smaller.

Survivors organisations seem more able than most to accept any sort of survivor of abuse. The very limited services that tend to be on offer are equally on offer to all survivors and no distinction at all is made between them. Perhaps much of this is due to many of these smaller organisations being set up and then often run by survivors. Abuse survivors generally know from the inside out what it is like to be judged and defined by the label 'survivor'. Perhaps this common experience is enough to make the difference.

The biggest problem faced by many of these smaller survivor organisations is that they tend to struggle financially from day to day. They are often completely unable to commit to any long-term planning and can fold overnight when the handful of volunteers which has kept it going just gives up the fight or move on to do other things with their lives. Many of them have no paid workers or very few paid workers yet they seem to carry out a very high degree of work. It is rare for these organisations to have a waiting list of any kind and the commitment they have to survivors is high.

BEHIND CLOSED DOORS

BEHIND CLOSED DOORS

All abuse is kept as secret as possible. In particular, childhood sexual abuse is kept as a very closely guarded secret. It has to be. The abusers, as with any kind of abuse, have a huge investment in keeping what is going on well under wraps. They want to hold onto their power and part of what maintains their power is the silence of their 'victims'. No matter what ideology or reasons some abusers might claim gives them the right or the excuse to carry out the abusive actions that are condemned by society, they also know that what they are doing is wrong. They know beyond all doubt that if their actions and the abuse ever were to come to light, they would face possible exposure, investigation, prosecution and potentially serious consequences such as a very long spell in prison.

So it is also with ritualised and organised abuse. This is kept so secretive that many people do not even believe that it happens at all in this country. Often because there are usually prominent and professional people involved in the groups and with what they are doing, they work much harder at making sure that people do not find out about what is going on. This usually means that they attempt, through various extreme measures, to ensure that any survivors will never talk to anyone, in particular anyone in authority, about their experiences. Or just in case any survivors ever do manage to talk about their experiences making absolutely sure that it is unlikely that they will ever be believed by anyone.

Many methods are used to silence survivors and for those who are involved in ritual abuse from an early age, keeping the silence is one of the first things that they are taught. Through indoctrination and brainwashing, young children are taught that they must not, under any circumstances, reveal anything to do with the 'religion' or the family, to do so would be dishonourable and a betrayal of the whole family. They are taught that what is happening in their lives is right and for a higher purpose and that they must be made 'worthy' enough to be part of it. Those who are deemed less 'worthy' do not survive or become part of the lower orders within the group. Children are shown by example what will happen if they ever try to talk out of turn to anyone.

Fear and pain is also used to teach the children the wisdom of not talking about private family matters to anyone. What happens behind the closed doors of the family home is sacred. The children are often tested to the point of torture to teach them to maintain total silence. In some groups,

electric shocks, deprivation of sleep, sensory deprivation and close to death experiences may be used to reinforce the silence with the child. Often the child is asked questions and encouraged to say something, then punished to the point of unconsciousness when they then try to speak. They quickly learn that they must not talk. These methods of enforcing silence and others like it are most often used as they seldom leave any marks on the body as evidence of the serious assaults upon the child.

Then there are the inevitable threats that seem to accompany all forms of abuse. With ritual abuse, the threats are usually followed through and backed up in a much more real and direct manner than would seem to always be the case in other abusive situations. The threat that telling will lead to a loved one being hurt will be a real threat of an action that **will** be carried out in a ritual abuse situation. So too is the threat to kill someone who might say too much or in any way threaten the survival of the group. This will already have been proven to survivors at some stage of their lives within the group. People are usually regarded as expendable for the sake of the group's survival and talking about the group or its activities would be very much viewed as a weakness to be thoroughly rooted out.

Then there are the bribes that are often offered. Some people, particularly the males, will more readily be able to gain power and wealth within a group setting if they are strong enough or ruthless enough. People who have the possibility of achieving something, particularly those who have very little to begin with, can much more easily be persuaded to stay silent than those with nothing at all to gain or lose. Some groups have been known to continue to buy the silence of survivors even after they have escaped from the group by making sure that the survivor has some financial dependency on them. If telling about the group was to mean a survivor was to lose their home for example, they would not be very likely to risk this. In this situation, survivors would be wise to stay silent.

A common way of maintaining silence about the group is leading a survivor to believe that the group has a child of theirs at its mercy. Most female survivors will have been made pregnant and had at least one child while still in the group setting. It is an easy matter for the group members to say that the child is still alive and well. If the survivor believes, rightly or wrongly, that the group has their child, then maintaining their silence is much more likely to be the case. The belief that somewhere there is a child, which might suffer badly if they tell or do not do what the group says, keeps many survivors quiet and in some cases allows the abusers to continue to abuse a survivor for many years.

Yet despite the training, teaching, threats and bribes, in time survivors often do reach a place when they will begin to talk about their experiences. Sometimes they are able to do so simply because they have become far enough removed from the threats, bribes and power of the group. If enough time has passed and a survivor has become more aware of their own power, they may find the strength to begin talking to someone. If the survivor has been able to relocate and stay safe for long enough, they are more likely to be able to talk as much of the conditioning, control and power will have lessened. If a survivor has been able to find a person that they can begin to trust, they may find themselves more able to begin the process of trying to talk.

Sometimes, survivors begin to talk in order to maintain their own sanity and they need to find a way to talk in order to heal from their own trauma. Some even talk because the effect of the trauma has broken through the constraints of their silence. Increasingly, though, survivors seem to be talking more to try and raise awareness of ritual abuse and to try and improve things for other survivors. All of what we know about ritual abuse has come from the survivors. There is no where else that it can come from at the present time. Certainly, the abusers are not going to talk about it or tell us anything except to say that it is not true and is all nonsense.

Most of the people that I have come across in my life and my work who have survived the experiences of ritual abuse, and begun to talk about it later in life, have experienced the abuse since very early childhood. Mostly they have been involved for quite a long period of time and had a great deal of difficulty in getting out of it. It is, in my experience, much rarer to talk to someone who was pulled into such abuse in later life, though on occasions it does happen that way. Perhaps it is the case that older people are much harder to control and the younger the child, the more chance of maintaining the silence.

It is very easy for abusers to involve young children in a group setting and abuse. Children have no power of their own in the world and do not have the life experience to know when something they are experiencing is not normal or wrong. They come to accept their own lives as normal, which it is of course to them. They have no choice in the matter at all. To them, no matter what they are experiencing, their lives are completely normal to them at that time. While young, they have nothing to compare their lives with and know no different.

They are also relatively easy to silence, much less likely to be believed if they do say anything or slip up and less likely to know that what is happening

to them is completely wrong or know what they can do about it. Generally speaking a child gets involved when a close family member or carer has been involved in the group or becomes involved in a group through someone else. This person then grooms and prepares the child before taking the child into the group at as early an age as they can. Many of the younger children learn how to dissociate and some even begin to be able to form different personalities to cope with the abuse. Because of this, they are often not fully aware of all that is going on and it would take a lot of work to fit all the jigsaw pieces of a child's life together and find out what is actually going on for them.

Most survivors of ritual abuse talk about a lot of the abuse taking place in their own home or the home of carers, with a parent or carer either knowing about the abuse or being actively involved in it to some extent. For the child who is living with this, the rituals and the abuse are often very much part and parcel of their normal daily life experience. To them, there is nothing abnormal in any way about their lives. Few, at a young age, would be able to contemplate any other kind of life than the one they are currently living. For them, life is normal until the time they have something different and better to compare it with. By the time they have something to compare their lives with they are generally very well conditioned to obey and have been taught about silence, honour, betrayal and the consequences of making a disclosure outside the family.

Often, the families that these children mix socially with are also involved in the abusive group. So too are childminders and others who come in contact with the younger child. This reinforces the conditioning and normalises the abuse and the rituals that are generally being taught to the young children. All a child will know is what the child lives. All the child learns, it learns from those in power and control and the child, like all children, will strive for love and attention and to 'be good' in the only environment they know. If there is something they do not like, they will be told that they are to blame, are weak or not good enough. The child will not question or blame anyone else for the life they are leading. The child will follow the lead of the adults and blame themselves for what they perceive as their own failings.

The home environment usually becomes the training ground for the child and it is there that the child is most likely to learn not to talk or tell and how to behave in group situations. Before any child can be used in a ritual ceremonial way, the adults must ensure that the child knows its place and will act in an appropriate manner at all times. As with any religion, the rituals are part of the worship and are taken very seriously indeed and it would be a terrible reflection on the parents or teachers of the child if the child did not

behave as it ought during an important event. A child would never be permitted to intrude inappropriately to any ritual by crying, demanding attention or making any noise out of turn.

It is in the home that children are taught many of the rules and values of whatever ideology is being followed by the group. It is in the home that the child is taught to accept what happens and taught how to behave appropriately. This includes being taught not to cry when afraid or hurt. Most of the rituals that involve children demand complete discipline and instant obedience on the part of the child. This has to be taught before the child takes part in a ritual. Often events are rehearsed many times over at home before the big event so that the child will get it right on the night so to speak. In order to make compliance certain, many younger children are drugged for the events. The adults do not want young children ruining their ceremonies and any young children present will be well trained and fully under control at all times.

It is difficult for younger children to be involved in ritual and organised abuse without a parent or primary carer knowing something about it. Younger children cannot readily hide the effects of extreme abuse. Some survivors talk of their childminder taking them into the abusive group. Other survivors talk of one main relative who spends a lot of time with them taking them into the group. In most cases though, it needs substantial and sustained access to a child to teach them how to behave properly and respond and also to ensure that no one sees or hears any evidence on or from the child concerned. Most of the survivors I have ever come across became involved simply because their family before them had been involved and they were involved as part of the continuation of tradition.

Where children are involved more on the periphery of a group, i.e. they are not taught or used in particular rituals; the main focus is then more on trying to make sure that the ravings of the child will not be believed. Abuse is then carried out in such a way that if a child tries to tell, anything they say will sound totally unbelievable to most people. Things such as monsters and spacemen might be spoken about by the child because that is their own experience from the child's perspective. Children used on the periphery of a group are often children who cannot talk or appear to make much sense. Children with behaviour, learning and/or communication difficulties are much sought after by such groups.

Survivors Accounts

Lee

"I became involved in Ritual Abuse when my mother started two timing my father with a much less nice bloke; they *(my mother and her boyfriend)* decided to take me along to the ceremonies. This started when I was about five."

Sheila

"I have no idea {how I became involved}. I was too young to know when and with whom it all started.

Has an early memory of being in bed with a family member who 'hurt' her.

Told parent who changed her nightdress who told her that the abuser was 'missing his wife'.

Kay

"Both sides of my family were involved in either one or two over-lapping paedophile rings. One was headed by my father's elder brother, with my father playing a major part and cousins joining in the rapes. They gathered at sacred stones and trained small children to be willing or at any rate docile prostitutes for purposes of profit or blackmail.

They practised gang-rape, torture, often with electric shocks, murder, mutilation and getting us to abuse each other.

Snuff movies were taken, girls held in underground captivity when pregnant and babies taken from them this happened to me at age fourteen.

They held at least one kidnap girl. Others of us were used for blackmail to gain positions of power in the establishment.

The other ring, with a cousin as a major figure, was totally into robes, hoods, chants, ceremonies, sacrifices, gang rape and terrorising children.

Memories of this ring come slower, but it was the full ritual abuse thing. Many men, 50 – 100 or so, came to ceremonies, some down a mine or mines. Apart from these two rings, other relatives abused me, another uncle with stinging derision.

Both my younger brothers and my mother were abused besides me. My youngest brother developed severe epilepsy and died or was killed at [age] two. My other brother was suicidal as a teenager and killed himself in his thirties. My mother was severely "manic depressive" and suicidal most of her married life.

Both sides of the family were part of the "establishment", with very powerful and influential positions held by my uncles and cousin."

Annie

"I was born into Satanic Ritual Abuse. I was conceived by two well known people. My biological parents were initiated in the group as children. It all started as I was still a baby. I was brought up in two parallel lives the cult life and the happy family Christian life. We went to church but also went to group meetings.

All my family was involved initially although one of my sisters has broken free to some extent. It is also in my circumstance a generational abuse starting back with grand parents."

Nat

"I think that the appropriate term for my involvement would be termed as generational participation. I knew of no other way of life.

It was there from the moment I was born until I, with help, managed to get away.

However, I am not sure if it was an entirely a family affair, in the sense that all members of my family knew what went on. Although if I was being honest I find it hard to think that any member of my immediate family could remain ignorant of the activities.

To people on the outside it may be hard to understand the complexities of a life where people around you are hell bent, excuse the pun, on a life of abuse, rape and torture, and manage to keep the very distasteful secret. I have to say it wasn't that difficult, if you wanted to remain alive, you kept the secret. But it wasn't easy, few things ever are. To be expected to pay lip service to the onerous ideology and 'faith' had to be maintained, regardless of the internal strife that this may have caused. It caused me a great deal of internal strife.

I hated them and everything they stood for, but on the other hand they were also my family and I loved them. At first it was the unconditional love of a small child. In the end it was more of a constructed idiom. They were all I had. I could not believe, for my own sanity, that they were all bad.

I know that this will be viewed as a very naive concept, but let me ask you this, what options did I have?

My family were the only reason I became involved. You don't choose to become involved and for a long time and to a certain extent I never knew that it was wrong. I knew just that I was wrong because I didn't like it. I knew that it wasn't for me. I used to think that I was adopted, that this really wasn't my family and that my real family would come for me and take me away from this. I could never understand my mother why she would want to be involved why she had married into it. I still can't understand why she stayed, or when she eventually left that she would want to leave her kids in that situation. I guess she espoused all the right values of survival of the fittest!"

Lucky

"I was born into a very religious family. Our religion was described by my family as one of the oldest religions in the world, which we all had to keep really quiet about, as those in society who were non-believers had always persecuted people who followed our particular religion.

The religion came from my father's side of the family but my mother on marrying him seemed content to marry into his faith. As a child I thought nothing of abuse as that was not how I viewed it at all. To me, my way of life was normal and in many ways I felt superior to the other kids and outsiders. They were stupid as far as I was concerned and they did not know the truth.

I was taught that I was superior and that even the lowliest amongst us was superior to any of the outsiders. All close family were involved but we were made to go to a Christian church as a cover. I was taught to look for the flaws in the 'soft' religion and to me as a young child I could see quite clearly that it had no power. I was taught to be disrespectful of all that represented Christianity. I was taught to desecrate the church at every opportunity and make sure that I did not get caught.

I was taught to be strong and to survive and in order to do that I had to be able to endure and learn. I never saw anything wrong with any of this until I grew older and noticed things were different in other families and for other people."

Ruth

"I was born in Scotland. I was lighter than a bag of sugar when born. I can't remember much of my life. I am going to start where I remember. I did not stay with my mother or father. I stayed with my grandparents.

My mother was never a mother to me that is why I wanted to love my kids and never do what my mother done to me. I do not want them to hate me as I hate my mother and father.

When I was staying with my grandparents they had sex with me. I did not know what they were doing to me was wrong till I was older and with what other kids said to me. It was not just my grandparents that had sex with me my uncle did it to me as well. I never wanted to hate any one but I do hate my grandparents and my uncle and my mother and father.

All I wanted was for someone to love me and not do those bad things. I never want any other kids to go though what I went through. But if you go for help to the police or to a social worker they do not help.

Once I came home from school late because the bus was late. My mother was so mad with me she just started to hit me. She had her hands around my neck, she was strangling me and I passed out. When I came around one of my mother's friends was giving me mouth to mouth. She was a nurse. She saved my life. But she did more than that she called the social work and the police. So the next day at school the police and a social worker came for me and took me away from my mother.
They took me out of school to a home where they took

photos of my body with all the marks. I did not want to stay at the home. I had to go to another school I was taken there every day in the mini bus. I hated it. I never done anything wrong but I was being punished. Every time I ran away the police would just take me back there. It was like a prison."

Jay

"I remember my father seeing them doing the bad stuff to me. But he never helped me. He just walked away and left me. He did not try to stop them or help me.

It is funny you only remember the bad stuff that happens. I was staying at my uncle's house. He came into my room. I shared a room with my cousin but that did not stop him. If I fought with him to make him stop he would lock me in the cupboard.

I was very scared and cold in the cupboard. I went to the police for their help to make him, stop hurting me. The police said they would not send me back to him and I would be safe from him. It was going to court but something went wrong.

Every one said I would not go back to him ever again. They lied to me. They did not help me. They just took me back to him. It made him very cross with me. It made it worse for me going to the police. That's when I stayed in my mind."

John

"It was friends of the family, catholic upbringing, forced to go to church. Even as a child it all seemed so fake. Smiles, deceit and then confession. The school was catholic. Everything was a sin. You had always done something wrong and had to be punished to get into heaven. I just wanted to be me and that was wrong. So I created people who liked me for who I was. I guess I'm just stubborn."

Helen

"My parents moved to Buckinghamshire when I was three years old. My father became involved in a satanic cult and I was abused in the cult from age three. The cult was unusual in that its members were all male. This was a group who hated, feared and despised women. The rape was always anal and I believe my father, as well as suffering severe mental health problems, was also very ashamed of his gay sexual leanings.

The lords, as they called themselves, used the local Salvation Army as a cover for the cult activities. I would be horrifically abused on a Saturday night and then taken to church to see the same people (this time without masks) on a Sunday. The Christian church introduced the idea of Satan, so to me, it is not so strange that the church was a cover for the cult. I am not suggesting that any one in the church knew, or condoned the cult, except the cult members."

Carol

"I became involved when I was sent to live with Foster Parents at roughly four years old. There were three other foster girls living there long-term also. It was an extended family affair. They had two older daughters, one's husband was high up in the Social {Work} Department (Top) and the other an Officer in the Navy. The eldest son of one was being trained when I got older, and when he came to the house was allowed nothing to do with me.

I remember the oldest girl coming to my bed in the early hours, with tears she hugged me, and kept saying sorry but she had to leave. I did not understand and sobbed into my pillow. Later I was told she had escaped with her boyfriend from across the road to Australia with his mother's help and was happy now with children.

Although the other two left the house, they have always stayed with the family. "Now I understand".

A KEY TO THE DOOR

A KEY TO THE DOOR

This society has failed repeatedly to protect its children, the most vulnerable members of any society. Time and again we hear of the death of yet another child either at the hands of a parent or carer or at the hands of a so-called 'pervert' loose in the community. Again and again, after the death, there are costly investigations and inquiries and lengthy reports written. Many times at the end of such inquiries, there are damning reports produced of the failure of all the agencies and individuals involved to protect the child. Repeatedly we hear of child protection systems letting children down, basic mistakes made, overworked professionals struggling under their workload and a system so full of holes that it is a miracle any children within it are ever protected at all.

Then there is the vast and ever increasing numbers of adult survivors of abuse, who after many, many years, finally find the courage to speak out about the horrors they lived with in their childhood. They too were failed as children. These people are however the ones who survived. What of those who could no longer cope and took their own lives? And what about those who were killed by their abusers? Even today it all still goes on. Many of today's children will become tomorrow's survivors. Until something radically changes in this society, we will continue to let the children down and fail to protect them. We will continue to bolt the stable door far too late, hold inquiries, write reports and then look for a scapegoat to blame rather than accepting that we are just getting it very wrong.

There is more that we could do. If only those in power could see that there is sense in perhaps looking more to the living for some of the answers about how to protect children rather than to the dead who can no longer talk. We can learn from mistakes made when a child is killed but we can also learn from others. In the living adult survivors of abuse there lies a wealth of information about abusers behaviour, what they do, how they do it, how they silence survivors and the many other complexities that accompany all aspects of all kinds of abuse. Survivors could, with just a little encouragement, expose many of the secrets of abusers and many hold the key as to how children are groomed, how they are made complacent and compliant and of the complex relationship and dynamics between the abuser and the abused. If we knew a lot more about these things, we would be much better armed in the struggle against abuse.

Yet, adult survivors are most often regarded as mentally 'damaged', in need of extensive services, liars who make up fantastic stories or as mere 'victims' whose duty it clearly is to report their abusers to the authorities and provide enough evidence for a prosecution. At best they are often pitied by many in society. At worst, the mighty myths prevail and they are regarded as a danger to children, permanently damaged or thought in some mysterious way to be to blame for the abuse they suffered as children. They are even blamed for not reporting the abuse they experienced. Survivors of sexual abuse are a dark, spreading stain on the conscience of society and an embarrassment to those people who prefer to think that only good and nice things happen in this 'perfect' society. Many people do not want their cosy world-view distorted by an unpleasant truth.

Society in its half hearted and somewhat ignorant way looks to study the convicted sexual abusers for the answers. Without a doubt, it is possible that some study of these individuals might have some worth for something. However, it must be remembered that these people have no reason to be truthful even to themselves. They are, by their very actions convicted liars. They are devious and manipulative and have little or no regard for the feelings of others. They have little humanity and no conscience. Most force their victims to testify in court. Few ever confess. And, in addition to all of this, let's face it, only the really stupid ones and the unlucky ones ever get caught and convicted. The numbers of those sex offenders who are actually convicted of their crimes are only the tip of the iceberg. Why then do we continue to waste time and resources in studying these liars and losers? The vast majority of abusers stay free throughout their whole lives and continue throughout their lives to abuse children, young people and those with less power than them. They never stop until they are stopped.

Survivors of abuse are seldom well supported and are frequently disbelieved by those around them. They struggle to get free of the abuse, and then struggle to come to terms with the effects it has had on them. Some survivors never do get over it and the effects remain with them until the day that they die. Yet, some survivors continue to break silence. This, despite the fact that to name oneself a survivor of sexual abuse is to invite being judged in terms of the many myths surrounding survivors of such abuses, not least of which is the highly mistaken belief that those who have been abused in their childhood will inevitably abuse others.

Despite the many difficulties, survivors still come forward and try to talk about their experiences. There is an increasingly better climate now for survivors to talk about abuse. People are wakening up to that fact that adults can and do abuse children. Things are slowly shifting in society and

there are more survivors now prepared to stand up and talk than ever before. Their usual motivation is to raise awareness of abuse and save other children from what they endured in their childhood. For this, survivors continue to expose themselves and their lives and this now increasingly includes survivors of ritual and organised abuse.

Society could learn so much from survivors. Survivors have little or nothing to gain by speaking out and more often have quite a lot to lose by saying anything at all. Most could tell communities and perhaps in particular teachers what to look out for in the children who are currently being abused. Most could say what might work best in trying to get a child to tell about what might be going on for them. Most could tell of the many ways that abusers use to gain and keep power and control over children. And probably all survivors could tell about how silence is enforced and maintained to protect the abuser. Perhaps some of this information could be useful in the fight against abuse rather than waiting for the next generation of survivors to come forward and the next deaths of children.

All of this also applies to survivors of ritual abuse. We could learn so much if we were to take off the blinkers of denial and disbelief and begin to actively encourage survivors of ritual abuse to come forward and talk about their experiences. If we ever really want to know the full picture we need to safeguard the survivors who can talk and share any information they can with us. We need to turn things around if we really want to know what is happening and rather than discouraging survivors and placing barriers in their paths, we need to remove the barriers and encourage them to tell. Part of this would have to involve a clear commitment not to prosecute survivors for acts of survival which may have been illegal but that they were unable to prevent or were forced to take part in, particularly as children.

Most survivors of ritual abuse will, as part of their own abuse, have been in some way involved to some degree in the abuse of others and/or in some form of criminal activity. This is yet another way that abusive groups can enforce silence and hold a high degree of power over individuals. Under the current criminal justice system, anyone in Scotland over the age of eight can be held responsible for their actions and any criminal activity they may have been involved in. This is the case even if this occurred while they themselves were being abused.

This means that survivors cannot ever properly tell their full story to the police as to do so would be tantamount to a confession of carrying out a criminal act. This could very possibly lead to the prosecution and the conviction of the survivor, particularly in the absence of anyone else to

prosecute or convict. The way things are at present it would not be in the best interests of any survivor to tell the whole truth. If we want the whole big picture about ritual and organised abuse, we would need to look at ways of permitting and even encouraging survivors to talk in a completely safe way without fear of prosecution.

Only with the whole truth, will we ever more fully understand what is really going on. A greater understanding of the many complexities and dynamics of ritual abuse would lead in time it is hoped, to the conclusion that the survivors will to survive crosses all boundaries. This includes boundaries that people will not normally cross until their very survival is compromised. We need to become very clear about who the victims are in all of this and realise that the ones to blame for the abuses that occur in this environment are those with the free will and the power. We need to create a climate in which the survivors can safely tell all that they are prepared to tell and maybe even a bit more than that.

If children who are currently being abused could only be identified and safeguarded sooner then the damage caused by the abuse could be greatly lessened. Adult survivors of all kinds of abuse often can, on looking back at their lives, identify occasions when it might have been possible for people on the outside to have intervened and helped them. It is no different for survivors of ritual abuse. Though telling would normally be much more difficult for survivors of ritual abuse, not all telling happens with words. Sometimes it is the behaviour or even activities of a young survivor that gives the clues that not all is well with the young person.

Many survivors can talk about signs of abuse that were missed by the people round about them, signs that, if only there was some awareness of ritual abuse, would have pointed towards a strong possibility that the child was being abused in this way. These signs can include children's drawings, strange behaviour and younger children being too good and too willing to please or more fearful than most children. A basic lack of awareness about abuse in general and in particular ritual abuse leads again and again to an inability to be able to fully protect the children.

Many survivors of ritual abuse talk with bitterness about those who failed to protect them. From the non-abusive parent or carer to the school-teacher who taught them or the policeman who dragged them home, most of the adult survivors I have spoken with felt completely let down and betrayed as children by many different people. Though according to the survivors there were often several signs of abuse, no one took any action at the time to find out more about what might be going on for

the child. Though this is in the past, unfortunately, not a lot has changed in this respect even today.

In this country, so much still depends upon the child talking and telling coherently about the abuse they are experiencing that it is nearly impossible to get to find out what is really going on and actually protect the child. Children and young people find it almost impossible to talk about abuse while still experiencing it. The responsibility of child protection should not be left up to the child. Everyone knows that child survivors can rarely talk or tell yet that is what the system demands before it takes action. Also, there is still the belief that the family is always best kept together even if the child does not want to stay with the family. The parents apparently have more rights than the child who must be able to tell about any abuse in order to get out of the family home. They cannot just leave and go to a refuge.

In order to provide for more protection for children, we need to move away from our criminal justice system and prosecution as the first step in protecting the child. The child should be the first and main priority and ought to be made central to all decisions, regardless of parental rights and any criminal activity that is suspected. The criminal activity should be regarded as a secondary priority and children's safety and well being, both physical and emotional, should come before all other things. This is definitely not what happens at the present time. Currently even if a child makes an allegation and then understandably retracts as the shit hits the fan then that is the end of the matter. Currently children who persistently run away from home are returned to that same home. If the child cannot or will not tell about whatever the problem is they are always returned home.

If there were only a greater awareness in the world or even openness to the possibility that ritual abuse might happen, perhaps more of it might be revealed or uncovered. Currently, it is still hard to reveal that you are a survivor of this kind of abuse because so many people quite simply do not believe that the abuse happens in the first place. As a consequence of this, they must then view people who say that they are survivors as either lying about their life experiences, suffering from weird delusions or in some way mentally ill. This particular, but common viewpoint makes it extremely hard for survivors to ever admit to being a ritual abuse survivor.

As children some survivors of ritual abuse do try to tell about what is going on for them. Some do the telling through extremes of behaviour as they cannot cope with their feelings and their lives. For some, their brains cannot

cope with the constant trauma and they develop illnesses, both physical and mental. Others become compliant and passive in the extreme as they struggle to find a way of surviving something that they cannot fight back against. There are often signs to indicate that all is not well with a child but no one investigates this. Signs of abuse are often present in abused children but if they say nothing then nothing is done. Such signs can be things like persistently running away from home, hyper vigilance, self harming, substance abuse and other behavioural indicators of problems.

Children find it extremely difficult to hide what is going on for them when they are being abused, even though they have been well taught and conditioned not to tell. They do not have the life experiences, particularly when very young, to know how to fully hide what is going on for them. Many survivors tell in adulthood of the terror they would feel on being asked by teachers in school about their holidays. Most would look for a way out of answering such questions rather than directly lying about it. Some would be so unaware of what a 'normal' holiday would be like that they would be unable to make something plausible up.

Avoidance of doctors, nurses, and people in authority and of answering direct questions is exceedingly common in the childhood of survivors of ritual abuse. Absences from school explained away by plausible parents or completely without any reasonable explanation are also common. Children who have difficulty socialising or playing normally may be well be 'victims'. Children who appear to be far too serious for their chronological years or who appear to be in some way 'out of control' are also possibly having some trouble at home. Troublesome children are more usually troubled and distressed children.

There are many, many indicators of childhood abuse and though we missed the child survivors of yesterday, we could, through listening to the experiences of adult survivors possibly find and help some of the child survivors of today. Thus we might help prevent today's children from becoming tomorrow's survivors. Those who have survived are in the best position to help us find indicators of abuse and thus identify children at risk and children who are currently suffering from abuse. Survivors might also, through their experiences be able to help design child protection and personal safety programmes for use with children, which will stand a better chance of working with children and young people to keep them safer and help them disclose any abuse sooner. Some of this is already happening.

Ultimately, we need to at least take the time to stop and listen with an open mind when survivors try to talk so that we do not fail the next generation

also. We need not to dismiss survivors as people who are damaged and with mental health problems. Though some may be damaged and some may suffer from mental health problems as a result of all that they have been through, it does not negate their experiences or make liars of them. We need expertise in order to learn and I would suggest that the expertise lies with the survivors many of whom would be prepared to help. Unfortunately there are very few signs that many are stopping to listen to survivors and there are few signs of many people open minds. We can continue to hope though.

Survivors Accounts

Lee

"Yes, there was very much a failure of society to recognise the abuse. An old woman, a neighbour of ours helped out by sometimes looking after me when I was ill so that I didn't get taken to the ceremonies, but I think that is all that she could have done. She was but one person.

Maybe I wouldn't have wanted help. My one experience of having a counsellor was certainly not encouraging. This was when my father died (when I was ten). I felt ready to talk about the experiences I'd had through my mother and he insisted that I was just feeling anger because of my father's death. I walked out of his office after about five minutes.
I didn't try talking to anybody 'official' again until I was fifteen years old.

If people are there to listen they should listen to what people have to say, rather than having some idea of what they expect the person to say. It would cause a lot less frustration for a start. Society can start by recognising Ritual Abuse for what it is. Not science fiction, something that is currently going on in parts of the United Kingdom.

Also, by not treating survivors of Ritual Abuse as long term damaged victims. As something to be hidden away and medicated, never to be let out into mainstream society lest they should damage the image of the all wonderful United Kingdom where kids (of course) never ever come to any harm from people they know. Not try to force survivors to talk, but to provide support when they wish it. To provide a more sensible way, also of allowing people to disclose information, should they wish to do so."

Sheila

"Don't know if it's as much that it failed [society]. Society as a whole didn't believe that it {Ritual Abuse} happened. If it did it was shut away. People give their children to people and don't ask any questions. Nobody questioned.

Yes I wanted someone to help. No one listened. Even when I told, no one listened.

People need to open their eyes and ears and listen. Stop labelling every kid with behavioural problems with ADHD. Is it masking other things?

Not sure that society can do anything except believe it is a reality. That it's always happened and is still happening today."

Kay

"My abuse, which is only now surfacing, was several decades ago when there were few social services. I just wish one non-paedophile relative had cared enough to see that a dead baby and two uncontrollable children meant something was wrong, but it was all blamed on my mother who'd had a breakdown and could be labelled crazy.

A primary school headmistress did get concerned. I was taught a terrible lesson in not talking, and she perhaps decided nothing could be done except care for me. This she did, saving my life at one point and giving me a bit of a childhood. At fifteen when I began to cry all the time (in the obliterated ritual abuse world I'd had my baby taken from me) I wanted to find a psychologist, but didn't know how.

I was at a boarding school, was told I had an "Identity crisis" and to meditate.

All my adult life I tried to get proper support for my depressed mother, but only slowly grew to dimly see that my father was against this. No relative ever supported me. The NHS (National Health Service) virtually collaborated with him for decades, and she had a rotten time. I feel someone in the NHS should have listened to her. He spoke for her to doctors, filled out forms for her, etc. Or they might have listened to me. Instead she and I were both regarded as unstable and my father as the heroic carer.

The NHS could treat survivors as people, not nutcases, which simply perpetuates our lack of confidence. It could be easier to whistle-blow on other suspected abuse. I found it too upsetting to talk to the police, which is where the NSPCC (National Society for the Prevention of Cruelty to Children) refer you. The media just hurt people as much as possible, instead of being constructive. A free press could make a lot of difference.

Annie

"I was failed many times as a child and adolescent. Initially by people reacting to my claims of abuse as being impossible due to my loving Christian parents. Then at one point my parents were taken to court for abuse and me and my sisters were put on the Child Protection Register. It took months for my solicitor to get the judge to say I was old enough and capable of making a statement and then after it was made any reference to ritualistic or satanic abuse was removed.

I wanted people to help, people wanted to help but those people couldn't understand and couldn't face what type of abuse was going on so they ignored it. Society needs to stop with the attitude that ritual abuse doesn't happen under their noses. Yes it does I was in it for years and I know it does."

Nat

"This leads me on to the failure of society as a whole to recognise either my situation or me.

The failure of society seems a big burden to put on society. I think that society and the many individuals in that society are naïve, and quite happily cosseted in the rosy glow of collective humanity. I think that many people use their own beliefs and attitudes, and reflect them on all people. They find it hard to imagine the absolute depravity that their fellow humans are capable of.

It may be that this dogged blindness to the reality of life is the reason that many in society cannot recognise suffering, and have difficulty in believing what many would deem the unbelievable.

I don't think I can blame society for not picking up on the many clues that I dropped from time to time. I did go through the school system; I guess that would give people ample opportunity to pick up clues.

I believe that even if my teachers or any others had recognised that something was wrong, I don't think I could have told them anyway. The control of my family was absolute, not so absolute that nothing could have been done, but absolute enough to terrify me into silence.

Silence, it's a funny word. You can say nothing but sometimes you give everything away by your silence. On being asked what you did in the holidays, you keep quiet, hoping that the bell will ring before the teacher gets round to you. All the while thinking, desperately trying to make up something while your mind fills up with the reality of the 'wonderful' summer holidays.

Did I get away before the teacher got around to me? Yes, a trip to the toilet and a complaint of illness. I managed to escape, until the homework was announced, 'write a nice story about your holiday experiences'. Nothing was picked up at school, as far as I was concerned. Despite the prolonged absences, the illness that invariably hit me on Friday afternoons at school, the absences on Monday mornings. Yes I think that there were many clues, but people and society as a whole did not, indeed do not have the awareness to either understand or pick up on clues.

I wanted help, but could not ask for it. In a lot of ways I did not know what I wanted help from. I didn't want to hurt either my family or my group; they were all I had. What would happen to me if I told? From a young age I was initiated in the torture and ultimate death that was inflicted on traitors. Staying alive is sometimes an onerous task, but it is one which the body and the survival instinct wins every time. I wasn't scared of dying per se, but I was terrified of dying by their hands. That and I didn't want to give them the satisfaction. My belief in this did change over time, and I wanted my life to be over, to escape from the group.

I think that society and the individuals within it should increase their awareness. Not only that but they should learn to actually listen and hear what children have to say. We live in a society that does not listen to children, let alone hear what they are saying. However, the groups make the truth unbelievable. They make children out to be elaborate storytellers, when all the children are doing is telling the truth. It is a truth that those in society do not want to hear.

I believe that a lot could have been picked up during my childhood. I went through primary and secondary school, and if people had known what to look for I wouldn't have been left with my family. Maybe that is a pipe dream too though. Can you blame anyone for not reacting, I don't think you can. Surely the ones to blame are the ones doing something, although the absence of help can be as distressing as the actual acts of abuse. But if people don't know what they are looking for, can they be blamed for not knowing?

I guess they can, but it was my job to make noticing as difficult as possible. But I was a young child and that wasn't as easy as I thought it would be, and if I am honest with myself then I am angry that people failed to see what was going on and failed to do anything to help me."

Lucky

"People in my childhood could have picked up on the fact that I was an extremely strange and very lonely child. They could also quite easily have noticed that I was often badly bruised, very hungry and unable to play or mix in any way with other children. They would never have guessed though at the extent of what was going on in my life, but they could at least have asked. How could they guess at the extent of my problems? Ritual abuse was never spoken about and as far as I am aware, no one would or could ever have known what it was. To me and the family and group, (everyone around me) it was not ritual abuse, it was our faith our religion and our duty. It was me who was out of step in not liking the things that went on.

The time was not right when I was young for the world to believe that adults might actually hurt their own children. The world was not ready for any kind of abuse let alone sexual abuse. There were no women's refuges, no battered and abused children and absolutely no possibility of parents involving their own children in any sexual activity. Rape crisis centres did not exist back then and many of the beliefs then would be that women deserved what they got and men had the right to do as they wanted anyway given as they were superior to women and children. That was of course a long time ago in the good old days.

Awareness has changed over time and it is survivors of abuse, mainly women, who have forced society to become more aware of what goes on behind closed doors. As a result, there are now a variety of services for women and children, training and awareness programmes, books and even story lines in soaps which all make people more aware of some of the issues of abuse. Though we are not quite there yet in terms of ritual or organised abuse, even that sensitive subject is beginning to be aired much more often.

With the greater awareness, there is more possibility now than ever before that survivors will be rescued younger and not have to suffer abuse for so long. Some survivors have already benefited from the increase in awareness and services, but there is still a very long way to go. Society does not really want to know about man's inhumanity to man and the real suffering of children and I can totally understand this. If I had a choice, perhaps I would rather not know these things too. Unfortunately though, society is going to need to know before anything can change for the better.

As a member of society, if I had a choice at all, I would rather believe that the world is kind and parents all are caring and nurturing of their children. I personally would rather live in make believe land and not know about ritual abuse. Unfortunately, while people choose to continue to live in make believe land, children, young people and adults who have no choices are forced to continue living and dying with ritual abuse. We need to all face up to reality whether we really want to or not"

John

"To be honest I think it's too late. It's either going to go full circle and be born again or get destroyed trying to save it. Society is fucked up and individuals are too self absorbed to worry about the big picture.

As for what could be done back when I was a child. I was a catholic growing up in a catholic family, going to a catholic school feeling the only thing I could do to be worth anything was become God himself. Anyone listening would have just made me feel like shit with some preachy advice about how lies make you go to the 'burny fire'.

Ruth

"A lot of people think we should be locked up because we are mad. But we are not mad we are just the same person. We have not changed in any way. So why do they treat us any different? We are human the same as them. But we had a very bad start in life. We did not ask for these things to happen to us. It was not our fault.

They were the ones who did wrong by touching us for their own pleasure. They are the ones who should be locked up for life not us, because they took our childhood away from us. We can never have our childhood back. Our lives are upside down not theirs so why should we be punished for what they did to us?

We should have been allowed to live our childhood and the rest of our life not in pain and horror about what happened to us a long time ago. There are times when I want to kill myself but do not because that would mean the abusers have won. We must keep on fighting. We must win. We must get strong to face them and ask them why they did those things to us.

I can't ask my grandparents because they are both dead. It is much harder to try and get over what they did to me. A friend said if I write a letter. Or I could go to their grave and ask them why. I will never know why they did it to me. My uncle is still alive I would love to ask him why. But I am too scared to ask him in case he does it to me again.

Every time I see him I am that frightened little child again. One day I hope I can face him and ask him why. Why did you take away my childhood? I never got to grow up like other kids."

Carol

"Teachers noticed and chose to turn a blind eye to the marks, and bruises, and thinness of my body, with constant sickness off school (a female teacher befriended us, and abused terribly almost daily, and waited in her car after school for me). We were told one morning that she was gone. Subject closed.

Did I want someone to help: I did not have the knowledge that I needed help as it was a part of my everyday life. I did not question that it should be different as I just seemed to be there for this purpose. The conflict and distress was too much to comprehend (I split).

It was not until my next school that I became aware of other girls lives, and families, were not as mine were, something was very wrong. Although I had been trained extensively in behaviour etc., I started to rebel against the system. A social worker suddenly appeared one day and threatened to put me in borstal, my face lit up "Yes please I will go it is bad here." He said, "I will slap your face for you, so be grateful for the roof on your head. He went and I never saw him again."

CHAIN REACTIONS

CHAIN REACTIONS

The reactions of people on finding out that someone is a survivor of ritual abuse vary considerably. A great deal depends on the level of awareness that the person has to start with, the openness of the person to learning, hearing and accepting and whether or not they have ever come across the issue before and in what way. Survivors who disclose what kind of survivor they are, are frequently met with disbelief and denial of their experiences. They are sometimes even laughed at and ridiculed. They are most often viewed as being in serious need of psychiatric attention or suffering from a mental health problem. None of this is all that surprising given that society as a whole still does not really believe there is such a thing as ritual abuse and indeed quite actively denies that it happens at all in this country.

Survivors are generally very cautious about the people that they talk to and very careful about how much they say. Ritual abuse survivors tend not to be the most talkative of people anyway and neither are they generally very trusting of other people. As a result of this, people might be unaware that someone in their social group, client group or even someone they work beside on a daily basis is a survivor. It is only through time and the building of a relationship of trust that the survivor eventually might tell someone something about the abuse. Once the survivor lets the information out with anyone, there is no taking it back and no control at all over what the person does with any of the information provided by the survivor.

Some survivors have learned, to their cost that on telling one trusted person, the whole neighbourhood soon knows all that there is to know about them. Unfortunately, such is the stigma of being a survivor of ritual abuse and all that accompanies this, that the whole neighbourhood knowing can sometimes prove problematic for the survivor. Not only do people in the community often then judge the survivor but more importantly for the survivor is the fact that the person whom they decided to trust has betrayed them. To learn to trust is hard for survivors and to then have that trust betrayed can be devastating.

For some survivors, particularly those who go the way of seeking help through a statutory agency, any information about them is most usually written down in their case notes and follows them wherever they go in their life. While this ought to be helpful to survivors in that they do not need to say the same thing over again and again to many different people, in reality, the survivor loses all control over information about themselves. Many people do not believe that ritual abuse happens in the first place. As a result when

they read the case notes that indicate someone is a survivor of ritual abuse, rather than questioning their own denial of ritual abuse, they often judge the survivor to be either lying, ill or deluded.

For others, though they may believe that ritual abuse happens, they sometimes also believe the many myths about ritual abuse and the accompanying myths about the survivors of ritual abuse. This too can be less than helpful to survivors. There is no way that a survivor can change the case notes about them though they can ask for notes to be added. This means that once the professionals in a particular agency know and write down the details of the abuse that the person has experienced, it will remain on their record forever.

It is very rare for survivors of ritual abuse to find understanding and acceptance from the first person they turn to for help unless they are very lucky indeed. What is much more common is that the survivor who seeks counselling or support often ends up teaching the counsellor or support worker. It is also common even for agencies who work with sexual violence to make policy decisions not to provide a service to survivors of ritual abuse. Even some rape crisis centres have sadly adopted this approach these days. Some Women's Aid groups will not take a survivor into the refuge once they learn about the type of abuse and will even ask a woman to leave once they find out what she is fleeing from. Usually this decision has come about because of a bad experience involving a survivor.

All of this is quite sad in that these groups and agencies which react like this have clearly lost the grassroots and feminist approach that once regarded every woman as an individual. Now, they too label and stereotype the woman as a Ritual Abuse survivor and therefore too difficult or dangerous to be offered a service. Some think that they cannot help because they believe that the survivor needs a more specialised service than they can offer. Even if this were to be true, given that there really are few specialised services available, the survivor is unlikely to get help from them. Sometimes the best help can be provided by a caring individual with no training but a good ability to listen to the survivor and help them find their own answers to their problems. Thankfully not all rape crisis groups or Women's Aid groups take this stance and some offer an excellent service to the female survivors that they encounter.

Survivors, when they escape from the group, tend not to have very many expectations of agencies and individuals. Over time and with support and encouragement this generally begins to change. The problem, which can then often occur, is that the survivor, if they find a caring and supportive

person, can end up with too many expectations from that particular individual. This is a common problem that workers in support agencies can encounter. Often, the more the worker gives, the higher become the expectations. Survivors who have never before encountered someone who actually cared about them can sometimes become rapidly dependant and even quite demanding upon the support worker in terms of time commitment and level of support. Experienced workers know how to set very clear boundaries and reduce the possibility of this happening, but less experienced workers often promise too much at the beginning because they want to help and inevitably without ever meaning to, let the survivor down.

Survivors tend to become very cynical over time. The more they access services as a survivor, the more quickly they tend to become disillusioned and cynical about what there is to help them. This is particularly the case for those who have had to seek help from mental health services. It is rare to find any survivors of ritual abuse who can praise any statutory agency or even think that the services that were provided by them adequate to their needs. This is not at all surprising given the lack of basic awareness and disbelief that is prevalent in most statutory agencies and in particular in mental health services.

Some survivors have been very lucky indeed and found quality support. Some have been lucky enough to find a person who would listen, believe and not judge them. Some have found a person or an agency with high awareness and also prepared to offer services suitable to the needs of survivors. Unfortunately only a few get lucky like this. This ought not to be the case and survivors ought not to have to rely on luck to get what they need and deserve. In time the increasing demands of survivors will begin to change this but it is a long and slow process and in the meantime there are many isolated survivors who are deserving of better services to help them escape from abuse and recover from their trauma.

Survivors Accounts

Lee

"People's reactions to me as a survivor: the official types: More sensible ways of allowing people to disclose information is needed. I read the books, got my society influence and decided I should go to the authorities when I was sixteen. I disclosed a bunch of information to the police only to be told they'd arrest my mother for a few hours and then release her. I was absolutely terrified. One of the people I was most scared of in my life was going to be questioned and become very angry, then be released knowing exactly where I lived. I wasn't offered any kind of protection, and suddenly the situation was turned and the police were making me feel like I was guilty for hesitating to give them more information. I begged them not to go ahead. It put me off authorities as bodies of society for life.

From my true friends over the years they have been supportive of me when I've wanted that support. If I'd just wanted to talk about the weather or whatever else, they haven't stopped me. They're the people that have said 'you can have your own life, you don't need a family'.

The authorities when I went to them, I wanted protection from abusers. I went to them because I believed it was the right thing to do (society influence), nothing else had worked. I had tried direct confrontation, apologising to mother for reactions that were perfectly justified and taking the blame which is not yours, telling your sister and knowing she'll only admit she knew what went on when she's drunk, and I was scared others would get hurt. I thought they would care more for my safety than my information. I was wrong."

Sheila

"It depends on the people. The majority of people won't know that I'm a survivor. People who do are close enough to accept me for who and what I am.

Not sure what people's expectations are of me. I don't know and I don't care. I suppose my hope would be for them to treat me as a person. Not to see me as a threat, for example, my G.P' (doctor) is scared of me."

Kay

"I don't tell anyone now. Only two friends will take my blurting stuff out. Everyone else who hears of the ritual abuse freezes and distances themselves, and I feel like a leper. The isolation of leading a split life is terrible, as my most important experiences and slow healing must almost never be talked of, except on the phone lines. Talking to people about incest was bad enough, even then half my friends felt I was hurting my father by not seeing him and pleaded with me to see him. Even the two friends who can accept the Ritual Abuse never speak of it, and one only half believes it, but is a great support. The other is amazing, has stuck by me and become a much deeper more rounded person.

Before my memories began to surface, I didn't want to know about Ritual Abuse, so I guess I understand people. I'd like to help raise the image of survivors from the media picture of pathetic victims. People who do help us on the phone lines are remarkable people, as is my therapist, when she's not being a pain."

Annie

"Most people don't know what to say and then you get those like a police officer I once tried to tell, who said, 'You've been reading too many Steven King books'. Even if he suspected that, you do not tell a young child that. A lot of my friends are shocked. People don't seem to expect that somebody that can hold down a normal life can be a survivor.

When people do find out they expect me to be a complete mess about it but I'm not so they can't understand and comments like 'if that had really happened you wouldn't still be smiling' really aren't helpful. My expectations of most people are to have them not believe me, and I think as a result of this I am starting to believe more and more people won't."

Nat

"It is hard to gauge people's reactions to you. I find that I put too much emphasis on how people see me. The range of reactions that people have is as numerous as they are varied. I have found that some people, even ones I counted as friends could not 'cope' with the fact that I am a survivor. They do not want to hear, and in the end I had to support them rather than getting support from them.

As I said there are many reactions, from thinking that you are too damaged, have mental health problems or out and out pity are some of the reactions I have witnessed from people. I have to say that I don't want to be seen just as a survivor. I am a person and a fellow human being. Any illnesses I have are a direct result of my abuse, this does not mean I have mental health problems. I certainly do not need any pity from anyone, I have survived something that I don't think many people could; maybe I should pity them?

Expectations

I think that one of the hardest expectations that I have had to deal with was that, once I escaped from the group, everything would be all right. Yes I got away from the abuse, but I lost everything. I lost my family, my home, my friends and also the situation in which I had coped for many years. Once the situation and the atmosphere of abuse had gone, I had nothing to fight against, nothing I needed to cope with. It was then that I believe the real nightmare began. I had to learn how to live in an essentially alien world, one with different rules and expectations, and to deal with the legacy my abusers had left me with.

To expect that someone will be healthy and happy when they leave an abusive situation reiterates the need for greater awareness. But if people need greater awareness, who is to teach them? Survivors will have to because no one else knows.

My expectations of people were at first nil. I had no expectations of anyone. I firmly believed that this was my mess and I would fix it. But when I had to interact with people, I found that I began to expect certain things. I expected people to believe me regardless of what I told them, not that I told them much. When I talked to the police this was the biggest expectation I had. I did not expect anyone to keep me safe. I believed that was something no one could do.

I think now that I have been away from the group for a few years, that I have greater expectations of people than they have of me. I place a good deal on trust, and if I am honest I find that the hardest thing to do, but I find that I can to a greater extent trust the people around me.

I think that I am still fiercely independent and would much rather do things on my own, but the saying that no man is an island definitely applies.

People's reactions...I guess it depends on who the people are. I haven't told many people that I am a survivor and I have told even less people that I am a Ritual Abuse survivor. The reactions I have witnessed not to me but towards other survivors have made me very reticent to divulge to many people that I am a survivor of ritual abuse.

I am not sure what people's expectations of me are, that I think is the hardest adjustment I have had to make. I have gone from the strictest rules and hierarchy, to having little or no rules and very few expectations. This is a hard adjustment to make, not knowing what people's expectations are and not knowing how you fit into this culture and essentially this new life.

In retrospect it seemed easier to know your place to know at all times what was expected of you and how you were to behave. But if I am being honest, you never knew what to expect because just as you thought you had one set of rules memorised, then they would change it. This was just so you got it wrong, so they could, as they saw it legitimately punish you for not knowing the rules.

I think the biggest chain reaction would have been the reaction throughout the group when I managed to escape. I so wished I could be a fly on the wall when they figured out that I was gone, not only gone but that I had gone to the police as well. But at the time, I was so worried and scared that they were going to find me and kill me that I never truly enjoyed that thought."

Lucky

"I have always found that the best way to deal with the reactions of other people is quite simply not to let them know anything. I used to tell myself that someday I would shock everyone by revealing all about my past but I think that would be a waste of time and energy. I have occasionally let someone know that I am a survivor but I am very careful who becomes privy to such personal information.

There have been a couple of memorable occasions when I made an error of judgement and told the wrong people about the abuse I had experienced in childhood. They quite simply took and used the information against me and it took quite a struggle on my part to be able to turn the situation around. Partly this was because I found it so hard to believe that anyone who I had trusted enough with personal and sensitive information would use it against me. They say that you live and learn!

The problem with sharing personal information of a sensitive nature is that once the information is out in the public domain, there is no way to take it back other than say that you have been lying about it all in the first place. I personally rarely feel it is relevant to give anyone information which can be used against myself at a later date. I don't think there is ever really any need for someone to know such stuff.

As for expectations of other people, I think I can safely say that I have none. I found that having expectations of people leads only to further feelings of let down and disappointment. A long time ago, I used to expect that everyone I met would be in some way abusive but am happy to say that I have moved beyond this now.

I suppose if there is anything I have expectations about it is that if I were to speak out I would not be believed by very many people. I do not expect this to change for a very long time to come. I will therefore keep my own council for a while yet."

John

"This is tough simply because it's still going on, the reactions and the expectations. As a child I told my mum about the abuse and she told me it was a bad dream. I wasn't even sleeping! Now when I speak about my abuse to others its one of two reactions I get.

1. They just ignore me, watch TV or change the subject or,
2. Preach to me about how it might not be real, it might just be in my head.

As for expectations, as I said growing up was to be a church goer 9am – 5pm., anything else wasn't acceptable. Expectations now are much the same except the church has been substituted by TV and work, football and drink, degradation and gossip."

Ruth

"Do not let yourself get down when they do not want to help you or to understand. There are people out there who do understand plus there are people now who say we should be locked up for life. They do not understand that we have been locked up inside ourselves all these years. Now we want to be free and happy. So why should we keep quiet any longer? We want to live and make sure that no one else gets hurt like us.

You must keep going and you will get strong. You will be a winner. Just like the rest of the people who went through what we are going through just now."

THE GREAT ESCAPE

THE GREAT ESCAPE

Most of the knowledge and information that we currently have about ritual abuse is provided by survivors who have escaped or been rescued from their group. This is partly because it is so hard for survivors who are currently involved to find a safe person to talk to and almost impossible for them to talk about what is going on for them while still living with the abuse. It is really only when survivors get away that they begin to talk about the abuse and share information. Survivors who seriously want to get out of the group usually do so because they hate the life that they are leading and disagree with the abusers to some degree. Once they recover from the trauma they are much more likely to want people to learn about the group and the abuse that goes on within it.

It has to be said that not all children who are born into a satanic or similar type of group and are abused within it, will want to leave it. Though it is almost impossible to leave a group, there is often an assumption that all would want to leave. This is not always the case. Many people as they become adults make the active choice to remain in the group. These are the people who become so conditioned by their experiences that they do not ever question the ideology or practices they have grown up with. These are also the people who will carry the religion, beliefs and accompanying abuse onto the next generation. Most of these people strongly believe in what they are doing and believe that they have the right to carry on. They also benefit from it all.

People's positions vary in these groups. They vary according to the structure of the group, the parents of the child, the decisions made at the child's birth and the perceived intelligence, ability and usefulness of the individual child to the group. Those people who find themselves 'lower down' in the hierarchy of power and abuse are the ones most likely to want to escape from the group because their abuse is often more overt that the any of the others. These are the people much more likely to be regarded as expendable and therefore more likely to be at the sharper end of extremes of torture and physical and sexual abusive activities. These are the ones more likely to become the sacrifices for the group and to be regarded through time as completely worthless to the group. Often the prettier ones, or those who look younger, may survive longer as they might be used in pornography and prostitution and thus they bring in some finance for the group.

behind
enemy**lines**

Yet these people who are at the lower end of the hierarchy are often the ones with the least opportunity to actually escape from the group. Some will not have been registered at birth and will therefore have no public identity. They seldom come in contact with any authorities and will not be registered with a doctor, dentist or school. They are often very closely guarded and some of them become so badly emotionally and psychologically damaged by the abuse that they do not even have the capacity to think about or ever seek to escape. Some give up entirely and accept their limited lives as best they can even to the point of believing that what is happening to them is right and that they deserve their lot in life. Others, a few, do seek to escape and some do make it away from the group. The evidence we have for this are those survivors who have shared their experiences with supportive individuals and in the pages of this book.

For those with the capacity to achieve higher positions in the group, particularly the highest positions, there is less likelihood that they will ever want to leave or escape from the group. These are the people who, in time, tend to gain to quite a high degree from the activities of the group. Though they may suffer a great deal as children while they are 'being taught' the ways of the group and they may suffer in the name of the cause, to some degree, the gains they receive more often outweigh the losses. As they grow up, they are granted more and more power and say in the activities of the group. Rather than being hurt, they can pick someone else who gets hurt instead of them. Given that those with higher position become the bosses in most groups, they are more likely to stay involved in something that they directly benefit from.

Even as children the hierarchy of power is rapidly learned and children learn to fight in whatever way they can for their own survival. If their survival is made dependant on the suffering of someone or something else, they learn to accept this quite quickly. Survival of the fittest becomes the real name of the game as children are constantly pitted against each other. The quickest and the cleverest rapidly learn that their own pain can be lessened as they gain in power. The stronger and more clever ones reach for and aspire to that power initially as a means of their own survival. No matter the position, if a child can survive long enough and become ruthless and clever enough, they can in most groups climb to higher positions of greater power.

Those who are 'destined' for position and power most usually achieve it because most things are balanced in their favour. Sometimes though the teaching and early training of these children has been so extreme that it has already broken their spirits, in which case they often become completely useless to the group. They can even become a liability to the group in that

they may be so mentally damaged that they might even talk. The group will make sure that these casualties are taken care of in the best way possible for the group. Even amongst those who are destined for position, there has to be some way of weeding out those who are in some way unsuitable and not strong enough to make it. Some become completely hardened to all forms of human or animal suffering in a way that the untrained 'lower' children could not ever contemplate.

The children from the so called 'lower' positions are much more likely to, in some ways, care for each other and tend to stick together against those destined for the positions of power. The children with positions to aspire to are often seen as the enemy by those with little hope of anything. There can be no friendships or even acquaintances for those who will hold power and they must be constantly seen to be worthy of this honour. Thus, from an early age, those children who are destined for power and position, learn to trust no one at all, learn they are totally alone in the world and learn through time to become completely self reliant.

They learn the basic lesson that to be powerful is to be in control. They learn that they gain tremendously though taking and holding power and they learn that the more ruthless they are, the more they will be feared and the more power they will then hold through that fear. They learn that fear is an important key to winning and that the only way to play anything is to play to win. By fair means or foul they learn to always win and thus survive. Such is the depth of their learning and the degree of what they have had to do to survive, plus what they have gained and what they are still to gain, that few seek to leave the group if they are in this type of position. However, some, a few do try to leave for a multitude of reasons. We know this from the testimony of some survivors who have shared their stories with us.

Getting away from any abuse situation is never easy and is rarely accomplished without considerable effort, planning and usually several attempts. For those attempting to escape from an abusive group of people it is even harder. Many survivors fight for many years to escape from the group and most often from their own family which is closely connected to the group. To attempt escape and then fail is a very painful lesson for any survivor to learn. The vast majority learn the lesson early in life and some learn it so well that they never attempt to leave again. Younger children are even encouraged to run away at some point so that they can be rapidly taught the error of their ways while still at an impressionable age.

Many survivors do escape from the groups and some are even allowed to leave under certain controlled conditions. Providing the group is certain that they will not be betrayed, sometimes it is more expedient for the group to allow a troublesome or too costly survivor to just leave. Usually there is still a great deal of control from the group and some survivors are forced to go back periodically to the group for certain rituals or ceremonies. For the survivor this is sometimes preferable to being involved all the time. Though the abuse continues, there is at least some limited freedom. Some survivors do not even regard this as abuse.

Few survivors get away completely and manage to stay clear of the group forever at their first attempt at escaping. Often the past lurks close behind them and for many they are constantly harassed, threatened and even attacked to remind them of the power of the group. Often this ensures that silence is maintained as the survivors fear that if they speak out, the violence will increase or they will be forced back into the group. The reality of this is that it is very unlikely that a group would take back someone who had already betrayed them to some extent by leaving. How could that person ever be fully trusted again within the group? This is particularly the case if the survivor is an adult.

Children are more readily forgiven their escape attempts. Indeed it is expected that they try. This can be used by the abusers to further control the child. They have much more worth than an adult and can be much more easily manipulated than an adult. It is so much easier to control a child than an adult who might repeatedly try to escape and may compromise the principles and reveal identities of group members. Secret organisations must at all costs maintain secrecy therefore they are unlikely to want a loose cannon amongst them. Survivors who try to escape cannot be trusted by a group and will seldom be privy to any information about a group or any of its members.

Survivors Accounts

Lee

"I got away from the group before I got away from my family. For me to be able to grow completely, to bloom, I had to get away from both. My father turned up at one of the ceremonies when my mother had a large knife to my throat. My father and I ran through the woods. The incident was never brought up, but my father got a lot of bruises that night. I was never taken back to the ceremonies.

I finally managed to break free of my mother in the year 2000, at age twenty-two. I spent years moving around the country, and ran away from home at the age of fifteen. I was blackmailed into coming back. I moved gradually further and further away from where my mother lived but until the year 2000 always went back to take care of her. I have come to the conclusion over the years that I am much more important than my family/ the group."

Billie

"I came from a very large family. Close family and extended family were all involved in Satanic worship and various other illegal activities. All of them participated in the sadistic, organised, sexual abuse of children. I was one of these children.

My first task in life was to learn how to cope with this abuse on a day to day basis and find ways to survive it. The next major hurdle as I got older was to find ways to escape from it. This I was finally able to do when I was in my twenties. By the time I got away I had become completely desperate. I was being subjected to frequent rapes and these were followed by several forced abortions. These were carried out mostly by the female relatives in the group.

It took me more than twenty years to recover from the abuse I experienced. These days I am strong but there are times when it is still hard. I am growing stronger every day I survive. These days I live my life more fully and enjoy my life better. I am no longer just surviving rather I would say that I am thriving."

Kay

"Leaving the house where my father knew where to find me, even though I'd not seen him for eighteen months, was the toughest time of my life. It also meant not seeing any relative, as he constantly circulates among them as a "grand old man".

I only managed it because I knew my brother had killed himself when dependant on my parents, and that my mother had wanted to get away from my father."

Annie

"I tried more than once to get away. I failed on many occasions. This failure is down to both the abusive group and me. I went on the run. I slept rough, and I went to refuges and to friends."

Nat

"It took me a long time to get away from the group. I don't think that was intentional, more of getting past all my teachers and anyone that could have noticed that something was wrong. Eventually, when I knew that I would not remain alive for much longer, I told someone the tiniest detail of my life. Things changed rapidly from there. I was taken to a support agency and I finally found someone who noticed and managed to encourage me to talk to the police. I know this may sound like a very hurried and drastic measure but retrospectively it was the only way that I was going to survive.

The abuse was reaching a very nasty crescendo and I had to make the choice of living because as I have mentioned earlier, the body and the mind have this innate survival instinct, which even I, could not ignore.

I think that to escape from a group requires more than a physical relocation, but this concept may be more appropriate in the safety section.

I did escape, but I guess it is true that all good things come at a price. I think that I paid several times over. I did not miss the abuse, but I had to endure giving statements to the police, medicals, and the knowledge that I would lose all that I was familiar with, family, friends and my home. Things were never the same again.

I got away from the group only with other people's help. I don't think I would have managed it otherwise. I was so thoroughly disillusioned with society and was so fully demoralised by the group I didn't care about what was going to happen to me. But if that statement was wholly true then I don't think I would be here today.

The abuse was getting more extreme I had every reason to believe that at any point they were going to kill me. This was never an idle threat and I knew that at any point they could do this. The fact that the abuse had become more extreme and sadistic only served to strengthen that thought. I guess I got scared, and didn't really want to die. It's not that I didn't want to die, that would have been an end to it all, its that I didn't want to die at their hands. I felt that at least my death would not be caused by them.

So I went and told someone, not the details, in fact as people tell me now I never really said very much in the beginning. I just said enough for people to listen. I never thought they would believe me or listen to me. I had tried when I was a teenager to tell, to get away but people hadn't wanted to listen then, or maybe they couldn't.

What is more important? I would have said the group, and in some ways I still protect them, but I don't think they are more important than other things. They are still more important than me. I haven't managed to shift that line of thinking yet, but other people are more important to me than they are. I have learned what it is like to live with people and not be hurt and for people to truly love me for who and what I am. They may not have lost all their power over me, but I feel it loosening as I have seen what it would have been like to grow up in a loving family environment."

Lucky

"I was very much a product of my upbringing. I thought only of myself and ran away even though I knew for certain that other kids would suffer for my running. At the time, I thought nothing of them or anyone else, all I had in my mind was my own personal survival. That was how it was and I wish I could say that I worried about those I left behind but the plain truth was that I did not.

I had tried so many times to get away and had always been found and dragged back home. Each time I tried, though I was punished for trying, I learned new things. One of the most important things I began to learn was that if I was going to make it, I was going to have to plan properly and trust and tell no one at all. Running blind was one of the most certain ways to get caught. When I left home for the last time, even although I was not certain at the time that it really was the last time, I was well prepared with plans of places to go and ideas for survival.

For many years after escaping the group, I continued to survive by thinking only about my own needs. I cared nothing about anyone else at all and survival became everything to me at all costs. It was only in later, less desperate years that I began to think about others and then I felt so guilty that I had done nothing except survive.

In fairness to myself, in hindsight, I don't know what else I could have done differently at the time. Sometimes the instinct for survival drives people so hard that nothing else gets in. That was a long time ago but as clear in my memory today as ever. For years I ran and ran and found it hard to think about anything as the fear was so great inside me.

It took me a long, long time to realise that I had actually escaped. The feelings, the memories, the desperation and the fear drove me for such a long time. Then one day I looked around me and wondered what on earth I was hiding from and I realised it was actually myself. I hated thinking about my background though it had made me who I now was. I fretted over all that I had lost rather than seeing all that I had gained and gradually began to look forward instead of backwards. That's when I really began to escape from the group and the abuse.

Getting away from abuse of any kind is a process and not just a single act. Even when you get away, because you are looking back over your shoulder all the time, you are not really free. As long as all the bad memories are flashing in and out of your head and your feelings are of panic and desperation you are not really free of it all. It takes time, effort and sometimes support to completely escape from the group."

John

"Nobody likes going to church and I always tried to not go but only succeeded when I was sixteen years old. As for stopping the grooming there were several instances where action should have been taken by my family but it wasn't.

I was cutting my arms when I was just a kid, going crazy when I couldn't take the bullying anymore. But the only real escape was high school. I took to drugs, fighting, staying at friends, drinking, anything to avoid the games and the pissed up violent arguments."

Carol

"An Attempt to Escape
I can remember trying to escape, running from a cellar underground, a night of torture and abuse. The dawn was breaking as I tried to run for my life, no clothes on, up this secluded road into the woods. I hid shaking and weak behind a tree watching three of them running, searching for me. "Where was I going I do not know" last thing I remember is a huge hand, it seemed, reaching over me and all went black. Of course I got caught and severely punished but "One Day I Would Make It".

The Escape

It was winter, and at nearly seventeen years old the care system had abandoned me a long, long time ago. I put a plan in action ~ day, time, and a short-term place of near safety with others around. I got home "Horror" they were there and suspicious. I shouted "I was leaving" world war two broke out and in the midst of it I ran for my hidden bag, but getting out the door my Foster mother grabbed my Only Boots. Terrified, torn shoes, I got to the city, my friend waiting.

The Women's Army: By now I had great sores round my face, a mess. The medical officer looked at my body while I pleaded to let me in ~ I was tough. "At least you'll get fed I suppose." He then put Money in my pocket for the train, a Bible, Food, and Boots were put on my feet. It was indeed Christmas.

He will never know how much he did that day.

What is more important~group or you?
There was a big world outside, and maybe I only knew my little bit of Island, but I was willing to take that chance and survive, rather then this life of control, pain, and horror. But Survival meant leaving the others behind and dissociating from that conflict. I have suffered by self-harm in many ways, but now it is time to try to forgive myself and grieve for the ones I HAD to leave behind. There was No choice."

SANCTUARY

SANCTUARY

For many survivors of abuse the ideal of a sanctuary to which they can eventually escape and find safety and peace of mind, is but a hollow dream. Some have dreamed about it during the more difficult times in their lives. Some have prayed for it. Some have hoped it might someday be possible to find it. Some have had no notion or concept of the possibility of any sanctuary ever. Some believe that there is no such thing at all and therefore do not even try to look for it while others strive continually towards finding some sort of a sanctuary. Most of the survivors who contributed to this book were somewhat sceptical about the notion of any sanctuary anywhere in the world and some saw it as having too many religious connotations.

One has to wonder if some survivors of extreme abuse tend to be realists or even so totally sceptical that they just cannot imagine what real sanctuary would be like. For those people who have never experienced a totally safe refuge and the feelings to match this, the basic concept itself can be an extremely difficult one to grasp. How is it possible to know or experience something you have never had? Yet some people do strongly feel the absence of something they have never had and even try to imagine what it would be like. Some survivors think that it is something that only other people can achieve, but not them.

As at least one survivor points out, the word sanctuary is somewhat synonymous with a religious notion of seeking personal safety in a church and of being shielded from harm by a strong religious body. For many survivors of ritual abuse this is a difficult concept to try and get their heads round particularly if there has been a particular religious aspect involved in their own particular experiences of abuse. Indeed, many abusive groups focus on trying to ensure that the survivors will not go near the dominant and hopefully non–abusive religion in their area. This means that many survivors are less likely to seek help from a church of any kind. For some because the word sanctuary holds religious connotations, they do not see it as something they would ever want to have.

Many survivors talk of having to go regularly to attend a 'normal' church. They talk of growing up in a family, which pretended to the world that they were all Christians and regular church-goers. Some talk of being abused in churches after the 'normal' religious activities have ceased and unknown to most of the regular churchgoers. Some talk of some members of 'normal' churches being involved in the abusive group also. Others talk of the abusive

group practising under the name of the dominant religion and abusing them within it using the church symbolism and different aspects of the religion to hurt and abuse them and other people. Some survivors talk of being taught about how inferior and weak the 'normal' and prevailing religion is and how hypocritical those who practise or believe in it are.

Perhaps those most likely to believe the survivors of ritual abuse and in particular survivors of satanic ritual abuse are those who hold a faith and a belief in a God. Those with a faith that encompasses the beliefs in the existence of both good and evil are possibly much more likely to believe that evil exists in the world. Fundamental Christians appear to be more readily able to accept that satanism exists and is practised in this country than other people who have no religious faith. Indeed some Christians have been listening to, believing and supporting survivors of ritual abuse for many years now. Those survivors who manage to get past any fears they may have of religion can get a great deal of help from people they do not have to convince about the evil that exists in the world.

In view of some of this, it is little wonder that abusers try to ensure that it is extremely difficult for the survivors to approach these institutions for help. Abusers strive to make it as difficult as possible for survivors to go to anyone for help. They make a point of teaching survivors that Christians are liars and hypocrites because they know that Christians are more likely to believe survivors of this type of abuse. It is the same thing they do to put survivors off talking to the police when they say that people in the police are involved in abusive groups. Abusers do whatever they can think of to minimise the possibility of survivors talking at all or being listened to and believed.

It is interesting to think a few thoughts about a possible radical change that could conceivably take place in this society and improve it tremendously. If there were to be enough awareness raised about the existence of ritual abuse and if the many non-abusive religious organisations could be brought on board on the side of survivors, they could possibly provide a very real sanctuary for the survivors. If enough Christians and other faiths, including their institutions, were to join in the fight against those who worship and believe in the complete opposite from them, we could perhaps really get somewhere. It would not matter if everyone did not believe that ritual abuse happens or not at first, only that they begin to join in the fight.

Imagine what it could be like if every church and holy place in the United Kingdom were to open their doors wide and invite survivors of all kinds of abuse in to stay there in safety. Perhaps if survivors were offered a guaranteed safe space where they could stay for as long as they wanted, a

real physical and spiritual sanctuary rather than a daily struggle to survive more might manage to break away from the group more quickly. Possibly many more would be able to stay away from the influences of the abusive group if they had a real sanctuary to protect them. If there was such a thing as a real mental, spiritual and physical refuge available then society might see increasing numbers of survivors come forward for help. If this were to happen, then, from a place of safety survivors might sooner find a voice.

Some survivors do not view sanctuary as a place at all but rather as a state of mind to sometimes accompany actual physical safety. As some of the survivors point out, even when physically safe, a person may still feel very unsafe. Just providing physical refuge does not always change how someone feels particularly if the person is feeling very afraid. Some survivors hold the view that real sanctuary is found on the inside of self and/or with people that are trusted by the survivor. For some survivors there is a feeling of having found some sort of sanctuary in the world after escaping from the group, though this is not the case for all of them. Some survivors do not view sanctuary as anything more than a word which means nothing at all to them.

Survivors are individuals and their experiences and views are equally individual to them. The views on the concept of sanctuary as expressed by the survivors who have contributed to this book are as varied and different as are the individuals concerned.

Lee

"Sanctuary: - that's an interesting word. I don't think where matters as much as who. I don't miss my family, those who are alive anyway. I have a bunch of good friends, and my own life now, and no guilty feelings for not being there to take care of my mother. Finding it hasn't been easy, but friends have helped a great deal, and so has self determination.

No one can make you more determined to do anything than yourself and from this comes empowerment when you no longer have anyone dragging you back down again. It can be found out side of the dictionary, but can take lots of self determination and some really good friends."

Sheila

"No it {sanctuary} doesn't exist anywhere except in the dictionary. If it does I haven't found it yet."

Kay

"The therapist who saved my life helped me get settled in a rented place. I began to feel safe for the first time in my life, with my father unable to find me though he did not try very hard. I was lucky in that I'd already lived in and had wanted to return to this city.

It was incredibly hard to start again, and without the therapist, trained in ritual abuse work, I could not have done it. There were no real support places or any support groups or drop in women's centres. Some old friends dropped me, and I'd no work."

Annie

"I've still not found my ultimate sanctuary but I am learning more and more that a sanctuary is anywhere you can escape to for safety. I now have more than one place. These range from my time spent on the phone to 'SAFE' (an organisation in England which provides support to survivors) people to hiding away on a website. I don't see it as a place to be I see it as a space to be.

It {sanctuary} does exist but it is hard to find and everyone has to make up their own definition of what sanctuary actually is."

Nat

"Sanctuary to me is a funny word to use. I guess because of the religious connotations it has for me. You know the thing in the old movies where the good guy who is wrongly accused goes and seeks sanctuary in the church. I found sanctuary not with an ideal, but with ordinary down to earth people. It was not the so-called experts or psychotherapists but with ordinary caring people who managed to listen without judging me.

It wasn't easy to find but when I think about it, I think that sanctuary found me. I think I was looking for it, without knowing what it was and it found me. Whether this is pure chance and coincidence or not or some kind of destiny, I will leave that up to the size of cynic you are.

I think it would be hard to find something that you have no concept of. You can believe that sanctuary the word means a safe place but if you have no notion of what a safe place either looks, or feels like, how can you know when you are in it and if it is really safe?

I can believe and did believe that sanctuary existed in the dictionary. I now believe that it exists both within and without me. I found it in people who were willing to care, to love and accept me and I think I am finding it within myself, although that is a long and slow and very hard process sometimes. But it is good to believe that something good does exist and can exist for you.

Sanctuary for me is a safe place, not just physically safe but emotionally too. It is safe not only physically but metaphysically too. You cannot create a sense of perfect sanctuary because it comes from within and without. You don't just happen upon it. It takes work and patience, not just from you but from the people that surround you, that are there for you. So yes I believe sanctuary exists not just for movie stars but for anyone who is willing to work for it. To know that things can be different, that you truly can be safe, it may not happen over night in fact it is impossible for sanctuary to be created overnight.

It is not just physical but a mental state, you can be in the safest place in the world have all the doors and locks between you and the rest of the world but that is just a safe place with locks. If you don't feel safe all the locks in the world are not going to create it for you.

Nell

"Sanctuary, always seems to hold religious connotations for me, have I found sanctuary? I don't think I have yet. I believe that you can find sanctuary or safety when you escape from the group, but even then are you truly safe? You believe that they are going to come after you, that terrible things are going to happen when they find you. You can be safe, you can be in the most secure place in the world, yet you can still believe that they will find you. There is no safety or sanctuary in the place where I need it most, in my head.

I don't believe that I have sanctuary. I don't think that finding sanctuary is or will be an easy task. I think for me I will need to move away from their belief system and formulate my own. I will have to have faith and belief in myself, to believe that I am a person as worthwhile as everyone else, I don't believe that. So is sanctuary merely a safe place? I don't believe so. I believe sanctuary is more than that. It is a feeling, a notion of safety, one that you believe in wholeheartedly. It isn't a safe place while the wolves are baying at the door. It can't be or we will all be stuck behind the thick doors of the safe place forever, never venturing out because we are afraid of the wolves that are behind the door.

I think it can exist out with the dictionary, although I think that the definition will be different for each individual. For me it is not only a place of safety it is a feeling of being safe and secure, knowing that they will always be out there, but that they can't hurt me anymore, because I will not allow it."

Lucky

"Sanctuary is for me a whole mental state, which lets me know that I really am okay at the moment. I remember when, for the first time in my limited experience I felt as though I had found sanctuary. It was a brief and fleeting moment but it let me know that such a thing could exist for me.

At the time, I was a young teenager and was in my grandmother's house when my parents came in unexpectedly and caught me there. I was in deep trouble. It was forbidden for me to go alone to my grandmother's house but I had gone anyway not expecting to get caught by them. I could tell that my parents were both absolutely furious and knew that I was about to suffer the consequences of my latest indiscretion. I found myself growing very embarrassed and felt completely humiliated that my grandmother was going to witness my punishment. My grandmother knew nothing about the abuse or the secret religion. I did not want her to see them hit me. I suppose I was protecting her from knowing what was going on.

My father's voice was raised and threatening but my grandmother cut right through what he was saying and she told him to sit down and shut up, which, to my complete amazement he instantly did! And then my grandmother, all four foot nothing of her, set about lecturing him and my mother about my lack of visits to her. Somehow, she turned the whole thing around and before I knew what was happening, I was allowed to stay the night that night in my grandmother's house and tasted peace and brief sanctuary. It was totally incredible and I sat up most of the night in her tiny spare room savouring the moment and the feelings. I had never felt like this before and could hardly believe that my little, seemingly powerless grandmother had stood up to my powerful parents and bought me a sense of sanctuary.

For me though that brief taste of something wonderful and so much better than I was used to made my life all the harder to endure. You can endure the most terrible things if you have never known anything else is possible. I now knew for certain that other people lived differently. I now knew that my grandmother lived very differently from me. I also knew that my parents, though powerful, were not god or Satan. They were not as powerful as I had thought them to be. They had backed down before a small elderly woman. I tasted something different for the first time ever. I knew that I wanted that feeling of peace and safety back more than I had ever wanted anything in my short life. I was determined that I would have this.

It was partly this that drove me and kept driving me with the thought that I could get away and be able to feel okay in the world. After I escaped I only had to picture my grandmother standing up to my parents to know that I must not give up or give in to threats. No matter how hard things became, I knew that there was something good out there in the world that I could have a piece of. This stopped me going back when things became tough. This made me fight and keep on fighting until I was totally free of them."

John

"I think safety is stability and is required sometimes in the form of support when we are totally suicidal. I personally don't believe in safety as life is always changing. Safe for me three years ago was being homeless on whatever drugs I could get my hands on and crying and cutting myself or violently punching the ground. I know now that I had to have that release, but it is no longer safe in my current situation.

Safety is a state of mind, and the system wants us to hide or come out. I feel I have been doing something different. Me when I was in the shelter place, I was a typical fucked up teenager. Into drugs, punk music, tattooed, violent and mysterious. But in reality, I was only escaping things that restricted me and embracing things that opposed that restriction. To the system it looks like I've given up hope, but deep down I know I'm stronger than the system at my very weakest because I haven't given up hope. I never gave up on humanity or god, it's all about faith, to achieve it you need to believe it."

Carol

"Sanctuary: Women and Men's Army, where on my eighteenth birthday we walked into an Army bar where my eyes met with this Male Scottish Army Trainee. A deep love although a turbulent marriage that was to last for twenty three years".

SAFETY

SAFETY

Safety means different things to people at different times of their lives. Many people who have never known the fear, brainwashing and reality of group life would find it difficult to believe that even on getting away from the abuse, survivors often do not feel safe. In fact, for many, the escape from the group leaves them feeling less safe than ever before. At least when they were in the group they knew to some extent where they stood. Once they have left, they can no longer see the abusers. They no longer know what is going on and what people in the family and the group are doing. They do not know what is being planned especially in regard to them. It is incredibly frightening to be afraid of something or someone but not be in a position to know where they are or what they are doing.

Survivors who escape from the group do have a fairly clear idea about what will happen to them if they get caught and dragged back to the group. They know that, at the very least, they will face extreme punishment, abuse and total humiliation. The imagination works away in most people and often increases the feelings of fear tremendously in such circumstances. Some survivors find the fear so difficult to deal with that they willingly return home in the hope of escaping from or reducing the punishment. For them, facing a known danger is easier to deal with than living with the constant fear of the unknown and fear of getting caught.

Survivors who get away from the group seldom get away cleanly or completely at first. Getting away from any type of abuse is a process and with ritual abuse it is much the same process. Most frequently survivors are harassed, threatened and even attacked when the abusers find out where they are living. It is not very difficult for the abusers to find survivors and begin to frighten them. Survivors are relatively easy to frighten particularly when they first get away from the group. This harassment can go on for many years and it is extremely rare for survivors to contact the police and complain about it. Yet this would be the one thing that could possibly put an end to it once and for all. Few survivors of this type of abuse could contemplate this course of action however.

This means that such abuse can persist over a long period of time and often has the effect of keeping the survivor silent and to some degree still under the power of the abusers. Some groups even drag the survivor back repeatedly and use them for some of their events or for prostitution or pornography. Again, this increases the fear, increases the power and control

and the survivor cannot rise far enough above the abuse to seek constructive help and support to break away completely. This way the abusers are able to keep the survivors subdued and accepting of the constant abuse. Survivors often accept this level of abuse as they regard it as much better than what they had experienced before.

Some do not get physically attacked but are kept in a high state of fear and terror by the constant threats, letters, cards with messages or phone calls they receive. Often these are more persistent during significant times when the survivor is understandably very upset already. Again, the survivor finds it difficult to ever feel safe enough to talk to someone or get support. A survivor who tried to report what was happening to the police would quite simply not be understood properly unless they were able to give all the background to what was going on. Though the survivor might be experiencing a degree of mental torture and extremes of fear, it would require some proper understanding of ritual abuse to appreciate what was actually happening. Unless people have some awareness of the issues involved, they cannot really understand why the survivor is so afraid.

It is easy for abusive groups to occasionally send a card with something in it, or on it, which they know will have a major impact on a survivor. The message sent would be a reminder of something and designed to trigger a memory or cause some distress. The key aims of such actions are most certainly to keep the survivor in a high state of fear and alarm. The real beauty, for want of a better way of describing it, of this particular form of harassing survivors is that it would be difficult if not downright impossible for the survivor to explain to anyone exactly why they are so terrified. Most people would not find a card or message a threat and would therefore find it hard to understand what is really going on. Few would be able to understand the meaning of any threatening symbols or be aware of the specific languages used by the group to get their point of view over to the survivor.

For many survivors safety is very much a state of mind rather than an actual place. But there needs to be a safe place to live also. Survivors need to be able to secure a place that is physically safe to see to their basic need for physical safety as until they are physically safe it is impossible to begin to achieve emotional safety. Like everyone else, they need a roof over their heads and locked doors as a starting place to safety. For some, actually feeling safe is a very long time in coming to them as they continue to try and deal with the trauma they have experienced and the aftermath of leaving the group.

It is common for survivors to move house repeatedly and keep on moving every time the abusers track them down. They expect to be found eventually

when they move but at least they may have had a few months of relative safety and peace before they are found again. Some survivors are so used to uprooting and changing address that they quite simply keep their belongings in bags so that they can move on as quickly as possible. Many live like this for many years and become so used to it that they accept it as normal and simply a price to pay for their personal safety.

Over time, issues of safety do change for the survivors. As survivors eventually get further and further removed from the group and the abuse, their needs begin to change. Often they begin to get some help and support and slowly they find their feelings changing. For some, their physical safety is no longer the main issue. Many begin to face up to their various fears and may look for ways to improve their lives. Survivors can and do go on to lead normal lives as they begin to recover from the trauma and find a sense of safety. They eventually begin to form a variety of relationships and friendships as they get to know and learn to trust people more. Often they go on to secure and hold down jobs, including professional positions and they can settle down in the same way as everyone else does. Many go on to have children of their own.

If the abusers are still anywhere near the survivor who has rebuilt their life, they may still try occasional threats. Sometimes the survivors will have moved to a position where they will defy their abusers and fight back against them in a more direct manner. They have reached the stage of no longer being afraid of them. Rather their concerns often become for their own children and others. It is often the fears for the safety of others, particularly other children, that eventually drives a survivor to think about taking the very difficult step of going to the police and making a complaint against their abusers. For some, even doing this feels extremely unsafe and given their personal histories, it is indeed a very risky thing for them to try and do. Nevertheless, some do feel strongly about the safety of others to attempt this course of action. Some feel that the only way they can safeguard others is to complain to the police.

It is quite rare for a survivor of ritual abuse to try and talk to the police because they fear for their own safety. Rather, most only approach the police at the point when they feel safe enough to do so. Few will go forward while they themselves at being threatened or attacked which is a great shame as they would most probably get help. Rather it is the concern that other children are still being abused that most often drives a survivor to try and stop the abusers. Though going to the police often has the effect of making the survivor feel quite unsafe again, many are prepared to try and expose the abusers for the sake of children who might still be getting abused. Unfortunately, it is rarely easy for the survivor to speak to the police, and is even rarer to get the abusers stopped.

Survivors Accounts

Lee

"The safety issues have definitely changed over the years. When I was a small kid it used to be if I kept my mouth shut I'd be okay. I didn't actually talk until I was four when I realised it didn't matter.

To keep safe for me for a long time was equated with keeping my mother happy. Living away from home was great for me because it gave me time for myself to be safe without worrying about my mother. I think safety is a combination of yourself and the people around you. I don't think we should hide, but hiding at times is necessary, or maybe just a little caution. Then again, it does depend on what hiding means?

If to hide is to allow yourself as safe a life as possible by changing one small part of you such as your name, I wouldn't count this as hiding. But if you get in a position where your life is taken over by doing things to hide, then this takes away the time that you have for yourself."

Sheila

"Trying not to come into contact with anyone from the past is safety. The safety issues haven't changed they are very much the same as before. I am still trying to get away from people who I'm not feeling safe with.

Safety for me is a feeling, and that feeling comes from people in the past. They told me that no matter where I was they would always find me. I don't think we should hide we should stand up and be counted. That doesn't remove the safety issue for me, I won't ever feel safe."

Kay

"I was very scared of meeting my father and of pressure by other relatives. Now I have begun to see the horror of my childhood and the things they did, the ambivalence has turned to anger. A year later, I think they may know where I am, as one or two odd things happen, but I feel stronger. I'm no longer torn into pieces by feeling I should help the old man, who I now see as a major criminal.

I think safety is also in the mind, in recovering my inner children, in gaining strength against adversity. Maybe it is also in deciding to speak out, despite my fear of getting eliminated in an "accident". In this I've been totally inspired by Laurie's introduction to "Where Angels Fear", and, because I write, feel safety may, as she said, lie in speaking out."

Annie

"My safety issues are still current as I still have problems. They have changed over the years but now issues include making sure I am safe and have access to support when needed.

There are other safety issues such as making sure that any injuries I have are cared for okay. My current dangers are the possibility of more abuse. I haven't really got safe yet but am working on it. I don't really know what safety is. How can any of us know what something is if we have never experienced it?

I find it hard to care about safety when it is something I know so little about. I don't think we should hide but I do think there are times we get forced to or need to for our own sanity."

Nat

I had just escaped a pretty tough situation, not only that I had gone to the police. But there were still people around who would have gone to great lengths to keep me from talking. The fact that I didn't move that far away from my hometown was a disadvantage as I could see them often.

I needed a safe place to be as well as I had effectively changed my life but lost it as well. I lost my home, my family and essentially my sense of belonging not only because I was breaking the rules surrounding talking, but also there was the betrayal I was committing to the group.

I had lost everything when I told. Before that there were attempts to get me to safety but the hold of the group was so strong. No, that's not strictly accurate. My sense of loyalty to my family was so strong that I could not imagine the very real sense of getting them into trouble and leaving them and how dishonourable that was for me. I had obligations. Duties that were mine and I felt as if I was betraying them.

The safety issues have changed. I have told and people believe me. I am not sure whether my group would so readily attempt to get me back. I am not sure how I would react to those attempts now anyway. Not that this has much to do with safety.

I believe that I am stronger than I was before, so in that, the safety issues have changed. But the people are less likely to want to attack or try to pull me back because time has passed and they saw that I talked. Okay, not extensively but that I talked and even talked to the police so they had to have concerns about their own safety.

It was hard to believe that I would ever get safe. I believed and still do to a certain extent that they were all powerful and that I would never be safe from them. That they would rule my life, whether directly with iron grip or indirectly through my fear and the way that I was letting that and still let that incapacitate me. It makes it so difficult for me to do the things that people take for granted. For example, to be able to walk down the street or go into busy shops and centres and feel okay about that. Be able to meet new people and not to be so suspicious that you can't talk to them without wondering about the hidden agenda.

Safety is more than a physical place although it is a vital component. You can hide in your head and pretend to be safe, but are in an unsafe place. Or you can physically be safe and not be in a safe place in your head. Neither of these is complete safety.

Can you ever be truly and absolutely safe? I believe so but I believe that by me talking, okay the little that I did say and the unwavering belief and support from others, all helped to get me safe. Me finally, and I mean finally after a long time beginning to believe that I could be safe, and feeling it.

It is okay for someone to suddenly whisk you away from an unsafe situation and to say here you are you are safe now. Everything will be okay, but will it could it ever be? I don't think so because safety surely is more than a place. Like sanctuary, sanctuary without the state of mind is just a safe place. Safety without one or other component is just an ideal concept that exists for some and not for others.

Safety is people, talking, a feeling, a state of mind and a place. It is security knowing that you are protected that you have the power to protect yourself and that they are as scared of you. I think that safety, true safety is an amalgamation of so many prerequisites that it is difficult to talk about the separate strands of safety. Is one aspect more important than the others? Without one can you be safe?

I think it is important to care about safety. Without at least a sense of safety we are paralysed by our fear, perceived, real or imagined. We cannot do things. We cannot heal grow or develop. That can only be achieved from a base of relative safety although that will be different for each individual.

We should always care about safety. Did I when I was there in the place in the situation? No I never knew what safety was. I never believed that I could ever be safe or that I even deserved to be safe. I believed it was safer for me not to be noticed not to attract attention to myself, to make myself as small and invisible as I could make me. I believed that safety was not getting hurt so badly. A good and safe day was avoiding questions or hurt.

Do we hide from safety? Yes I think we sometimes do because we can't quite believe it exists or that it is there for us or that we can have what people take for granted. Maybe it is easier to hide? I know that for me it was easier to hide from people, from safety, because the consequences of what leaving and being safe meant were too much too massive to handle.

I think that if we have found something that, to us means that we are safe, that makes us feel safe we shouldn't hide from it. Safety allows us to heal, to be ourselves, to find out what we can achieve. Safety is everything including feelings, people, places and more importantly the way that we feel about situations. Safety and the feelings associated with it can help to keep you safe.

The safety issues have changed, from when I first got away to now four years later. It is hard to believe that I am still breathing four years later. That the fears I had have in essence proved to be nothing. I think hindsight and retrospect are great things. I can remember how scared I was in the beginning. I was scared that they were going to get me no matter where I was. That I was going to be subjected to the most horrible death for being a traitor and for running away. But they never really materialised. I got the little threats the presents, the cards, but then they stopped. Was I really that worthless? I guess so, or maybe it was because they were all scared, scared of me. Now that was a huge concept that I have never really come to terms with, but then again I did show that I was willing to go to the police. They were scared of me, scared of me talking and telling about what they did to me.

As with sanctuary I think that safety has to be a state of mind as well as a place. You can be thousands of miles away, be in the safest place in the world and if you don't believe that you are safe then you never will be. I think most people believe that safety is merely a place, that once you are in a safe place it is ok now. It never was for me, I needed to believe that I was safe, that they could never hurt me again, and that has taken a long time, and will continue to take a long time to come to terms with.

I got safe first by being out of the situation, and then by seeing that they couldn't do much to get at me. There were the cards and presents through the door but beyond that nothing, although I still have a hard time believing that I am truly safe, I am getting there with it.

Hiding, I hid for a long time, or at least I tried to, not wanting to go out, not wanting to be noticed, but they took away a large chunk of my life. Should I let them take away more of it? Sometimes I think yes, I need to hide for a while. I just need to lie down and just simply breathe in order for me to continue to exist. I don't think that I am hiding from them anymore more that I am hiding from myself. But I don't believe that we should have to hide, but maybe for some it is a necessity."

Lucky

"I never really thought about safety as an important issue before. To try and think about it now is not an easy thing for me. I do wonder if there is really such a thing or even if it is something that I would want to have in my life all the time. I am now in a place of safety and certainly feel safe but that is not always enough. Certainly, when I stop and think about it, it is great that I have managed to keep my children safe. I sometimes think I personally prefer a little danger though in my life.

I am at heart a risk taker in my life. I always have been and probably always will be. I get quite a kick out of taking risks providing I am in control of the risk factors to some extent. I will probably never change and will someday become the kind of old age pensioner who frustrates and infuriates the young drivers. Actually I possibly do this already to some extent. I would be the type who would get happily into my electric wheelchair and 'rush' headlong into the traffic in front of the young drivers to slow them down and just annoy them.

I probably need the buzz of taking risks to survive with my mental health intact. It certainly feels that way. Life feels way too calm and boring sometimes and I have a tendency to start stirring things up a bit when I get bored. Perhaps my background is the cause of this or perhaps I was born this way. I know I do not like or want a quiet life. That kind of life would not feel real to me. I would be worried that I might grow complacent. I prefer to be on my toes and ready for anything that might happen. Life is unpredictable.

I believe that I live in a very dangerous world and that the illusion of safety is everywhere. It is not real though therefore

I cannot believe in it. I look at the little houses where people sit inside behind glass and wood and brick and consider themselves to be safe. How could they really be? A stone goes through glass and wood burns with very little encouragement. Safety such as that only lasts as long as civilised people stick to the rules of a civilised society. I am fortunate enough to know that civilisation is a very thin veneer on the surface of a seething cess pit and some people stick to the rules only as long as it suits them to do so. Either that or they are afraid of the sanctions if they break the rules and get caught. The way I grew up, no-one stuck to civilisations' rules and there were no sanctions put on them because they were too clever and cautious to ever get caught. That's how I know about the thin veneer.

I feel okay about the absence of safety for myself. It is what I am used to. In some ways I feel as though I am better equipped for survival than many people as at least I know the truth. At the same time I have created a very safe world for my children to grow up in. I do not want them to know too much about the real world as yet. There is time for them to know more when they are older. I wish all children could grow up with safety and the veneer firmly in place".

John

"I've always known, even as a child that sanctuary is something you create, believe in so much, then practise so hard to make real that somewhere down the line you can't remember if it's real or not because it seems to be helping. Sanctuary for me is punk music, writing and drawing, listening to Pink Floyd when I'm too wasted to think, or if worse comes to worst, cutting my arms.

They are all temporary though and I'm currently still creating a sanctuary/rehab idea that isn't. The idea is based on destroying apathy and exposing truth, two things I think are important if survivors are ever going to be accepted as strong people and not just the outspoken whistleblowers on such communities that silently endorse abuse."

Carol

"Safety: Although they knew where I was through the Army, I was physically safe. Abroad all was well, but returning to the south was not. They telephoned and cunningly lured my unwitting husband without my knowledge into returning to the family. By then I could not quite remember what the danger was, only an intense inner fear of it. A secret I not only kept from him but from myself also.

What safety means for me is: Staying many miles away physically, knowing and accepting that I can never visit my real family again (once only in secret) as there are so many issues.

Emotionally it goes through my mind when I pick up the phone and nobody speaks, but I guess you don't fully forget even though you know you are all right."

HELP AND SUPPORT

HELP AND SUPPORT

When trying to flee from any abusive situation survivors need quality support. Even when a survivor has finally escaped from the abuse and found safety, they need to have access to good quality services. This is even more essential for survivors of organised or ritual abuse as there are many abusers, survivors often have little or no practical knowledge of life and the stakes are very high indeed. For some it is only when they reach safety that they become overwhelmed and the symptoms of trauma sometimes rise to the surface. Those who receive quality services and support are much more likely to succeed in getting away and staying away at an earlier point. They are also more likely to recover from the effects of the trauma much more quickly.

There are some services for survivors of abuse. Unfortunately most statutory services are at best inadequate and at worst quite damaging to many survivors because they have such a limited understanding of ritual abuse and many do not seem to be prepared to learn. It has to be said though that in some parts of the United Kingdom there are some improvements happening as some individuals within agencies are beginning to listen to survivors and learn from them. Those who have encountered survivors through their work or leisure tend to be more open-minded and aware and some individuals are simply more open-minded to start with. On the whole though, as most survivors have commented on here in this book, statutory services are currently the services to be avoided. Hopefully this will change.

There are several telephone help lines available in the United Kingdom, which now offer a specific service for survivors of this kind of abuse. At least with these support services, the survivor is believed when they talk and the awareness level is kept quite high amongst the volunteers offering the services. As with most voluntary agencies working with abuse survivors, few if any of these help lines are adequately funded. They all appear to operate on a shoe-string with volunteers often paying out of their own pockets to keep the services open. None of this is at all surprising given the current climate of disbelief in this country and general lack of awareness about abuse in general. Few resources are directed to abuse survivors of any kind.

An increasing number of private therapists and counsellors now offer to provide a service for ritual abuse survivors. Some of them are absolutely excellent and according to some survivors they have quite literally been life-savers. Some give their time and services free of charge but not many are able to do this. Most who claim to have experience in the field of ritual

abuse have gained their experience from working with the survivors. The real irony in here is that most usually the survivor pays the therapist to listen to them and the therapist learns from the survivor talking. In effect, the survivor is often paying for the privilege of teaching the therapist something that then provides the therapist with the credentials to offer services to other abuse survivors who also pay them! Thankfully not all are like this and there are many caring individuals who support survivors simply because they care about them and for no financial rewards. At the same time, therapists do have to make a living.

There is an increasing focus on self-help and it is interesting to see the growing numbers of survivors who are supporting each other in a mutually agreeable and highly beneficial way. Though self-help can be fraught with potential hazards, for many it seems to work quite effectively. For some it is the only effective support that they have. More and more survivors are using the anonymity of the Internet and the chat rooms and message boards to help one another in an effective manner. Survivors are the real experts on abuse and it is perhaps not all that surprising that they are able to offer each other a great deal of support. The Internet would appear to be a very safe way of giving and receiving information and providing survivors always follow some basic safety rules no one can find out who they are or where they are currently living. As long as survivors remember that abusers can also use technology and you do not ever really know who you are talking to while on line.

There is no question that only the survivors of this type of abuse can ever really know what it is about. This means that in the first instance, it is they who are the ones who are raising the awareness and providing all the teaching on the subject. It is only they who can describe the full extent of the teaching, religion and all the trappings that often accompany the abuse. Few can ever tell about it all, as the trauma of telling can be too much and sometimes there is no way that every detail can be provided. There are also some things that people prefer never to talk about with anyone. The only way the world can ever really know about secretive and organised abuse is if survivors talk and tell about it and that is what is beginning to happen to some degree.

Workers can learn quite a lot through supporting survivors even when survivors are not quite at the stage of talking. They can learn about the intense fear, the extreme flashbacks, the hypnotic trances, the panic attacks and the degree of the trauma. Unfortunately, not all of this is a positive learning. Some agencies only encounter the most severely 'damaged' individuals and therefore end up believing that all survivors are like those

they have encountered in their work. To quote one mental health worker, "all survivors of ritual abuse will at some point be sectioned under the Mental Health Act and detained in a psychiatric hospital." The sad thing is that this came from an experienced worker who actually believes this to be the case. Perhaps this worker needs to meet the survivors who have not been in hospital, have never approach psychiatric services and have never suffered from any mental health problems at all. Then again, she might still think that as long as the survivor lives there is still the certainty of it all happening as she has predicted.

Also, in Dundee more recently, perhaps because there is a lot of awareness raising happening in the form of training, conferences and book publications, there has been at least one deliberate attempt to cause serious difficulties between agencies and sabotage work being done. As mentioned earlier in this book, we recently encountered a person claiming to be a survivor who went around numerous agencies, made serious allegations against workers in different agencies, took up a huge amount of time and resources and generally caused huge problems in the area before moving on to do the same in another area.

Unfortunately many agencies in Dundee now believe that this is how a survivor of ritual abuse presents and operates and some now refuse to work with the subject or with the survivors. Agencies and workers need to communicate with each other and learn to see people as individuals rather than judging them as all the same. They also need to realise that part of the backlash in dealing with this type of abuse will continue to be deliberate attempts to put agencies off working with the survivors and trying to sabotage the work and the working relationships. If people who are thought to be ritual abuse survivors are seen as causing problems or are regarded as being far too difficult to work with, no one will want to work with them.

Agencies, particularly statutory agencies need to start offering quality services to all. This includes survivors of all kinds of abuse. Many claim to offer such services but the simple fact that survivors do not use their service is a clear indication that the services are in some way not accessible to them or not helpful to them. It is remarkably easy to put a survivor off using a service. I once heard a police officer state that they did not believe that ritual abuse happened. "I don't believe any of that shit." To quote the person concerned. This remark was said in the presence of two such survivors though the officer did not know they were such survivors. Is it any wonder that these survivors did not go on and talk to that police officer after hearing that being said? Would I as a support worker then suggest to any survivor of this type that they ever attempt to speak to this particular officer? I really do not think so!

Survivors Accounts

Lee

"Lots of help and support seems to be provided by 'official' types who in general don't have any understanding. They have the general idea that all survivors of Ritual Abuse are long-term damaged victims and that anything they hear should be kept confidential after telling the police and all the other authorities they can think of.

Support is useful when it can be provided by those who can empathise, who don't try and shove some explanation down your throat or stick you on a bunch of pills. I think survivors can provide the so called 'professionals' with a great deal of insight, though one particular doctor makes me wonder what they remember from all the years of learning they are supposed to have done. Did their tutors not mention listening and empathy anywhere in those six years?"

Sheila

"A clinical psychologist provides my main support along with a few good friends.

Yes I need the support as no one has all the answers to all of the questions as to why these things happen. But to have someone to talk to who is not judging [the survivors] has been helpful. It helps to put things into perspective. (slightly)

Survivors themselves need to learn to be more open and honest with the support group that they're working with to get the most out of it.

Yes, we do need to teach others. We're the only ones who know what we need.

Yes it is difficult to deal with agencies. We can't be honest. There are too many people to deal with and you aren't able to explain your problem/situation all at once. I don't really want to anyway."

Kay

"I get therapy and call up the SAFE and SERICC help lines. (Support help-lines for survivors) My therapist really got me through last year with practical support when I was homeless, and this year we've been surfacing the past. Although I've had a lot of therapy in my life, as I haven't been able to get along without it, this is the first time I've been able to begin this work. As the horror story unfolds, stress lifts from my life and I don't need to write every day to stay sane.

The help lines are great and have helped me get through terribly tough and despairing times, when I felt I couldn't go on. It is almost like having family. It is often difficult to get through, as the pressure on the lines is so great, and it is difficult not to get dependant on them. But they're fantastic.

What would really help is somewhere to just be when you felt rough, or just anyway. I haven't found any drop in women's centres in London. A support group would be like a dream. There are none in London, even for incest survivors, let alone us, but I hope to start one.

Since the Ritual Abuse surfaced I can't talk to the Samaritans any more. To have someone just saying, Yes", or "How does that make you feel?" when you're talking about gang-rape of a four year old is really awful. You need a human reaction, or you start to feel it must be all your own fault. I think people do have natural reactions, but it is trained out of them.

And we need safe houses desperately. I'm sure that would save a lot of lives and souls."

Annie

"Help is provided in so many ways, some positive some not so. My help comes from a mixture of volunteers, other survivors, and professionals. I certainly need support, and most of my current support is really good and very helpful. More available ways to tell on abusers with out having to go direct to police would be helpful.

I feel it is only the survivors who can teach. How can somebody who has not been subjected to torture teach another how it feels? They can't. Some agencies are great. I've had really positive outcomes from some and others don't understand. Each one of us has to look for an agency we trust and can work well with as we all react individually to different types of agency support."

Nat

"Help and support: who provides it? Is there supposed to be a magic answer to this question?? Like is there an illuminated expert that you want me to name? I can't because... are there any experts??? Well, except those that have survived and come out the other end. I believe that there are people that have expertise. This book and the others before it show us that much.

I think that everyone to some extent needs help and support whether to get help to get out of a situation or to deal with what has happened. Then on some level whether practical or emotional, physical or spiritual, people need help and support. Even if that is as basic as someone just listening and believing the things they are saying.

Who provides this help and support? I think people who are ordinary caring individuals such as volunteers and workers in voluntary agencies. Statutory workers don't want to know. They don't even want to hear the words. They think they are the experts, but they don't do you the honour of actually listening and hearing the things you say. There is a mental block with hearing the words and equating it with the human being they have sitting in front of them. It's their loss. They are the ones with the problem. The help and support from some voluntary organisations is good, with time and worker commitment being a problem. More is needed. It always is needed, more workers, more awareness, more acceptance.

Should the survivors be the ones who teach? Why? Why should we help you to help us? What makes you think we know what needs to be fixed? Or if anything is broken, what makes you think that you will be the one who can listen and truly hear and then fix what may or may not be broken. It hurts to talk. It hurts more to teach, but we do it because there is no alternative. What option do we have? If we need help or support from people then we have to teach workers how to give that support, how to help us and what the issues are. But even when we say, do you pay attention? Do you actually want to hear? Want to learn?

It is difficult to approach any agency because you are unsure of the response you are going to get. I was lucky. I got a good response from the people I told and put in touch with a voluntary agency who had awareness of the issues. I had such a good experience dealing with this support agency that my view on this is coloured. For others the experience is a bad one, and one I think that needs to change. I would not ask for uniformity but just honesty if you can't handle something why do it?"

Nell

"I don't think that I would have survived had it not been for the help and support that I received from the voluntary support agency, as there was no other help available for me out there. People did want to help and try to help but it wasn't enough.

The hardest thing I think is asking for help and being able to say enough to get the help that you need. I think that in fairness it is a subject that is often seen but rarely talked about and people don't understand or know what to do. But similarly survivors don't know what to ask for.

I think that there is a conspiracy out there. I believe that there are many conspiracies out there. The backlash, the conspiracy to try to discredit every single survivor that escapes. The conspiracy of silence that surrounds and pervades the statutory organisations, the... 'that doesn't happen if we don't talk about it' conspiracy.

Dealing with agencies such as income support, benefits, housing, council tax and health is a minefield of conspiracy a true hotbed of intrigue. To run the gauntlet of the benefits system you have to have support. Anyone without good support you would not be able to live or survive away from the group.

It can at first be attributed purely to poorly managed systems, delays and incompetence, but after six months with no money, these start to wear a bit thin. So do we believe there are conspiracies? Well of course, weren't we part of one? It was one that both sides wanted to maintain, the conspiracy of silence and to some extent disbelief. But these can be and are broken down all the time. People are breaking these circles of conspiracy."

Nik

"Help and support, I was lucky in this respect, I got good help and support, but I believe that there is a definite gap in services for ritual abuse survivors. I believe that they should have their own services, like T.R.A.S.H. (Tayside Ritual Abuse Support and Help), and that survivors should be part of information networks. After all we are the ones who have the knowledge. Why are we excluded from so many organisations? Maybe it is because of the fear? I am not sure. Maybe because they think that we are damaged beyond repair and that we couldn't handle what they are talking about. I would have happily switched roles while I was in the group, to show what I could handle.

But not many people have the knowledge. They don't know how to support or help, which I guess leads on to the 'should I teach them how to help and support me?' question. I think that in some cases yes. Not just for me, but for those that come behind me. If people are willing to help but lack the necessary knowledge then I would be willing to help them to understand and gain knowledge. But in fairness, you don't require knowledge in order to be supportive of someone. There isn't going to be a test at the end of the support session to see how much knowledge you gained in that session.

I/we need supportive people, not Einstein. You don't need knowledge in order to listen, just a couple of ears, even just one would do. We don't need you to give us the answers, because sometimes there isn't one, and most of the time, we have the answers. We just need a different perspective, a new way of seeing things, not a definition of what ritual abuse is. We already know what it is, we lived it remember!"

John

"Who provides support? Survivors do!

Do you need it? I don't need anything except my will to survive but there are times when to have that will power I need to talk to someone, usually around twilight. The fact that there is no one there is a challenge, so maybe I do need help (joke).

Is it any good? It's good for what it does. It offers empowerment and advice like a job does. Personally I need help that isn't based on earnings or medication. It's an issue of trust for me.

What more is needed? People to quit working and stop being sheep and start showing things they themselves never had.

Should we (survivors) be the ones to teach others how to help us? No, I think that there is a great understanding between survivors, it's humanity but I don't believe in duality such as teacher/learner, doctor/patient. It's just another form of manipulation so subtle it goes unnoticed. Empowerment is the only thing that can be taught and it can only be taught by a survivor that truly realises just how far sexual abuse goes in the way of shaping societies. After all there's no point empowering a survivor only to be duped by doctors and judges.

What was/is it like dealing with agencies. Is there a conspiracy do you think? I think it's impossible not to believe in conspiracy theories. If you try to disprove them for piece of mind, you end up proving them and if you simply put blinkers on and disbelieve, you end up like most 9am – 5pm people, moaning about getting shat on by the system before handing over cash to feed it and cause it to shit on them again. I think the phrase that sums it up for me is, 'just because you are paranoid doesn't mean that they are not out to get you.'

My own way of dealing with it is thinking like those in power so as to try and see where they are heading with a seemingly trustworthy cause. If I can see where they are going, it can't surprise me and also I get a head start in trying to stop it. Everything is just a test and the only way you win is by being totally honest, because even if the system tries to stop good people, all it does is make us stronger and wiser."

Ruth

"Every one said I would not go back to him ever again. They lied to me. They did not help me. They just took me back to him. It made him very cross with me. It made it worse for me going to the police."

Rose

"But if you go for help to the police or to a social worker or to a counsellor they do not help. You are alone in this bad big world. You just want the world to swallow you up and make the bad things to stop."

Lucky

"I think I was very much in need of support after I first got away from the group. I never found any though. I was completely unable to trust anyone enough to ask for support and in many ways was far too busy trying to survive from day to day. There was not a lot of support about anyway when I was younger. Even organisations such as rape crisis and women's aid were not about at the time. Or, if they were, they were not easy to find. I doubt very much if I would ever have approached anyone for help though.

As the years went on, there have been other times when I could have used support but I think I have just become so used to doing things for myself that I no longer ever think of seeking support from anyone. I mostly find that friends and work colleagues are great support. Not to talk about horrid or difficult things with but just to be there for each other. It is enough for me to know that some people really do care about me and I care about them.

I do think that there needs to be a lot more support and information services for survivors though. Survivors need to have the choice of a range of different organisations so that they can choose whatever is best for them at any particular time. The needs of survivors do change and the services should reflect this fact. The most basic need that any survivor can ever have, particularly at first, is somewhere safe to stay and food and clothing. Even this is really hard to get at first and if you do not know where to even start getting help, what can you do?

I think survivors do already teach others about ritual abuse. We teach every time we are in any kind of contact with other people. It may not be a formal teaching or training, but it is teaching nonetheless. Some survivors as they heal do a lot of work trying to raise the awareness of people. I think that survivors, as long as they have healed a bit, are the best people to teach as they are the ones who know the most about the subject. We do have to be careful though that survivors are not exploited.

Dealing with agencies of one kind or another has always been a bit of a nightmare for me. I am thinking here of statutory organisations such as health, police, housing, Social Security and social work. I learned very early on in my adult life to just not try to engage with any of these agencies as a survivor. I would be very reluctant to ever let any of these professionals anywhere near any sensitive information about myself. My own experiences have taught me that these agencies are highly prejudiced against ritual abuse survivors, if they even stop long enough to believe you in the first place. I have always had problems with these agencies so I just avoid them now.

It has sometimes been hard not to think that there is a conspiracy or at the very least, some abusers in high places. So many times has there been a mix up with records, information and a total mess made of things, particularly when dealing with statutory agencies that I am forced to conclude they are at best incompetent and at worse, it is all very deliberate. I now make sure that if I have to deal with any of these agencies I keep copies of everything and make sure there are witnesses available for any meetings I need to have with them. The number of lies they tell is unbelievable but I suspect they lie to cover up their mistakes more than anything else"

DAMAGED BEYOND REPAIR?

DAMAGED BEYOND REPAIR?

Many people who hear about ritual abuse are so appalled at what they hear that they find it difficult to believe that people can endure such extreme abuse and horror and actually survive these experiences. Because most people (or so I am told) are lucky enough to have had a non-abusive childhood they find it difficult to understand. Many people who have not had experience of violence, particularly extreme violence, cannot imagine what it is like to cope with it on any level particularly on a daily basis. Because very few people can imagine surviving through days of rituals, torture, brainwashing and terror, they find it hard to imagine how it is possible that survivors can survive such things and even manage to remain sane.

When some people first hear about organised and ritual abuse and begin to listen to what is actually being said about it, they can find it a struggle to come to terms with the things that they are hearing. Their natural inclination is to not want to hear about it and not want to believe that any of it is possible. This is an entirely normal reaction. People have a tendency to judge everyone by their own moral standards and ideals and good people just cannot get their heads around the concept that people would behave in such an abusive manner towards other people and in particular towards their own and other people's children. It is extremely hard for good people to come to terms with the reality of ritual abuse, or indeed any sexual abuse, happening in their own community.

When people do begin to take it on, they often feel a great deal of sympathy and pity for the survivors. Again people judge most things by their own standards and as they hear of the acts of violence and abuse, they try to imagine their own reactions to it. Most believe that they could never have survived such things. They cannot imagine coping with such a terrible life. They cannot conceive of how a child might manage to grow up and survive amidst such continuous horror. By the same token, many people often cannot understand at all the loyalty that many survivors feel towards their families despite the abuse they have experienced. Few people can really understand the complexities of the relationships, the group dynamics and the range of feelings that often accompany many abuse situations. Ritual abuse is even more complex when it also encompasses a system of strong beliefs and even a faith.

Due to much of this, most people often expect survivors of this type of abuse to be extremely damaged and seriously disturbed individuals. Certainly most

people would expect them to be in great need of psychiatric help. Even when survivors present to police, social work or health services, as soon as they say the type of abuse they have experienced, workers thoughts swiftly turn to the need for mental health services. No matter what the survivor is in contact with a particular agency for, the assumption is quickly made that, because of the abuse, there must be mental health problems of some kind present. Yet, this is not always the case.

Often it is actually the worker who is struggling to hear what is being spoken about and workers frequently become overwhelmed and distressed by hearing about ritual abuse. This is regarded as completely normal as in fact it is very distressing. If on the other hand it is the survivor who becomes distressed while talking about a problem, there is often an assumption made that a doctor must be immediately called. Though it is normal to become distressed while talking about difficult issues, people who witness this distress most often cannot deal effectively with it. Many people tend to want to make things better for the survivor but often it is they who are actually struggling and not sure what to do or say for the best. If they telephone for a doctor, then they at least can feel that they are in fact doing something actively to help the person. Most survivors of abuse would be expected to be a bit upset if they are trying to talk about difficult things. It does not inevitably follow that they have a need for medical help.

Often survivors who are seeking help and support are directed to mental health services as it is assumed that this is the most appropriate agency to help them. This is in fact not always the case. If the survivor is attempting to leave the group for example, they are more likely to need the assistance of the police or even in the first instance the housing department or women's aid if it is a woman. If the survivor is struggling to access services, they may be most in need of an advocate to help them achieve this. The ideal response regardless of which service the survivor accessed first would probably be to carry out a standard assessment of needs and then direct the survivor to the service most likely to be able to meet those needs at the time.

Many survivors learn through time not to mention the fact that they are a survivor of ritual abuse until they are more certain what the response is going to be. Having dealt too often with the reactions of others, they learn to say as little as possible about the abuse. For some survivors to have reached the stage of being able to say what it is they have survived is a positive step but people's reaction can be so detrimental that they sometimes find it easier not to say anything. Sometimes though it is too late to say nothing about it as some agencies will have already recorded such information in their notes. These notes then follow the survivor round and many professionals who

read the notes then assume that every problem the survivor has stems from the abuse that they have experienced.

People often completely fail to understand the many and varied coping mechanisms that children develop in order to survive their abuse. Most have no awareness and no idea of how people learn to cope at an early age. Children know only what they live and when things get tough for them they have no means of escape other than how they learn to deal with things in their minds. Thus many children learn while still quite young to dissociate from the abuse, to different degrees. They learn how to switch off to the pain and to control their emotions. Some of them learn how to compartmentalise their minds and put things into boxes. They even learn how to swiftly lose all memory of a recent and traumatic event so that they can carry on as normal. Thus even quite young children are able to go to school, behave in a fairly normal manner while in the community and hide what is really going on for them at home and in other places.

While living with extreme abuse and torture, most people find ways of coping and the daily struggle to survive is all that they can think about at the time. While in survival mode sometimes there is not even the space for a thought and pure instinct is all that exists at the time. However, when people escape from the group and the abuse, this is often when they have problems and symptoms which they have not had before begin to manifest.

Once safe from the abuse, symptoms of post-traumatic stress often appear. For the survivor who has never known safety there is a whole new world opening up to them but few at the time can appreciate this fully. Often flashbacks and panic attacks begin to make every waking moment a nightmare as the brain attempts to make sense of the memories of what has been happening. Often the survivor has trouble with eating and sleeping also. The fear of being found by the abusers torments the survivor and a high state of hyper-vigilance is often maintained which can be very draining for the individual. Some survivors become so distressed that they develop different phobias. Many have psychotic attacks during which they can see and hear their abusers all the time even though no one else can see them. In time many survivors can become extremely depressed and even quite suicidal. It is usually through this very difficult time that many survivors need most help and support.

Sometimes the coping mechanisms developed by the survivor that made survival possible while living and surviving in the group, actually end up working against the survivor who is trying to learn how live in an abuse free world. Dissociation that has led to the creation of separate personalities

189

being formed in the one individual can begin to cause the survivor problems. If, for example, there is no internal communication between the different personalities a great deal of internal conflict can arise. Some of the personalities may seek to return to the group. Others may wish to die or self harm. The things that previously safeguarded the survivor to some degree, such as having many different personalities, which do not know of each other or communicate with each other on any level now makes the survivor unsafe. It is hard to function if you do not always know what you are doing on a day to day basis. Many survivors need help to understand what is going on for them with this and help and support to sort this confusion out.

There are some injuries that can never be put right for a survivor and physical scars on the body cannot be unmade. For many survivors, there are permanent physical injuries. Some survivors are rendered physically disabled by the abuse they have experienced and this is usually permanent though sometimes there can be some improvement through medical intervention. Neither can the memories of what has happened be undone. What happened to the survivor happened and nothing can ever change that basic fact. If there was the slightest possibility of getting some false memories of a better variety, many survivors would possibly welcome this and go and get them. Sometimes the mental trauma the survivor has suffered leads to mental disability of one kind or another.

Survivors can recover from the trauma they have suffered. They can recover to different degrees depending on the severity of the abuse and the individual capacity of a person to recover. They can learn to deal with and come to terms with the memories, the panic, the fear and the feelings that endlessly surface for them. They can work through most of the memories in whatever way works best for them and they can unlearn the coping strategies that no longer work effectively and learn new coping strategies that do work for them. Survivors do survive the abuse and they do survive leaving the abuse. They are extremely strong individuals who have survived things that many did not. They can also survive the healing and the recovery. Very few survivors would ever agree that they are permanently damaged beyond repair though some would agree that there are some things that cannot be repaired.

All survivors are individuals and though experiences may be similar for many of the individuals their reactions and how they deal with what has happened to them is unique to each and every one of them. So too it is with the healing. There is no one way to recover and heal from any trauma. Each survivor chooses their own path or stumbles across it. Some choose to talk about the things that have happened to them, others choose to write

or draw and others choose to quietly think things through by themselves. What works well for one person will not automatically work well for another and survivors need as many choices as possible in this. Also, survivors, like everyone else, need different things at different stages of their lives. Survivors do hold their own answers to their own healing and if they can gain enough confidence in themselves they will soon take charge and show themselves to be the real experts in their own lives and their recovery.

Survivors Accounts

Lee

"The effects of such abuse are harmful but they can be overcome. I'm not much of a believer in pills unless the person concerned feels that the pills are actually helping. Survivors survive.

I've been lucky enough to have good friends who have given me support when I've wanted it. I don't think that we need 'professional' support it can sometimes do more harm than good. I'm a great believer in finding what works for you as an individual. If it's professional support or friends and artwork, it doesn't matter as long as it works for you.

My sleeping, eating, trust has remained okay though physically I suffered from a lot of childhood illness which may have contributed to my physical disability."

Sheila

"I hope that someday I will be ok without eating and sleeping disorders and without repulsion against some kinds of foods. It would be nice to think that someday we can trust people and that we'll feel less fear, but I'm not convinced that any of it will ever happen. But at least if we trust ourselves then it's a start.

I think the abuse has caused damage but I don't believe that I'm damaged although I have many problems emotionally/physically to deal with. We definitely do not need pills."

Kay

"I am sure we can heal, given one tenth of a chance. We have all the strength of our survival so far. But we have a lot to learn to get along in the world.

I get bullied easily, hurt easily, cannot read papers since the Afghan bombing, get furious or murderous at sexist or pornographic ads, have a pile of allergies, sleep so light it causes problems, etc, etc. Physically in your fifties the body does not take stress well, and I've begun to get knee problems and am intermittently on crutches.

Emotional and physical problems combined are tough. Sometimes it's just a battle. At others the very extremity of need can force you into development. When immobilised, I discovered sculpture and singing. All of it pushes me into a spirituality I never knew. I meditate, pray, and, at best, try to totally accept my life as my job on this earth, which gives meaning and fulfilment.

At first I only heard of one woman healed out of 1,000 listed. Then I met another and the chance of healing doubled. Now I've learned of a third."

Annie

"Physically apart from external scars there are internal ones as well. Scars which need treatment but due to the abuse you feel too scared to go and ask for medical help. Even little things like typing this hurts due to the repeated use of wrist chains and restraints. I don't think we are damaged as much as being hurt. In some cases I do believe we may need pills especially if the abuse triggers off severe depression or sleep disorders but I don't believe that being a survivor is an illness and therefore it does not need treatment with pills.

I hope one day I will be okay. I look forward to the time where I can turn a tap on or fold a towel with out horrendous memories taking over. I look forward to when the word secret becomes something special rather than something horrible. I look forward to the day when I find out what care really means and what safety is. Yes I will be okay it will take time but I have to be okay. I think trust and fear will always be a problem for me but in time I will learn to manage these."

Billie

"I think that all survivors, of any form of childhood abuse, whether it is sexual, physical or emotional, or all three of them, carry an enormous amount of hurt around with them, inside their hearts. It is a bit like being bereaved but nobody has died and you feel the grief all the time. If grief could kill, then I am sure that I would have been dead many times over.

I'm sure abuse kills lots of young people every year through being unable to cope and committing suicide. I first thought of suicide as a way out, when I was eleven years old but I decided against it because I did not think that they had finally silenced me. If I had died over what they had done to me then I would not be here today to write this. I would not be able to join in the fight for the rights of other survivors of ritual abuse who are younger than me and therefore more in need. Let's hope that each generation has a better chance of escaping at a much younger age, than we did and a better chance of recovering at a younger age than we did too. The younger they get away and get some help, the better the prospects are for them.

Some of the children, abused by the group that abused me died or were killed. I did not actually know many of them on a personal level. They are strange, nameless, ghostly little figures that haunt me still and probably always will. I do grieve for them.

The people who I trusted and were closest to me are all people who I lost through telling them the truth about the abuse in my life. I never told about the ritual abuse at first because I was afraid that my friends would not believe me and that I might lose them. I should have continued to keep silent. But if I had then I would have been denying my past experiences. Why should I in order to save the feelings of people who had a good childhood.

Isn't it bad enough that we were as badly abused as children and young people without having to be abused all over again by the mental health services that are meant to be helping us. My encounter with that lot nearly finished me off. They think they know so much but actually they know nothing at all about this kind of abuse. They did not help at all but made it worse. I would never go to them for help again.

The misery and suffering caused by ritual abuse is huge. It goes very deep and penetrates right into every corner and aspect of your life. Little by little, we have to face it, in our own way and in our own time. We can recover from this.

For the survivors who did manage to kill themselves, I hope that they are finally at peace at last. For those of us who are still battling on, their deaths, serve as an important reminder that we need to continue the fight against the evils of ritual abuse and those who perpetuate it.

We owe it to ourselves and we owe it to all those whom we once knew. We owe it to those who were murdered by a group, or were driven to kill themselves. If this was the only option that they felt they had, then there are simply not enough options available to people. We need to create safe places for survivors to get help, so that suicide does not become, the only way out. There is so much more that could be done to help and it does not all have to cost a huge amount of money"

Nat

"Damaged beyond repair: are we? Some of us will be but surely then they cannot be called survivors because to be damaged beyond repair states that there is no hope. You are essentially dead. If you are dead you can't be surviving.

Who makes the judgement that we are damaged beyond repair and is that a measurement that exists? There are times of despair and despondency where yeah you believe that there is nothing. There is no point but does that mean we are damaged beyond repair? No I don't think so. To think that would be admitting defeat, concede the battle...

I got ill. I still get ill sometimes. Does that mean that I am damaged beyond repair? I hope not. There are effects from the abuse. I would think that if anyone went through abuse like that they would have side effects from it. Trust is the major factor. There essentially is none. Not even for yourself. There are so many effects that can be debilitating. I have trouble sleeping and eating. I have major trust issues and my way of thinking can be very 'unusual' sometimes. I hope that I am not condemned because I get ill sometimes from the effects of my abuse.

I think that pills and doctors are okay for those that are happy with that course of action. And they can and do help many people. I got annoyed with the pills because suddenly because I had left a bad situation I suddenly had major chemical imbalances in my brain that needed medication to fix. I like how suddenly these imbalances can suddenly appear from nowhere. How the issue of abuse can be swept aside in favour of the more tasteful underlying mental illness.

I think we need to trust ourselves. Trust ourselves that we know ourselves better than anyone else. Do we need the pills? I think that if they help why not. We deserve all the help we can get and if they help then why shouldn't we take them.

I believe that we are as strong, intelligent and as capable as everyone else. There is nothing that can be done that I can't attempt too. I am as capable as anyone else. I get ill sometimes I know, but I am working on that and we can become and do anything we want to do. Anything we put our minds to. We have survived this far. We survived the abuse, we can survive the healing and we can survive the doubts of other people.

This is my life I already let people take some of it from me I will not let everyone else do that too. I am capable of a lot of things hopefully of great things. Don't disregard me before I have had the chance to prove myself. Not to you, but to me."

Nell

"Damaged beyond repair, I hope not, otherwise what would be the point in getting away and living. I think some people believe that we are. They believe that because of the extreme trauma that we suffered that we will never be okay. I can't believe that. I fought to get away from the situation. I need to believe that it was worth it. I need to believe that I have something to offer. I need to believe that I am the same as everyone else. I need to believe that I will have a life that will be fulfilling. That one day I can go to sleep and not have the nightmares. That I will eventually be able to believe in myself enough to trust others.

I think that professionals, especially health professionals believe that pills are the answer to the effects of abuse, any abuse. But is there actually a pill that can alleviate all the effects of abuse? Yes there are physical and emotional effects of abuse, I don't deny that. But I can remember that suddenly I had a chemical imbalance, where did it come from, when I walked through the door to the doctor's office? I think that it is harder for other people to hear that you have been abused. They have this amazing urge to want to make it all better. The problem is that they can't. We need to feel the feelings go through the crap to come out of the other end. Otherwise, will we ever get through to the other side?

When I was there (in the group) I never needed pills, to put me to sleep, to wake me up to stabilise my mood, but as soon as I got away, then I needed all these pills. I can't say that when I got away I was in the best shape, but I sure didn't need to become a pharmacy either."

John

"We are totally broken in every way but I think that is our beauty, the pure honesty of it. For example, I could say that my paranoia is only due to the fact that when I was being sexually abused I was being lied to with a smile. I instantly mistrust people who smile. Maybe that explains why I believe in conspiracies but at the end of the day, does it really matter because the end result is I don't trust people with smiles. I can't change that.

What I can do is think, 'why would anyone be happy in this fucked up world unless they are totally oblivious of it?' and with the media as it is, you can't be obvious, so in conclusion happy people are people who don't give a shit. This correlates with my experience and also the fact that I am depressed. So the whole thing is actually self rectifying, like it was meant to be."

Helen

"I really believe deep down, that I can heal fully from what happened to me, and I also believe that I have not got anything that other people haven't. So for me, it is possible for everyone who has been ritually abused to recover fully.

I will never know what it is like to be a person who has had an unabused childhood. But I have already survived the worst a human being can do to another. The only thing I can compare it to, is the way the Jews were treated in concentration camps. I have survived as a child with no adults to protect me, no safe place to run to, with only child skills to cope. If I am that immensely strong to still be alive, I can do absolutely anything. My survival is incredible and I know that I am capable of anything I choose to do, and what I choose is to be a loving, joyful woman who lives life fully.

I have had the most amazing help and I think that is the most important thing in healing the wounds of ritual abuse. I have had twelve years of counselling with a person who was prepared to, at times, give me twenty-four hour support. She showed me complete acceptance and taught me about personal boundaries. We literally went back to my beginnings and I lived it all, this time with a loving caring healthy adult by my side. My counsellor, for a while, took the role of a 'good enough parent', so that I could, in turn, learn to look after myself. I did not know when I was hungry or cold. I had to learn the basics and then slowly and painfully relive the abuse and then take care of myself gently and lovingly.

I don't think I could have got to where I am without my counsellors amazing understanding, skill and love. The wounds I have were inflicted by people who were supposed to take care of me. They were healed by someone being there for me in a healthy and non-abusive way.

So yes, I believe we survivors can heal fully. Yes we were and are damaged in every way imaginable and I really believe nothing is unmendable. I may always have some inner wounds and that means I will have to take extra care of myself, and I am strong at the broken places.

I am more than I would have been if my experiences of childhood had been different. My goal is to take the crap and turn it into roses."

Lucky

"The effects of my abuse will always be with me as I will never forget what happened or forgive those who did it to me. This does not mean though that I am damaged. I do not believe that I am any more damaged than someone who grew up without abuse. Certainly I can do as much as anyone else and sometimes a very great deal more. I hold down a steady well-paid job, raise a family and have lasting and meaningful relationships with people. I have friends and socialise as much as I care to. I, to all intents and purposes am not so very different from other people. Certainly no one could ever say I have a mental health problem because I do not.

There are a few differences with me however though these differences are not immediately visible to the outside world. One of the main things that makes me different from many people is my awareness. I know the bad things that happen in the real world. I have no illusions at all about anything. I am seldom surprised at the things human beings get up to or do to each other. I am also a total sceptic. Bet you would never have guessed that one?

I appreciate life much more than many people. I listen to people moaning about the most incredible things and find them naive in the extreme. Perhaps it is just the nature of human beings that they must have a good moan about everything and nothing. It does seem such a waste though. These people know absolutely nothing of real suffering. This is not a bad thing at all. It is in some degree good to know that some people have had a good childhood and a relatively good life but they really ought to learn to appreciate what they have more. Then again, most people take the things they have for granted and it is only when they lose something that they suddenly appreciate it.

Being a survivor made me determined to make sure that my own children were fully protected. I had to carefully balance protecting the children against all the evils I knew were out there in the world against allowing them the freedom to grow and develop fully. They needed to take risks in order to learn but it is so hard when you want to protect them from everything. It was and still is a very difficult balancing act to maintain and I am certain I am still learning. Being a survivor has also given me a greater empathy with others than I suspect I would otherwise not have had. Though not damaged permanently, my world view is perhaps very different from a lot of other people. I have no veil over my sight.

I have always avoided doctors and as a result have never taken pills to assist me through some of the hard times. I have on occasion in the dim and distant past used illegal drugs to help take the edge off a bit. At the time I thought that they helped me but when I look back I know that they only gave me some temporary escape from the thoughts and feelings I was having at the time. When the effects wore off, all the bad stuff was still waiting in my head to be dealt with. The drugs never made it go away they just covered it for a little bit of time. Then I had to deal with the problem of the drugs also.

I will confess to not having a great deal of trust in other people and that is probably as a direct result of my past abuse.

However, I see no reason to trust someone I do not know even if they are a professional. Just because someone wears a white coat does not mean that they are a good person or worthy of someone's trust. There is nothing wrong in taking the time to allow a relationship of trust to grow and develop with people. I am not generally hurt by people as I tend not to let people very close until I know them well enough to know if I can trust them. I take time and therefore do not feel as let down as many people around me when people are not as honest as I hoped they would be. I am an excellent judge of character and usually get it right with the people I think it is okay to trust."

Carol

"It has affected every aspect of my life. When it first came up it literally turned my world upside down with shock and horror at what I was experiencing, from being an outgoing social person who worked, had friends, (but not without problems) I became a virtual recluse suffering from all the symptoms of severe P.T.S.D. (Post Traumatic Stress Disorder) The dizziness was so bad I could hardly stand up, taking to my bed for long periods at a time, dissociation, terrible body pain, and I could hardly talk without my body shaking uncontrollably, and fear surrounded me constantly. I later took to drinking to get me through, and would lock myself into a room unable to control the self-harm I wanted to inflict upon myself. I ended in hospital, then having to go on anti-depressants.

I have had to take a long time out, and it has been unbearable, and painful, and much learning and hard work is required to start healing, "cry you must" I am off the pills and can get through most days now with few symptoms, "yes" there are times when stuff emerges that I need help with and it is difficult to get through, but now I have stopped worrying about tomorrow because today is not bad, not bad at all."

BACKLASH

BACKLASH

It is never easy for a survivor to get away from groups and families who are involved in organised or ritual abuse. There are a number of reasons for this. Firstly there is the simple fact that there is not just one abuser for the survivor to contend with, there are many and the survivor may not even know who they all are. The survivor is unlikely to know everyone who is in the group or is associated with the group and as a result knows that one of their abusers could in reality be anyone. For all they know it could be someone who works in housing, health or social services or even in the police. The survivor may even have been told that one or more of their abusers works on one of these agencies. This makes it harder for the survivor to trust anyone and access help from the agencies they most need.

Then there is the fact that to leave a group is effectively, from the group's perspective, to betray them. Survivors often become extremely fearful of what the group members will do to try and stop them getting away and staying away. Survivors will have been taught and will believe that those who try to leave the group are severely punished and will face almost certain death through torture. Because of this, the fear of getting found and dragged back often renders survivors helpless to think or to take any action to safeguard themselves. Some become so afraid that they may decide to return to the group of their own free will before they are found by the group. This way the punishment will not be so severe and they can make out as though they were not actually leaving the group at all but were taking a break.

Some survivors have been kept so much under control that they do not know the most basic things that would help them to live in the outside world. They have never been allowed to get to know any of the ways of the outside world. Some are not registered at birth, have never been allowed to go to school and have never been allowed the freedom to go anywhere or do anything without the abusers being present to dictate to them and control their every action. These survivors are completely owned by the group. This is quite deliberate to try and ensure that escaping the group will be very difficult. It would in fact be almost impossible for one of these survivors to leave. The best hope one of these survivors would have is to be found and rescued but this is unlikely to happen.

These survivors have never had the opportunity to live independently or learn about such things as accessing services, finding safe accommodation or finding out how to get money. Some do not know how to go shopping,

how to budget or even how to make decisions for themselves. They often have no education other than what is needed to be part of the group activities. Without a great deal of help and support, these survivors cannot possibly succeed in getting away from the group and staying free of it. Part of the problem here for these survivors is that they would not even know it is possible to leave, that a different life is possible or how to access help and support in the first place. It is most often only through sheer luck that any of these survivors get away and find some support.

In addition to whatever individual problems a person might have in trying to leave, find support and somewhere to live, get money and find a way to cope in an abuse free world, there is also the constant and persistent problem of the abusers to contend with. They are always there to some degree in the mind and the memory of the survivor. Long after escaping from the abuse, the control exerted through brainwashing, hypnosis and fear persists and to some degree dictates the actions of many survivors for many years to come. Frequently and almost inevitably, the abusers find out where the survivor is living and/or working and they then become a very real problem for the survivor.

The abusers in any kind of relationship of abuse have a vested interest in keeping their victims suppressed, under control and if possible, completely silenced. All abusers who are known to their victims do this to some extent so as to safeguard themselves from the consequences of discovery. The greater the criminal activity committed by the abusers, the greater becomes their interest in ensuring that they keep power and hold firm control over their victims. When we look at ritual abuse, we find that not only are most moral laws broken, but more to the point, some serious criminal offences take place as an integral part of the abuse. In many ways, that is the point!

On top of that, people who get organised in groups to carry out abuse have usually invested a great deal of time, energy and money into 'training' people how to respond to them in the way that best suits the interests of the abusers. Most of their 'victims' have been carefully groomed and trained from infancy to obey and accept all that goes on in the family, the faith and the group. They are familiar with all that is expected of them and have been taught to stay silent and complacent at all times. They have learned to accommodate and accept things that most people would find intolerable. They have learned to accept their fate and frequently think that they deserve no better from life. They have become well trained assets for the group to use in whatever way they choose. In strict business terms the abusers are very loathe to lose out on this type of long-term investment. Add to that the simple fact that the abusers would much rather get away with

their crimes than be caught, and possibly convicted and sent to prison. According to the survivors, many who are involved as abusers are seemingly respectable people and many often have respectable positions of power in the community and the prosperity which usually accompanies this. Many are professional people with well paid jobs and the standard of living to match this. They quite understandably seek to maintain their high standard of living and the 'god-like' power they hold over some of the individuals they choose to abuse. Is it any wonder that the abusers do everything they possibly can to maintain their positions of power and control over the survivors?

Abusers do not ever let go of their 'victims' easily. They cannot afford to just let them go. For a start, if 'victims' were allowed to just walk away from their lives, other 'victims' might get similar ideas. They might think that they too could just get up and leave also. The abusers cannot afford to lose any, never mind all of their 'victims' so they must make it as hard as possible for anyone to get away from them. They must prove to those they control that they will severely punish any who try to leave them. They must show beyond all question of doubt that it is in people's best interest to stay with the group. They cannot ever risk being seen as weak or soft by anyone, especially other group members. In order to keep hold of their power and authority, they must fully display it and wield it as often as possible and most certainly in the face of a rebellion such as anyone trying to leave the group.

Also, they cannot ever take the risk that a survivor might someday report them to the police. Though they will have done a great deal to try and ensure that a survivor will not approach the police for help or even talk, they rarely take any risks. A survivor who succeeds in escaping from the group is potentially a huge threat to the group. If they were ever to tell and name any names, heads might roll. As it happens though, the survivor is, in reality, rarely a very high risk due to the high degree of conditioning, control and fear that survivors experience. Most survivors also lack the ability to talk about anything that happened to them for many, many years. Even if they did manage somehow to break through all the conditioning and talk, they are unlikely to be believed and much of what they say will be attributed to them having developed mental health problems.

Then there is the lack of awareness in the community, lack of services in general and total disbelief that most would face if they ever did try to break their silence. The likelihood of survivors talking and informing anyone about the abusers is very slim indeed. Nevertheless, abusers do not care for anything that might potentially be a risk either now or in years to come and therefore try to ensure that they maintain the silence of the survivors forever. If they could simply kill the survivors they would but they cannot always

take the risk of murdering someone. When survivors are accounted for in the world, it is too risky for the abusers to try and just make survivors disappear. They then have to employ other tactics.

Abusers need survivors not to talk about them at all. This is one of the reasons there is often a repeated and sustained backlash against the survivor who escapes. Many survivors who get away are attacked, harassed and threatened, often for many years after they have escaped. The attacks often carry on until the time that the survivor is finally prepared to make a stand and let someone know what is going on for them. The abusers will stop if they think that there is any chance at all that they might be seen or caught in the act. They will not take the risk of discovery.

It is a shame that survivors do not realise that they could get the harassment to stop sooner if they were only to contact the police for help. The abusers do not want to be identified and would try to do nothing that might lead to anyone making any allegations that might be substantiated. They want to ensure that they are invisible therefore the second they believe that someone has reported them to any authority such as the police, they will vanish from sight. Though it is a frightening thought for the survivor to think about going to the police for help, and they may have good reason for such caution, it is the one thing pretty well guaranteed to stop any more direct attacks upon them. This does not necessarily mean the abusers will give up, only that they will be less direct about their threats in the future. They are like all bullies, at heart they are simple cowards who when confronted deny and hide away from any possible consequences they might have to face for their actions.

Those who support survivors are also occasionally attacked, harassed and threatened. There is often a more subtle approach to the threats received by supporters than those received by survivors. This is because those people who support survivors are far less likely to believe that the abusers are all powerful and are more likely to report any attacks on them to the authorities. The abusers know already that most people who are not survivors of this type of abuse and who are threatened or attacked will normally go to the police instantly. Most people would consider this the only course of action. The abusers are therefore more likely to be much more careful in what they do or threaten to do to the supporters. They do not want to risk any investigation or anything that might suggest the survivor is perhaps telling the truth about what they fear, but they do want to cause fear and alarm in order to further isolate the survivor from any support. It does not take all that much to put some people off supporting survivors and often threats are enough to effectively achieve this end.

When workers in agencies receive threats or are actually attacked, it can mean the complete withdrawal of a service for the survivor and indeed sometimes for all survivors of this kind of abuse. For example, sometimes survivors who have fled to Women's Aid refuges have been asked to leave the refuge after threats were made by an abusive group to workers or other women in the refuge. The levels of fear can be quite high already in a refuge and the threats from the abusers often tip the balance and cause absolute terror. The survivor is regarded as bringing too much trouble to the door in the shape of numerous, faceless baby-eating abusers who strike terror into the imagination of all. People become so afraid that it is believed that in the interests of the other residents in the refuge, the woman has to leave. Sometimes it is.

Some of these Women's Aid groups who have had this type of experience now even refuse to take ritual abuse survivors into the refuge at all. Some feel that they are not equipped to deal with some of the issues surrounding women fleeing this type of extreme violence. It is understandable that people get frightened and react strongly to threats from abusers but it is sad when agencies and workers overreact and the survivor suffers as a direct consequence of this. Thankfully not all Women's Aid groups react like this, only a few. Some react by raising their own awareness about organised and ritual abuse, training their workers and helping the woman find additional support so that she can cope with what is going on for her.

The backlash or just the fear of the backlash can severely affect survivors for many years after they have escaped from the group. So too, as has already been stated, can a survivors network of support be affected. People who support survivors can often become so afraid that they can no longer continue to do the work. Most supporters are not survivors themselves and unlike survivors they often have no experience at all of how to cope with the constant threats, fear and violence which most often accompanies ritual abuse. Some people even cannot cope with the survivor beginning to talk about the abuse, even on a superficial level. It can be relatively easy for the abusive groups to frighten off kind hearted but very naive supporters.

Not all are so easily frightened off though. Some workers and agencies are prepared in the first instance to take on any type of abuse with varying degrees of success. When agencies and individuals begin to raise awareness and join the fight back against ritual abuse, they often also experience the backlash. A number of agencies have fallen foul of the backlash in a variety of different ways. Some have been thoroughly discredited in the media. Some have faced law suits. Some have been forced to close down or re-brand themselves. Some have had workers

threatened with violence or even physically attacked. Some agencies, because of the severity of the backlash, have completely stopped working with survivors of ritual abuse. Some continue the work but are very low key about it and never mention the words ritual or organised in relation to their work with survivors of abuse. Others disregard the backlash and keep on publicly working with the subject and with the survivors of it.

Though the backlash itself is often expected by agencies, it rarely comes from the expected direction. For example, in October 1994 the local rape crisis group in Dundee, which I was involved in as a volunteer at the time, organised a three day training event to raise awareness of ritualised and organised abuse. This was to be the first ever event of its kind in Scotland. The event was widely publicised and there was a huge amount of interest from many different agencies and from all over Scotland. Places on the training were limited to one per agency and the three days were fully booked in no time. So many others wanted to attend that we could have run this training event about three times over and still have been fully booked.

As an organisation we had to discuss the possibility of a backlash and we thought we had done as much as possible to protect ourselves from it. We discussed keeping workers confidentiality, working in pairs and getting to and from the training event safely. We spoke about the various things that could maybe happen if abusers wanted to do something to discredit or disrupt anything during the event and we felt we had covered most of the avenues. Yet, when the backlash came, actually during the three days, it was from such an unexpected direction that we were left reeling from it and felt completely uncertain about how to handle it. As a result, we handled the whole thing very badly indeed.

On the second day of this unique training event, the main organiser of the event was subjected to a prolonged attack at home which lasted throughout the night. The attacker was a woman who was a rape crisis worker from another centre, and was attending the training event. During the assault, she carried out several intense rituals, including calling upon Satan and various other deities. There was no doubt left as to the attacker's involvement in an abusive and probably satanic group. During the attack, many threats were made against the worker and her children. The attacker knew many personal details about the family and in particular about the children and pets in the household and detailed exactly what would happen to all should work on raising awareness about ritual abuse continue.

The strange events leading up to this attack, the extremely weird things that happened during the attack and the totally incredible things that

happened afterwards as a direct result of the attack and attempts to complain about what had happened, are almost unbelievable. It would be hard to try and describe in any detail all the things that happened and expect to be believed, yet, the aftermath at least is evidenced by many letters exchanged about it and minutes of the many meetings held about it. A great deal of what happened during this time is provable. All that happened at that time happened as a direct result of trying to raise awareness of ritual abuse in Scotland.

The person who actually carried out the attack and made the threats was, at that time, a rape crisis worker from another rape crisis centre in West Scotland. It was not Ayr! Neither was it Glasgow! That it was a rape crisis worker at all was totally unbelievable and completely unexpected. No one could ever have suspected that they were at any risk from a worker in the same field. And certainly no one could imagine being attacked in such a ritualistic way in their own home by someone who was effectively a colleague. Rape crisis workers were supposed to be women who helped female survivors of sexual violence. They were not supposed to carry out violent attacks on other women! It was unbelievable. On top of all that, how she had managed to get as much personal information about the event organiser and her family was, and still is, a complete mystery.

When a complaint was instigated against this abusive worker by the Dundee group, the group from the West refused point blank to accept a complaint from the Dundee group. They insisted that the woman who 'claimed' she was attacked, make the complaint personally. Eventually, after a great deal of persuasion and thought, the woman did just this. She was instantly met with open hostility and threats. The rape crisis centre the attacker worked for stood by the alleged attacker completely and totally refused to even accept any complaint against her. They also threatened legal proceedings against the woman who was attacked if she did not back down and stop complaining about what had happened to her.

They refused to hear, see or discuss in any way any evidence whatsoever against their own worker and simply denied that there was any case to answer at all. This was despite the fact that there were many witnesses to some of the worker's bizarre, very drunken and extremely aggressive behaviour earlier in the evening in a pub and beyond. Though no one witnessed the actual attack on the worker herself, the events leading up to it were witnessed by many people, and showed the general abusive direction that things were moving in at the time. So much so that the woman who was later attacked expressed at an earlier time some concern and fear of attack to no less than four people who were present in the pub and later in the car taking people home.

Yet the rape crisis group concerned did not want to know about what happened and indeed reacted aggressively to any suggestion that something might have happened at all. They were accountable to no one it seemed and just not prepared to accept any complaints from anyone about their worker. It turned out that the worker concerned had a bit of a history of people making allegations against her. It was an unbelievable way for an organisation which was supporting survivors of sexual abuse to behave. One seriously has to wonder why any organisation working with vulnerable people would act in this manner.

The attack by this worker was not reported to the police at the time, though with hindsight it probably should have been. It was thought that much of what had happened would have been met by disbelief and it would have been difficult to explain all that had gone on to people who had no understanding at all of ritual abuse. To be completely honest, talking to the police at that time was not even thought about at all by the woman concerned or the Dundee rape crisis group. The worker who had been attacked was extremely traumatised for quite a long time afterwards and it took her about three years to go back to working to raise awareness about ritual abuse in Scotland. The backlash on this occasion caused a major setback.

There was also the problem of being very concerned about bringing the rape crisis movement into any kind of disrepute. Publicity about one rape crisis worker attacking another was a totally unthinkable thought. The Rape Crisis Network became involved because the alleged abuser was a worker in another rape crisis centre and the Dundee group refused to attend any meetings that this particular worker might attend. This meant that joint meeting of the rape crisis groups could not properly go ahead. As it was, it was difficult for all of those who were involved to fully comprehend what had actually happened and the things that continued to happen as a result of the original attack upon a worker. It took more than a year for the dust to settle and the main outcome was that the rape crisis centre whose worker had been accused of the attack was simply asked to leave the Network as they were deemed to have broken policies agreed by all.

There were serious consequences of what was clearly a backlash against trying to raise awareness about ritual abuse in Scotland. There was not only a hard lesson learned by myself and those around me, but also a hesitation to be as open about the work as previously. A book which was written in 1995 was not published until 2001 and it was not until 1997 that the next series of training and awareness events about ritual abuse were organised. Though the work continued, there were many delays as a direct consequence of the attack and its aftermath. The backlash on that occasion

effectively slowed the work that many of us were involved in and made all of us much more cautious about what we were all doing to raise awareness. Some individuals who had worked with ritual abuse survivors became too afraid after this and stopped working with the issue of ritual abuse entirely.

There have been other examples of the backlash both for the organisations and the individuals who support survivors, raise awareness and fight back against ritual abuse. Sometimes the backlash is direct as in the example I have just provided but on other occasions it is much more subtle in nature. Things happen to workers such as their cars being damaged or interfered with, pets deliberately stolen, injured or even killed and on many occasions, statutory workers suddenly being removed from cases they have been involved in and survivors being left isolated as a result of this.

Despite all of this though there is one good thing about the backlash, at least for the agencies and workers concerned. It is the fact that if we were making no progress at all in relation to this type of abuse there would be no backlash at all from the abusers and their allies. The backlash is a fairly clear indication that the abusers are getting a little bit worried about what we are up to. If we were being completely ineffective, they would not have any cause to worry and would not try to stop or discredit us. They would not need to do anything. So perhaps to some degree at least we need to take the extremely positive message from this and learn to regard the backlash as some measure of our continuing success in exposing ritual and organised abuse.

Survivors Accounts

Lee

"I have experienced backlash from my family, though not now that I've been entirely out of contact with them. I hope there won't be backlash now I'm out of contact with my family. I don't know what'll happen if they find me. I'm hoping they won't cause I really like my life."

Kay

"Being older it hasn't been an escape from abuse as much as an escape from contact with my father, one of the ringleaders. At first, when the incest surfaced and the Samaritans encouraged me to write to say I was advised not to see him for a month, then three, etc., he wrote often and phoned once. Each time I would be almost destroyed by feelings of guilt, but slowly from his letters I began to see he did not care about me but only himself.

After I left home, there were letters from him and emotional blackmail letters from relatives. I expected people would try to kill me. But nothing has happened. The only odd thing so far is a man joining my sculpture class and doing a sort of creepily amputated body, and last week edging up on me."

Jill

"The backlash since getting away has been ever increasing attempts to undermine me, my confidence and my progress. I rejected them and their religion and their money and their life style and their status.

I rejected them in every way I possibly could. I did not understand their religion or their beliefs. I certainly did not like any of it in any way. I did not like their life style and their status seemed empty and futile to me. So I left them at the first possible opportunity. I escaped from them.

But I was only a child. I desperately wanted love and acceptance. It never came from anywhere. I eventually looked for love and acceptance elsewhere because I needed it so much. I found love by doing the opposite of what they lived and believed. They tried to force me to do things I did not find in any way acceptable. I fought back against them. I still do fight back.

They still want me back but I've stayed away from them since escaping. Occasionally they still try to get at me. Occasionally they really get to me. Sometimes they get close. They can hurt and upset me sometimes but they won't ever get me back. I would rather die than ever go back to them or let them have anything they want.

They even tried to get to my children. I fought back and they did not get them. I threatened to expose them if they dared to touch my children. They did not touch them. They tried to trick me again and again and sometimes it worked. They tried to frighten me and I was very frightened on occasions. Then they tried to threaten me. I felt threatened. But I did not back down or give in to their threats. I never will back down as there is no going back. They have already done their worst."

Sheila

"Backlash? They know where I am. It's not a problem."

Annie

"Backlash includes further abuse, a sister getting attacked and disbelief, labels of illness and fear and uncertainty. I do expect backlash, I have no reason from past experiences not to expect it. I expect to be hurt whenever I get found."

Nat

"The backlash? I'm not sure about this question. I have had trouble with things since I escaped. Money and health problems are just a couple of examples but whether these could be put down to conspiracy or a part of the backlash I am not sure. I think that the backlash is inevitable. The more people want to talk about ritual abuse, uncover it and expose it to the world the greater and louder that the backlash is going to be. They (the abusers) need to have and maintain their secrecy. They can only survive with secrecy so any attack on that will invoke an attack from them.

I think that there are many ways that the backlash happens. On a personal note the easiest way to get back at a survivor is to mess around with things like income support, benefits, housing and council tax. These people come from all facets and strata of society they have every possible job. This is an easy way and is extremely effective at harassing the survivor who if not very strong or who does not have a good support network would inevitably crack under the pressure of this kind of attack. Missing paperwork, misinformation can all lead to severe delays in getting benefit. Payment dates and the like messed up. It is very hard to live on no money at all for long periods of time.

I think that every survivor expects a backlash from the moment you escape until the moment it happens. You expect it because you believe you have done something wrong. You have betrayed your group and your family. It is like believing that you deserve to get a hard time. Even though you do not want that hard time you give it to yourself. You wait for the backlash and wait. It's a bit like waiting for the sky to fall down. Sometimes it will happen. I am not dismissing anyone who has been on the receiving end of the backlash. But for the most part they are too scared to directly attack the survivor in front of witnesses. They are too scared that they will be named and that people will start to listen to the people who know what goes on."

Nell

"The Backlash; I haven't experienced that much of a backlash. There were the cards and letters and presents from my family that set me back a bit, but they dwindled and eventually stopped coming through the door. I expected a huge backlash when I got away. I never was very far away from my family and was scared that they would find me, take me away and try me as a traitor, as I should be. The thought of them finding me was more terrifying than the thought of what they would do. I knew what would happen. I had seen it. There was no mystery in that. It was the not knowing that was hard. Not knowing what they were doing and what they were going to do.

Do I believe that they are looking for me? I am not sure. I think that they would take their chance, if they could. But I am pretty well accounted for now. They would have a lot of explaining to do if anything happened to me. I am glad in a way that I have so many people that would start asking questions if anything happened to me. I have been away for four years now. I would find it hard to go back."

Lucky

"Over the years the backlash I have experienced has changed. I think this may, in part, be due to the changes in me and how I respond to things now and also due to changes in the way they try to attack and silence me.

When I first ran away from the family as a quite young child, I was caught, brought back and punished. I learned not to run away unless I would be absolutely certain to get away for good. The fear of getting caught again and punished again was too unnerving to cope with. I was too afraid to try again for many years.

I did manage to escape when I got a bit older and for many years, as they could not find me, I was physically safe from them. I did not ever feel completely safe but there was no direct backlash against me. Then one day they found me. At first the threats were subtle though frightening. There were phone calls and messages through the letterbox. I was followed and threatened with violence. Then I was actually attacked. I think they had been testing to see if I would tell anyone or do anything about the threats up until then. I was forced to go with them and was held captive by them for over a month but they could not really go too far with me as I was now accounted for out in the real world. People would ask questions now if I vanished. The questions would need to be answered.

I now had a full time job and people who knew me. People would now question my total disappearance and there would be an investigation if anything really serious happened to me. I knew this to be true. They knew this too. They knew how far they could go with me. They knew I would not tell on them, but I knew though they could hurt me they could not kill me. Over that month there were times when I seriously wished that they would. Eventually they let me go. I went home and packed. I moved to another town and found a new job.

As time went on I began to realise that I had some power. Though they had tracked me down again, they were more cautious. It took me a long time to realise that I had any power of my own and occasional threats and minor attacks from the group made sure that I remained silent. One time when I did begin to break silence, I was physically attacked and that shut me up for a long time.

I found, in time, that they pretty well left me alone if I did nothing and stayed silent. It was only later that I realised that silence protects only them and even though it is hard, it is better to be able to talk about things when you need to. I also found that the more people actually know about you, the less the group will bother you in the end. It took me ages to get to this but then I tried naming names and making sure they knew that I had. That was the end of all direct assaults. After all, if anything now happened to me, everyone would know who to look to first to ask some questions."

John

"The backlash is everywhere. The fact is that you have to be part of 'the mental health club' before anyone official listens to you. Then they try to medicate you, when you eventually manage to speak to another survivor and are supported enough to empower yourself to swallow your pride and neurosis and acute schizophrenia and actually talk to the police, simply to be treated as a person who has just reported a stolen hubcap. Show your true emotions and get handcuffed and put in a cell for no reason. Before you know it you are a borderline psychopath with a criminal record with absolutely no chance of being taken seriously. All because you played by the book, saw the doctors, saw the police. Fuck the system and fuck going by the book. There is no justice. Abusers are treated like victims and survivors are treated like criminals.

The backlash is simply having to survive in a fucked up world that everyone just accepts. As for what I expect when the shit really hits the fan with this project I am working on. I expect to be killed just like others. It will be made to look like suicide. But bring it on. I know what happens after death. Still, I only think like that because I am a meglo-maniac with a persecution problem (joke)."

SURVIVOR

ISSUES

SURVIVOR ISSUES

For survivors of any abuse there are many different issues which change over time for them. As the circumstances of any survivor's life change over time, so too will the issues and problems experienced by them change. Life is not static for most people and over time different issues become less or more important to any individual. Survivors are not a homogenous group. They are all individuals with individual thoughts, feelings and issues which do not remain static.

For the survivors who are currently still being abused, basic day to day survival would probably be the only thing of any real importance for them. Survivors in this position of necessity have to focus all their energy on staying sane and alive day by day. Issues for them might focus on finding ways of getting enough food or sleep. It might include focusing on making sure that the abusers are kept calm, happy and appeased. It might also include finding ways of tending to any injuries they receive to make sure that their wounds do not become infected. With on-going abuse the issues are often simple and basic. When the base line is survival there is little room for any other issues to penetrate.

Some survivors may be struggling to survive the abuse and may become so desperate that they begin to look for ways to get out of the group and get away to a safe place. They may know that they are soon to be killed. Escape becomes the only issue in the mind of the survivor at that time. Attempts at escaping are seldom successful though when attempted through such desperation. By far the best results in escaping are achieved when a person has the time and ability to plan properly. Unfortunately not many survivors of ritual abuse will be able to find the time to plan.

Even if the survivor is able to think and plan and maybe stash some money, important documents and a change of clothing before fleeing, they will stand a better chance of success. If the most important issue is to escape and stay away, the more prepared a person is the better it will be for them. Finding a safe place to hide is essential, particularly in the early days. A little thought before running can sometimes help the survivor focus on thinking about where to go and where the support networks might be. On first escaping the issues begin to change very rapidly.

After a survivor gets away other things often become more important. Initially survival will still be an issue but this is more likely to revolve round safe housing, money and keeping themselves physically safe. Staying safe sometimes means going into hiding or moving again and again as the

abusers continue to find them. Few survivors get away easily or cleanly the first time and most survivors have to work very hard at staying clear of the group. The most common occurrence for the survivor who has recently gotten out is to be found by the group and attacked or threatened on more than one occasion. Safety and staying one step ahead of the abusers is often the most common issue for survivors at this time.

For some survivors there is the difficult issue of trying to stop themselves from returning to the group or the family. The temptation to return to what is familiar to them can be overwhelming particularly at certain times of year. So too are the constant reminders and incentives to return. Then there is the programming to deal with that often forces survivors to return. Most do so the first time. Some return because they have no awareness of themselves and one of their personalities takes them home. Often there is some sort of hold that the group has over the survivor, such as a child of theirs. It is common for survivors of this type of abuse to believe that a child of theirs is still alive and 'safe' with the group. They can then be coerced into doing things they do not want to do in the hope that it will save their child from too much harm. The link to the group is kept open with this type of incentive.

As time goes by and the regular abuse and life within the group comes to an end, the issues change again. Though staying safe is often a lifelong endeavour, and survivors may still have some problems with the abusers, over time, there is no longer the daily fight to survive within the group. At this stage, survivors often begin to look around for help and support in order to begin to heal from their personal trauma. Survivors begin to move beyond a baseline survival and often begin to see and accept that there could perhaps be more to life than what they have had up until now. Some begin to find hope.

Many survivors of extreme trauma experience major problems with their physical and mental health. They often suffer from flashbacks, panic attacks, depression, mental health problems, physical health problems, etc. Some try to cope with the help of people close to them or they may seek support and advice through statutory or voluntary organisations. For a while the issue becomes one of trying to find good help and regular support preferably from someone with a high awareness of the issues of ritual abuse. This is never an easy task to achieve. Survivors often have to work very hard to find a suitable agency with awareness and often spend a lot of frustrated time searching for quality support. Often they think they have found someone but through time become disappointed and feel let down due to the person's low level of awareness about ritual abuse. It takes time and effort to find qualified support.

As survivors move beyond base-line survival, move towards greater personal safety, manage to find some therapy and support for themselves and get used to the many and varied frustrations that abuse free life brings, they often begin to create their own families and own set of friends. This brings a whole new range of issues for them including those of trust, child protection and managing relationships with friends, partners and children. All of these bring their own set of problems and even bonuses. Survivors are normal people and as with all normal people, once some of the more basic and practical difficulties of their lives are removed, they can go on and lead a normal and fulfilling life.

Many people imagine that survivors of extreme abuse will suffer from long term complex problems and illnesses, and indeed, some do. Some continue to suffer from the effects of the abuse until the day they die. Others do not. People are individuals and as such they vary in how they are affected by any abuse and they heal at different rates and in different ways. Some people appear to be able to move on very rapidly from an abusive life while others struggle for many years to heal and move on in their lives. There is quite a high degree of disability among ritual abuse survivors but there is also a very high degree of recovery from the effects. The bottom line is that all survivors are individuals with different needs, different reactions and different responses.

The issues that survivors deal with are as varied as the issues that anyone else deals with. As parents they worry about protecting their children. As parents who are also survivors they probably worry more than most parents as they know just how abusive people can be. Though survivors may have a slightly different perspective from many people in thinking about and dealing with different issues, this is most usually due to their additional experiences and awareness. They are still normal people dealing with the same and similar issues as everyone else.

Survivors Accounts

Lee

"It's strange to think at times I was very protective of my mother. The important issue for me is having my life and being able to do what I want to do. Now that I no longer feel guilt for not being there to take care of my mother I have time for my self. I am as I grow older finding it easier to speak though I do still pause at times and find it difficult to speak in large groups. I still feel like my writing and reading skills are somewhat ahead of my speaking skills."

Sheila

"The important issue is that it's not happening anymore, and to know that it's not my fault that somehow I didn't make it happen.

I have multiple phobias e.g. agoraphobia, closed/open spaces, men, people in authority (police, Doctors, dentists, social workers).

Yes issues have changed. The most important thing for me now is to protect myself and my daughter."

Kay

"The most important issue for me is therapy. For about twenty years now therapy or the search for it has dominated my life. It seems to me incredibly hard to get a good therapist, and also I'm incredibly lucky as my brother and then mother left me some money so I could afford it.

Medical needs have been a huge issue. I find the NHS (National Health Service) very dismissive of physical problems, which are often worse because of my poor immune system. Again I've been grateful for the money, as I got invalided out of the job market a long time ago. I often feel I must survive in order to pave the way for people who've not had my luck in recent years with money.

Isolation has always been a huge issue. It is very tough to force myself out to go to things, but I am trying to do so more and more. Finding that I'm a Ritual Abuse survivor has helped, as well as hindered, as I now have total respect for myself."

Annie

"Making sure I always have at least one person who understands and believes, whether this be an outside or an inside person. Making sure I always keep in touch with real life such as doing house work and food shopping.

I still have physical and emotional problems as a result of the abuse. I also have so called disorders, which are supposed to be a problem but are not. I still have fear, and I frequently fall back into the victim trap. The issues haven't really changed that much over time."

Lucky

"Over time the issues I have had to deal with have definitely changed for me. At first the only thing in my head was getting away, hiding and surviving on a day to day basis. I was afraid most of the time and found it almost impossible to cope with the nightmares and flashbacks that were my constant companions. I avoided people as much as I could and chose solitude rather than trying to learn to trust anyone. The main issue in my consciousness was to stay out of sight and finding ways of surviving that would not bring me to the attention of any authorities.

As the years went by the issues slowly changed. In time, I recognised how lonely and isolated I had become and began to risk getting to know people and risk having relationships. Friendship became important to me and my friends became my new and okay family. Increasingly I knew that I was missing out on a great deal. All the time I did not feel any sense of belonging anywhere. I felt totally different from the rest of humanity and I very desperately want to fit in and be accepted by people. Though I knew I could not dare tell anyone about my background, I did find more and more that I was beginning to want to share some aspects of my life with someone.

In time, I found a partner and eventually had some children. The kids were now the most important thing to me and their safety became a huge issue for me. I was so determined that my family and others like them would never get to my kids, that I became very over-protective of them. It was so hard to let them take normal risks and hard to realise that I had to find some sort of balance between protecting them and letting them learn and take some risks for themselves. As they got older and more aware I gradually began to relax. They were always sensible and were very well taught about personal safety.

One of the hardest things was seeing my children grow up and realising just how small and helpless I must have been when things had happened to me. I would look at my seven year old child and remember being that age. I found myself raging against the people who could hurt a child so young. In many ways, it probably helped me heal as I began to realise all that had been denied me as a child. I worried with my own children that somehow being a survivor might affect them adversely. I worried that I might deprive them without even knowing that I was doing so. As I had not had a normal upbringing I worried that I might get things badly wrong with them. I used to buy and read all the parenting magazines I could get my hands on to try and make sure I was getting it right. I suspect that I over did it.

When my kids grew up I knew that they were well adjusted and that I had done a good enough job with them. I had time on my hands again and again the issues shifted and trying to help other people like myself has now become an important issue for me. The best help I feel I can offer at the moment is to help raise awareness about this type of abuse. Perhaps if enough people know about it, it will change something for someone. I would hate for anyone to ever be as alone as I became when I first escaped from the group. I would also hate others to not have quality support and access to help when they want and need it"

Nat

"I would say that safety was and is an important issue for me, as well as being believed. Because they always said that no-one would believe me and to some extent that was true, I always felt that I had to monitor what I was going to say to people. Sift through it and take out the unbelievable, make things more palatable for the listener regardless of who that was. So belief and trust were and still are important issues.

I think that the issues have changed over time; safety is no longer as huge as it was. I want to be treated like everyone else although I know that I am not the same as everyone else. I know that my past has affected me and that I get ill. I know that people take trust and love for granted and it has taken me a long time to get to that place where I can to a certain extent trust people and love them.

I can do that with other people but I have found that I can't and have great difficulty in trusting or loving myself. I don't and I can't. Although I have got to a place where I believe that people see things in me that I can't see or don't want to see, which I took a long time to get to.

I still believe that I am not as worthwhile a person as anyone else. The belief system that was instilled is turning out to be more difficult to overcome than the safety issue. I think that there a lot of issues that face survivors everyday. I think that these issues change over time and can change as we deal with them."

John

"The important issues are freedom, expression and truth. The system is against all of these. They are not encouraged. Sexual abuse is just the malfunction of such repression and suppression in a physical body. There is only one real issue which is destroying the system by feeding on it to create something better.

I am a big believer in turning negative into positive. I get my cash from the post office every fortnight and use it to create something better in myself and others. I am a total parasite on the system. If only there were more parasites with vision then maybe there would be no structure to the sexual abuse. Apart from that, always being me and staying alive are the only issues I deal with daily."

INSIDERS

INSIDERS

Disociative Identity Disorder (D.I.D.) is a term that is often used to describe a condition which is generally characterised by someone having, or believing that they have, more than one personality within them at the same time. The person has two or more distinctly separate personalities. The personalities often have their own individual names, separate memories and individual characters. Sometimes the personalities are not regarded as human and/or are regarded as part of the cult or group. The personalities in some individuals are often in conflict with each other and cannot agree about anything at all. Sometimes, in some people, the personalities do not know anything about each other and/or do not communicate with each other in any way. Occasionally, there is no problem at all between the different personalities and they all work together well.

This is often referred to as multiplicity, multiple personality disorder or dissociative identity disorder and regardless of the name of the condition, it most usually comes about as a result of extreme and ongoing abuse which happens to someone at an early age. It is not, in the opinion of most survivors and many of their supporters, an actual disorder; rather it is most often regarded as a creative way of a young child learning to cope with extreme abuse. The child, in trying to deal with many painful and difficult things, which are so extreme and incomprehensible, that creating another person to deal with the abuse, becomes the only way out. The child just cannot cope with the abuse any more but they have no way to control or end it; therefore someone else is created to cope with what is happening. If this works for the child and succeeds in distancing them enough from the abuse so that they can cope with life, they will continue to use it. This often results in many personalities being created.

Not all people who are survivors of ritual or organised abuse have multiple personalities and not all people who have multiple personalities have lived with or experienced ritual abuse. Though not all ritual abuse survivors have multiple personalities, many, and perhaps most, do. Most survivors of ritual abuse do talk about having a range of different personalities or inside people who came into being in their childhood usually as a result of very extreme abuse. Survivors when they become more comfortable with themselves, talk about the voices they hear inside their heads, their inside people, their alters and their inside family. Many survivors are comfortable with having more that one personality but some are not.

When a child is being abused, he or she often learns quite rapidly that the only way to survive and stay sane is to dissociate self and identity from what is happening to the body. This 'out of body' way of dealing with abuse is very well known to survivors of all kinds of abuse. When the abuse is severe and sustained and the child has to take an active part in the proceedings, the 'out of body' experience is sometimes shifted into the child creating another part of self that exists to cope with what is happening to them. The child can switch between selves to keep going. In this way, the child can still function and do all the things that have to be done within a group abuse situation, and indeed a normal setting such as going to school the day after extreme abuse, but the child no longer has to cope alone.

For the child who has experienced the isolation of abuse, not having to bear it alone or passing it on to someone else, even a not quite real someone else, can make a tremendous difference to them. It makes no odds whether or not all of this occurs only within the mind, which of course it does. But, if it works for the child, then it means that the child is more likely to survive and that has to be a positive outcome. This is, in the main how multiplicity probably occurs. Though there is one brain and one body, there can end up being various, very different personalities existing within the one person. Sometimes the personalities are so different that it becomes difficult to remember that this is all the same person.

The child may dissociate again and again and create more and more personalities to cope with the continuing abuse and so find new ways of distancing self from all that is going on for them. The child may also not want to remember the details of the abuse or even who the abusers are and therefore may take a larger step away from the nightmare that is their daily life. They may even create for themselves a personality who is a 'normal' person who lives a 'normal' life which is more like the kind of life that everyone else has. This personality then knows nothing about the abuse and lives, albeit narrowly, in an abuse free zone. This part of the personality would probably end up having no knowledge at all of any of the other personalities.

As the child grows up, if splitting into other people within the mind has worked positively for them, then they continue to do it. For them, this is normal and it can help them stay in control and help them function in their daily lives for a very long time. The only thing disordered about any of this is the abusive group and what they are doing to the child and to other children in the first place. It is often only when a survivor finally escapes from the abusive group that the whole multiple personality way of being can become a problem for them. Being many different people who do not necessarily communicate very well, if at all, with one another can be majorly

problematic for a person trying to live in an abuse free world. When the abuse stops, the survivor still has their coping mechanism and this coping mechanism may no longer effectively work for them.

In this country, multiplicity is, at best, dismissed by medical people when they are treating survivors of ritual abuse, or at worst seen as an illness or disorder that needs to be cured. In the United Kingdom it is hard to find a professional who will call it anything other than a personality disorder or a borderline personality disorder. Professionals always seem to like to keep the word disorder in all their diagnoses. Multiplicity is most often treated by medics with heavy duty sedatives and anti-psychotic medication which quite simply cannot and does not work for this condition. It is an example of medical people trying to treat symptoms of something they do not fully understand while not being prepared to listen to the experiences of the survivors. Treating the symptoms of having more than one personality by sedating the survivor seems a very bizarre approach for doctors to take.

Multiplicity, which is a coping mechanism which has actually saved the life and sanity of a person, soon becomes something to hide and be ashamed of, treated with medication or electric shock therapy and/or be viewed as madness or illness. As medical people seek to force the condition to meet their narrow medical models and seek to find suitable labels of their own to stick on the survivor, they also seek to 'cure' it with pills. Many survivors become mystified as to how they could have survived their abuse and appeared sane and mentally healthy but suddenly on going to a doctor they become labelled with a disorder and suffer from some sort of chemical imbalances of the brain that only medication can help.

Yet for many survivors who are multiple, in time they can learn to accept themselves and their own creativity. They can learn to communicate within themselves and can learn a great deal about themselves and how they have coped. Some can even get to the stage of being glad that they are multiple because they have so many skills and personalities to draw upon. Many go on to use this skill to their full advantage in their home lives and in their careers. Many people who have multiple personalities never go near the doctors or therapists but find their own ways of coming to terms with their coping mechanisms, their lives and the abuse they have experienced.

The abusers often deliberately use the survivor's ability to dissociate to their own advantage. Some abusers force the survivor to dissociate through creating a situation of extreme pain and fear and then try to dictate the characteristics of the personality that is formed as a result of the dissociation. Survivors in this position are very vulnerable and are often very suggestive.

Sometimes, the personality formed is regarded as belonging to the group, because it is believed that the group created it. This is not true. They did not create it at all though they may have contributed to some of the characteristics of it through the suggestibility of the survivor.

Unfortunately, the survivor who realises that this personality exists may fully believe that it is a part of the abusive group. The abusive group will almost certainly have found ways to reinforce this belief. This may be taken as far as the 'cult created' personality being regarded as an internal spy or saboteur. Yet, this personality is still all part of the same person who is surviving and it is all a part of the creative coping mechanisms that the survivor had to find or create.

Survivors use whatever means and methods they can and have at their disposal to stay sane in what is often an insane and cruel world. They often do so instinctively. Most are far too young at the time of the first abuse to rationalise or find a logical way of coping therefore they are forced to rely on their own instinct. They draw their strength from whatever source they can find and sometimes they have to find ways of holding onto the thought that someone else rather than them is there in the situation and someone else cares for them. Often survivors who are enduring extremes of violence cannot believe in themselves anymore and need to believe in someone or even something else. Which ever way they do it, does it really matter if it harms no one yet helps the survivor to survive the things which ought not to be happening to them in a so called civilised country?

Survivors Accounts

Lee

"The other part of things that's given me strength is that I feel my father's spirit is part of me. I don't have inside people per se, but this part of me that gives me determination that seems to come from my father. Maybe this is bizarre but its part of what got me where I am today so it can't be bad or wrong. So I think as long as it doesn't do you any harm, especially if it's helping you survive then it shouldn't matter if it's normal (sorry to disappoint all those psychiatrists out there)."

Sheila

"Insiders. Yes, they're part of me. Yes, it's normal it's a part of me. It's how I survived. They're there to help me get through the day."

Kay

"I don't think there's such a thing as "normality". I think we're all different, and we who were badly abused as children split to survive. It is just how we are. I do hear of multiples spontaneously integrating to one inner child. It seems the best thing is to just go along with it all. My inner kids are often terribly funny, very loving or caring, besides being very brave. I love them - most of the time."

Jill

"I never developed any kind of multiple personalities or dissociation, simply because I did not need to. I had found other ways of coping that are maybe not so very different in some ways and I had invented an 'invisible friend' or two. These friends were my safe people and I trusted them with my many and various problems. I lived in my imagination most of the time as it was a safe place to live and my friends and I created our own world to live in. It was a far better world than the one I really lived in. I suppose this is another form of dissociation. My friends took all the 'shit' not me.

I was brought up as a Satanist but there were Christian people around me too and they were just as bad. I could not really see any difference between the Christians and the satanists. They just all merged into one for me. They probably were one and the same.

I hated religion of all kinds. But I was really glad to have these invisible friends with me. They were always there for me as I carried them inside me at all times. No one ever knew about them. It was my secret weapon against them. I had a kind of faith about it. I believed there was someone or something there and therefore, there was someone and there was something. I used to wonder if that was what it was like to believe in god or satan. All of them were only there just because someone believed it to be the case. It seemed like it was a bit too much like my imaginary friends.

I did whatever I had to do, to survive at the time and no more. I became extremely depressed and very suicidal at times. I thought about suicide many times but never really went too far down that particular path. My imaginary friends would not let me as they needed me too much and I was too afraid that I might not succeed and might end up stuck in psychiatric care. This totally terrified me. Psychiatrists were in the abusive group, or at least I was often told that they were. I had also been threatened so many times with being locked away for the rest of my life in an institution and told what they would do to me there. I was told that they would just keep filling my head with electricity and I was so scared of electricity that I could not cope with the thought. Attempting suicide would be in my head from time to time, but I never actually tried it for myself.

Dissociative Identity Disorder is not a disorder at all in my opinion. It is a very creative response to an impossible situation that cannot be escaped from. It is a bit like my imaginary friends except on the inside. Professionals give symptoms a name so that they can be superior and they always have to put in the term disorder as a matter of course. What survivors who suffer from this need most is to be treated as normal human beings, which they are. Professionals are too quick to give labels and prescribe controlling medication. People become quite desperate to get help and yet often the survivors have their own answers to their own healing."

Ruth

"I have not had a good life at all. Having M.P.D. is very hard work. Every one of the personalities has their own memories. My alters help but sometime they get very angry about what happened to us so they take it out on the body by hurting, taking drugs or taking us back to the ones who hurt us. We have to change every thing in our lives. It is very hard for some of the personalities to understand that what we are doing is for the best."

Rose

"Then I started to hear the voices in my head. I did not want to tell anyone about the voices because people would think I was mad and get me locked up. I was not mad and if it was not for the voices I would not be here today.

At first it was just one voice and that was all right with me, but it did not stay that way for long. I did not want to tell anyone about the voices. I was too scared to tell anyone at first. Then I started to tell the people I loved about the voices. It was good telling them. It felt as if I was free. I did not need to hide them any more.

Just after I told them that is when it all went very wrong with some people. I tried to tell them that I was just the same person. But a lot of the friends I told did not see it like me. In their eyes I was mad and I should be locked up. It was very hard for me. I told them because I loved them. I did not want to tell them any lies.

It got worse. The personalities were coming out fast and each one had new memories from my past. Things I could not remember. It hurt so much that I wanted to die.

The personalities were taking over my life. I could not handle my past. My memory was coming back to haunt me. I just wanted it all to stop and leave me. Every time I was getting back on my feet another personality would come out. That would put me back a bit.

Each one is very different and holds different memories. Some were good and very sad. Some of them were very difficult. They would take over the body and take it away. Half the time I did not know where I was."

Tess

"Being Multiple has a good side and a bad side. The good side is I have many friends and they understand what it is like being scared. They are always there for you. The bad side is they can take away the body and they bring the bad memories with them.

We should not be scared about being Multiple. But we are because not a lot of people understand about Multiples. They think we are mad. But we are not mad we are just a person. So why do they treat us different? We are human the same as them. But we had a very bad start in life. We did not ask for these things to happen to us. It was not our fault."

Annie

"Well I have dissociative identity disorder (I have more than one separate identity). I have many inside people and friends. Some are good some are bad. I have some like Lyn. Who is closer than a sister or a friend. We talk together. We share our pain and fear and our hopes for the future. She helps me look after my little insiders.

We do fun things together like play online games or monopoly. I love my insiders. They're the closest thing I have to a family and in my way they are family. They protect me and help me when the going gets too tough for me to handle on my own and when they need to; they take me out and step in so they get the pain rather than me.

They are here because at times when the abuse got too painful for me, they came to help me cope. I think all people have more than one identity except with some people who have suffered from severe trauma these identities split further and yes I do think it is a normal reaction to trauma."

Lucky

"I never thought it was anything other than normal to have more than me inside me. For me, or should I say we, it did not become a problem until I realised that I was in some way different from other people. Though it took me ages to work out what was so different, in the end, I thought that I must be absolutely mad to be the way I was.

I was okay up until the day that a friend told me that she thought I was like someone she had read about. She told me she thought I maybe suffered, I ask you...'suffered!' from multiple personalities. I was shocked! I felt completely nuts! I thought my friend must be completely nuts. It took me ages to think about it and work out for myself that, yes there were a few of us, but so what? I realised that dissociation was not something that all people did.

Who can say what 'normal' is? By whose standard do we judge a person? I will not be judged by people who know nothing about my life. In the end, I could only go by my own experience in the world. I am normal for me. I am a product of my life and my experiences and I have, in my adult life, hurt no one and nothing by being the way I am. I have never needed any medical or psychiatric services nor have I ever been diagnosed with anything. I function very well in my daily life and have done so since healing from the trauma. I hold down a well paid job and have successfully raised my family. I may have inside people and be able to hear them but I am a whole person.

Perhaps I am lucky that internal communication is not a problem at all for me. It never has been a problem at all. Many survivors who are also multiple seem to have problems with inner conflict between personalities and seem to have a basic lack of internal communication. This has not been the case at all for me, or any of us. We worked together as a team in order to survive the really bad stuff that happened. It was always us against them. We still work together in order to survive the past and enjoy the good stuff and everyday life and we have a good and fulfilled life these days. I do not feel that there is any kind of disorder anywhere in my life now. All the disorder that there ever was anywhere near me was what abusers did in the past"

John

"M.P.D. is just a label to make doctors feel superior. I used to think I was schizoid, but now I think to myself what is personality and how is it even able to stay the same throughout the years without being absolutely self destructive when change happens.

I don't see M.P.D. or D.I.D. as disorders. I see them as part of my evolution enabling me to see not just two sides of the coin, but the edge as well and how it must spin always if life is to go on. It's just another case of abusers trying to destroy us but actually making us stronger.

I have ten personas but I am aware of most of them, which is slightly confusing. Most of them I like or can put up with but there are a couple I fucking hate. Not because of deviant thoughts as I realise now that they are just memories trying to surface. I hate them because they are quitters. They are morally devoid and godlike dictators. I don't get them very often but when I do, I just try to do weights or guitar.

I don't like having two at the same time that are really opposed to each other. I usually end up cutting myself. I don't know why they are there or if it's normal, but saying that deep down I do but will only reveal my true feelings in my project. Deep down I'm proud that even as a kid, I was creatively more superior to my multiple abusers. How weak must they be? Getting beaten in this power game by me!

Having multiple personas is needed I feel, even in everyday life. Speaking to a victim like a survivor helps empower the victim to become a true survivor. And, acting like a victim to those who might be out to manipulate me, helps me to see if they are givers or takers, helpers or hinderers. M.P.D. is just soul expansion. As long as you have a true unbreakable spirit, nothing else matters."

THE
UNBELIEVABLE

THE UNBELIEVABLE

At present, the denial of the existence of ritual abuse and all that it involves is powerful and enduring. The reaction of the press to any hint that ritual abuse might possibly exist in a civilised country such as the United Kingdom is swift and often extreme. Survivors are ridiculed, professionals are attacked and castigated and alleged offenders are rapidly turned into poor innocent victims who have been 'got at' by the unfeeling authorities who listened to 'mad and made up stories'. In the rush to sell newspapers by pointing the finger and accusing and counter-accusing, there is no room left for questioning whether or not there just might possibly have been any hint whatsoever of abuse happening in the first place, let alone ritual abuse. The over-reaction of the media is often enough to stop all investigations in their tracks and muddy the waters enough that we never quite get to the truth of what was going on in the first place.

It is difficult to talk about the subject of ritual abuse. Survivors find it painful to talk and almost impossible to describe the extremity of the abuse that they have experienced. They know that it will be hard for people to listen and believe them but on top of this they tend to want to safeguard their supporters from the whole horrendous truth. It is also very hard for supportive people to listen to the details of this type of abuse. Though these supporters are very caring people, or perhaps because these supporters are such caring people, they often find themselves quite deeply affected by what they hear from survivors. It is very hard for people who have been brought up by caring parents and family to understand how it is possible for parents to allow or even do abusive things to their own children.

Further to this though, there is also what some people refer to as the 'weird stuff', which is often associated with ritual abuse. Hard as it is for survivors to talk about the details of the abuse, it is almost impossible to get anywhere near talking about some of the more bizarre aspects of the things associated with it. Most survivors of ritual abuse are very loath to talk about things that they know for certain they will be ridiculed about. Survivors are not stupid people. Stupid people do not usually survive such abuses. Survivors know that if they try and talk about some of their actual experiences they will be further discredited. Yet these 'weird' and seemingly impossible things are also part of their lives and their memories. Let us try to talk about some of it here.

Many survivors talk about the 'magick' that they experienced in the abusive group. Many of them do spell it with a 'k' at the end and seem to regard it as something very different from the magic 'tricks' we see performed by magicians. There is, with some survivors, an almost superior view regarding their kind of magick as opposed to magic tricks. Though generally survivors seem to fear the 'magick' greatly, they still often seem to regard it as a superior form. Many add the letter 'k' to indicate that the magic is completely real and not done by the use of any tricks. Many believe, mostly because they are taught to believe, that the 'impossible' and magic things that the abusers were able to do were done through the use of supernatural powers. These powers are often believed to be gifted to the abusers by satan or that they get them by tapping into the dark forces of nature. Some believers in this type of magick study for many years to become proficient in its use.

For the most part, many survivors believe in the power of the magick because their experiences are real, vivid and in some ways totally unexplainable unless the particular belief system they have been taught can explain it for them. People usually need an explanation of what they have experienced, particularly if their experiences do not appear to fit within what is deemed possible in the natural world. Survivors may have experiences of such things as seeing people 'die' and then come back to life, or have seen demons, or experienced fire that does not burn or experienced out of body events and none of these things are believed to be possible in the real world. Survivors know this and need an explanation that they can live with and understand to some degree. They are intelligent people who know what is possible in the natural world and what is not and they, like any other thinking person, look for an explanation.

This is exactly what the 'magick' sometimes does for a survivor. It puts all the difficult and unexplainable stuff in a box so that the survivor can make some kind of sense of it. It must have been the 'magick' or it could not have been at all. This can be a kind of explanation which can sometimes satisfy a survivor. It is also an explanation that many will be familiar with in growing up with ritual abuse. It is the only explanation they have and indeed the only one that they are given. Otherwise, when a survivor thinks about some of the more 'incredible' things that have happened to them, they end up feeling completely mad. Trying to tell ordinary people about any of it and face absolute disbelief can make a survivor feel even more nuts. Yet the survivor remembers it all very clearly. Using the explanation that it was all done through magick can make the memories more manageable for many, at least for a while.

The belief in supernatural powers and dark forces can also cause a great deal of long-term difficulties for survivors. Often survivors believe that the abusers can read their minds and can track them down through the use

of their magick. Sometimes survivors believe that they can be hurt or manipulated at a distance by the magick. This belief, whether it is based on fact, experience or teaching, can lead to many years of fear and high levels of anxiety. This in itself, without any intervention from the abusers can make survivors lives a misery and can even lead to physical or mental ill health. It can be very difficult for survivors to shift their belief systems and/or find ways of protecting themselves from the indirect threats of the abusers' magick.

Whether or not this magick is real or not is not really for this author to comment upon. I do not have the right to tell any survivor that they are wrong in their thinking or in their beliefs. Neither do I think anyone else has that right. When survivors begin to look into making sense of their own experiences, some of them think that perhaps drugs and mind altering substances made them believe certain things to be true. Some end up believing that they may have been tricked and some believe that the abusers have extra powers which are supernatural.

Survivors are not crazy or stupid and they themselves will come up with an explanation for themselves that works for them and explains things best for them. It really does not matter what the rest of the world believes about this aspect of the abuse. Neither should this aspect of a survivor's story in any way discredit the survivor or what the survivor is talking about. The person who has experienced the abuse is the one who most needs to find a way to live with and make some kind of sense out of all the memories and the feelings. This includes them finding ways of making sense of the 'weird' bits of it all.

Colours are often very important to many survivors of this type of abuse because colours are often used in many groups to signify different people's position in the group, their station in life, the time of year and the different types of ceremony being performed. In the same way that the Catholic priests and other dignitaries in practising a faith such as Catholicism dress up in different coloured robes at different times of year, so too do abusive group members. The colour of robes or other clothing they use may even reflect, or mirror those used by other religions. In the same way that some religions use different coloured robes at different festivals, so to do some abusive group members.

Some survivors, because of the association they have with particular colours, will never wear clothing of a certain colour. Some of the associations that some survivors may have are around the belief that certain colours are only allowed to be worn by people of a particular position and status in life. Some survivors limit what colours of clothing they wear, as they believe they are

only entitled to wear particular colours as befits their rank or even lack of rank. Some feel that wearing some colours of clothing is beneath their own station and therefore would make them appear or feel inferior. This often extends beyond the group and the 'religion' to what is worn in the outside world. People who have been born or raised into a position of greater power are less likely to be constrained by the choices of colour than those people who are regarded as lower down the hierarchy.

Sometimes there is a fear of a colour because the survivor links that colour to a particular abusive act, extreme trauma experienced when the colour was prominent or punishment when surrounded by the colour. Colours such as purple or combinations of red and black or gold more commonly can upset a survivor and trigger them into a flashback or even cause them to dissociate for a period of time. Seeing the colour, particularly in a specific way, for example a cloth rather than a pair of socks, may remind a survivor of such things as the cloth that wrapped the holy book or the cloth that covered the altar.

Sometimes a colour has come to represent a time of year or an event and the survivor struggles to cope with the memories that seeing the colour (or combination of colours) brings up for them. For many survivors the experiences they have had have been so traumatic that the colour is almost imprinted on the brain and seeing it inevitably triggers the memory. Survivors, being creative people, often find ways of dealing with these memories and flashbacks. Sometimes the time of year coupled with seeing the colour, or colours does it. Abusers know this and often use this to get at the survivor who has escaped. Abusers often deliberately trigger memories in the survivor to try to force them to return to the group or even just to make them feel they are mad or unable to cope.

For some survivors, the lack of basic awareness in the world about the importance of the use of colours in the abuse means that they are sometimes hampered in getting support and help. It can be hard to build a relationship of trust if a survivor is surrounded by the things that lead to uneasiness and discomfort for the survivor. Though it is impossible for a supporter to be aware which particular colours (or even objects) might be of importance to a particular survivor, at least having awareness that some colours may have some significance, means that the right questions can then be asked. Supporters may be reluctant to ask at first but what harm is there in asking a person if there is anything in the room which makes them feel uncomfortable or unsafe? Or asking the survivor what, if anything, would make them feel safer in the room. It is harder for a survivor to talk if there is a feeling of unease or discomfort.

Survivors are often very reluctant to talk to outsiders about the colours used in groups or about their significance. Not only is the detail of the survivor's religion often regarded as a close secret that must be kept at all costs, but there is also the disbelief that outsiders often give out at any mention of the importance or significance of such a thing as a colour. Because colour is not generally regarded by most people as something of importance it is often dismissed or not even thought of value even if a survivor does try to mention it in any way. Survivors are usually taught by the group not to talk about such things anyway and this teaching is often reinforced by the disbelief or lack of awareness of the outside world.

Few survivors ever talk about astral matters and those few who attempt to talk about it are most usually swiftly silenced by the reaction of those they try to talk to. Yet, some grow up with the belief that when they sleep or when they dissociate, part of them goes to a different place called an astral plane. The belief might also include that while on the astral plane they may be subject to attack and may even be killed. The belief might also include believing that if one is killed on an astral level, the body also dies. This belief is often taught to some survivors from quite an early age. They may also be told that people who escape from the group will be tracked on the astral level and punished for leaving. Some survivors who may have escaped and been brought back may reinforce this belief by things that they say.

The world in general does not share this belief and many would laugh at someone who said they had been attacked in this way or that they feared they were being tracked down in this way. Survivors may, if they trust enough, begin to talk about hearing the abusers in their minds and they may talk about communication through mind talk. Most people would dismiss this and further deny the survivor their own experience and beliefs. Just because someone has not personally experienced something does not mean that it does not exist. Also how can a survivor be properly helped and supported if there are things they cannot talk about because other people do not believe it to be possible? Supporters need to try and keep an open mind.

Other things that are often not talked about because of the disbelief in society are some of the wider things that go on both within the group and outside. A group may decide to involve some of their children in prostitution for example. They may use the children to make money for the group or even to find like-minded people who respond to the advances of a young child. Some children are taught how to make advances to adults and some become highly sexualised in their behaviour. The children, young people and also some adults may be used to make pornographic films, including snuff movies. Survivors sometimes do talk about highly sophisticated equipment

being used to shoot explicit movies involving animals, babies and young children. They also talk about experienced film crews being brought in to shoot the scenes.

Then there is the usually not ever talked about human trafficking that is associated with groups. This involves children and young people being bought and sold and being moved round this country and others. Some of these children are not registered at birth. Most of the children are regarded as the property of the group to do with as they like. Though people seem able to accept that this sort of thing may happen in other countries of the world, few will address the fact that it also takes place in the United Kingdom and even in our most civilised Scotland.

Perhaps one of the biggest barriers to survivors of ritual abuse being believed in anything they say is the belief that we live in a civilised country where abuse does not happen. Yet, we now seem to be more able to accept the prevalence of domestic abuse and increasingly child abuse. Organised abuse is a step further and few can take this step. Many people cannot seem to believe that in a so-called civilised country such as the UK, extreme abuse can happen and people do organise to continue to abuse others, including and especially children. Perhaps some people cannot believe quite simply because they do not want to believe that these things are possible in their own backyard.

Sheila

"The unbelievable? It's real, it happens. People really need to open their eyes and see that it happens."

Nat

"The unbelievable is the mystery and magic, the things that, are so hard for people to hear and ultimately to believe. In some ways it is hard for me to understand how and why these things are so hard for people to believe in. The trappings the pomp and circumstance of the groups, are all evident in this world. Maybe it has more to do with the disbelief that these events, occur in what people perceive as civilised places, and not in some foreign land where people do not know any better.

There are as many trappings and mystery in the organised Christian religions and that is accepted and believed by people. But as soon as you start talking about another religion, where people dress up, chant, burn candles and perform rituals, it suddenly becomes unacceptable, and more importantly unbelievable.

Maybe it all comes down to experience, and what you know. Maybe it has more to do with the hurt that is inflicted rather than an unwillingness to believe in the 'unbelievable'.

I have to agree that some things are to those who have not experienced it 'unbelievable'. However, there are so many parallels in this 'world' that it is hard for me to understand the 'unbelievers'.

There is a hierarchy in this world. There are those at the top, those at the bottom, and although there is no uniform that makes this apparent, it still exists.

Those at the bottom fulfil and execute the wishes of those at the top. There are rules, a system into which you have to fit, and most religions and ministers, wear robes of varying colour to denote their power and position. Are the two really that different in appearance at all? Or is it the 'god' that these people worship and the hurt that one causes? Surely that is a subjective argument as I am sure many people will claim to have been hurt by all religions.

So what is it that makes one more believable than the other? Maybe there are differing degrees of acceptance, of the ability of people to understand and accept? Maybe the challenge to their view of the world that Ritual Abuse puts forth is too much for people to cope with? And so to remain sceptical and unbelieving protects them from having to review the way their world is, what goes on and the effects that this has on their fellow human beings. If, however, people remain unbelievers, what then are the effects on those people who have experienced, who have lived with this and all the unbelievable components therein?"

Annie

"I believe in rituals very much. I have had nineteen years of watching them. I think the rituals are just the ways a group of sick individuals feel they can exert power and control over others. I believe in out of body experiences and feelings. I can normally tell if a group member is within walking distance from me by an uneasy feeling inside. I also get this feeling around other survivors."

Lucky

"What is actually unbelievable to me is that fact that no one believes that my early experiences are real. People prefer to believe that the world is a lovely place, full of kind people and fluffy white clouds. It must be wonderful to think like that and actually believe that. It must be great to have only experienced this. My reality sucks but it is my reality!

I grew up believing that some of the people in my group and family were so powerful that they had supernatural powers. I would sometimes see them doing the most unbelievable things. I would see them bring forth a 'demon from hell' and name it to control it. Sometimes they would name it as me. I would see them have injuries, which would miraculously heal. I would see them apparently bringing people back from the dead. As an adult I now know that most of what they did was most likely illusions and tricks but I have to say that many of them must have been very elaborate tricks, as I still cannot work out how they managed to do some of the things they did. As to why they did it? I can but assume it was to create a sense of power beyond the norm. Anyone that powerful would be hard to rebel against or stand up to.

I also believed as a child in the astral abilities and mind reading abilities of the 'higher' people around me. Not only did they seem to know things they could not possibly know but they seemed to know what was about to happen even before it did. We were taught about the astral plane and taught how to stay safe when we were there. There was no question about believing it all. It was all I knew and had been taught. There was no reason to question any of it until I got away. After I escaped the group, the beliefs I held in their abilities made it very hard. I believed they could track me both physically and on an astral level. It was terrifying. Only time was to change this for me.

A person has to believe what they see and hear and are taught. How else can you make sense of the world without going completely mad. As a child there is no reason to question what you are taught and many reasons not to ever question the very powerful people in your life. Questioning only began to happen with me a long time after I got away and became safe. Even then, it was hard to make sense of many things. In the end, I just had to accept what had happened to me as a child and come to terms with the fact that much of it was hard to make sense of and some of it had to be tricks. I am not prepared to believe now that they are all powerful."

John

"I could easily write a book on all this stuff. Perception is an individual thing and people experience things in their own way. My experience and perception is that the most unbelievable things do happen. I think they, the abusers that is, deliberately make some of the things they do seem unbelievable so that no one will believe the survivor. There were things that I can remember very well but when I think about them they are, even to me, almost unbelievable. I am more distant from things and reality is different now. This makes my old reality seem incredible.

I believe that is what every true survivor has done somewhere down the line. Some will call it 'being a good person' or simply 'surviving' but the real fact I believe is that this survival is on the astral level and we have been good spirits from the start, groomed and abused to break that spirit before it became too strong. Needless to say, the abusers failed."

Helen

"Any thing outside our sphere of experience can be unbelievable.

It is very easy to trick children especially frightened and stressed children. My understanding is that in many cults or paedophile rings, clever and scientifically researched brainwashing goes on. As someone who was brainwashed, I know how difficult it is to sort out real happenings from manipulated ones. The cult's survival depends on trickery and the child's confusion.

Some of my memories I question not because they are unbelievable, but because I can now see that the cult could easily have made me believe something was real when it wasn't. Having said that, if I had not experienced this abuse myself, I would not want to believe that it was possible for human beings to do such terrible things to another. I can understand that people, who do not believe ritual abuse happens, are afraid of facing the possibility that we, as collective humanity are capable of such crimes.

I witnessed many 'unbelievable' things in the cult. Magick is only something that cannot be explained. As a child there was much that was unexplainable to my child mind. Looking back, I see that the rituals and the events that took place were cleverly designed to make me, and others, believe that the members of the cult were all powerful and that Satan was omnipresent. In a sick sort of way, it was like a cleverly performed abusive pantomime. I also believe that I was opened up and damaged psychically by the abuse. I believe we are more than physical, emotional and mental, and some of my wounds are on a spiritual level. My abusers used any power they could tap into.

The only thing I find completely unbelievable about my childhood is that no one outside the family or cult questioned why my behaviour was so bizarre or why I was terrified all the time."

WORLDS APART

WORLDS APART

People, who grow up in an abusive and hidden culture and with a secret religion, often need to learn how to lead a double life. They live a life which has extremely important rules, rituals, responses and ways of being at home and with family which they must get right at all times. Sometimes there is even a different language used within the family or in the group. What we must remember in all of this is that the earliest formative years will have been spent growing up in this culture without much in the way of input or involvement from the outside world. This home life and culture is completely normal for the child who lives it. Obviously this does not apply to all survivors of ritual abuse but it does apply to many of them. Normal is what a child lives and all that he or she knows at the time.

As the child gets older, they are, in the same way as all children, gradually introduced to the wider community. They are also taught how to behave and respond in this setting. This is not such a strange concept and actually applies to all children with responsible parents. The main difference is that there is for some a huge difference in culture, language and systems of beliefs. This is not a completely alien concept and we only need to look at second or third generation immigrants in this country to see how well children and young people can adapt across cultures at home and in the wider community.

Children from different cultures learn very rapidly to adapt and can function well in the community speaking one language and obeying the cultural rules and then on returning to their home can instantly revert to a different culture and language. With the young second or third generation folk from different backgrounds there is not the secrecy and abuse issues that are experienced in ritual abuse, but the cultures and religions at home are often very different from what is regarded as the norm in this country. Yet, these young people adapt well on a day to day basis.

I am not likening ritual abuse to the experiences of people from other cultures here but am trying to explain in a way that most of us are familiar with, how people can live simultaneously within two or more cultures and religions. No offence is intended here to any non-abusive person, faith or culture. This is a strong parallel though in seeing how well children and young people can bridge across two or more cultures and can easily learn and apply them appropriately in each of the individual settings.

Survivors of any abuse learn how to stay silent for many years and certainly while they are still dependent children. This is even more the case with survivors of ritual abuse. Not only is the child defending the abusers, though it would be rare for any child to see the person or people in that light, but they are defending the faith, the culture, the family and the whole belief system which they are born into and is their life. Children are taught loyalty and the consequences of betrayal of the faith, not only for them, but for all who are involved in it. This is an exceptionally heavy burden for any child to bear and most do keep a very strict loyalty to the family and stay silent.

It is only on leaving the family and the group that survivors begin to see and acknowledge just how very different the outside world is from the world they grew up in. For some, depending upon their position in the group hierarchy, they will have had more experience of the outside world, but for many, it would be very restricted. Some survivors who get away just cannot cope with what they see as the double standards and lies of the society we live in. Some prefer the 'truth' and 'honesty' of beliefs in 'the strong can do what they want to' attitude from back home. Some even return to the family in which they at least know where they stand rather than face the uncertainty and apparent hypocrisy of the outside world.

It is also extremely difficult to move away from a life of almost total dictatorship and control to a life in which you are forced to make decisions about everything all the time. If you have never been allowed or able in any way to make a decision, it is almost impossible to do so. Even things that many people would regard as simple decisions are hard for someone in this position. Such decisions as what you want to eat for your tea becomes a nightmare if you have never had to consider this before or in fact do not believe that you even have the right to make that particular decision or any other. People who have reached adulthood never having being allowed to make a decision for themselves, struggle in this world.

Leading a double life is not easy for anyone but many people have to find a way to do just this. They do succeed. Learning to live and get to know a new culture and way of being in the world is not easy either for anyone but again, many people have to find a way to do this as it is in some way preferable to what has been in their past. Sometimes survivors learn how to copy what other people do until they learn the rules in this society. The survivors who find it easiest to adjust are those survivors who have had most contact with the outside world. Those who have been kept hidden away from sight or those who have had really strictly controlled and very limited outside contact will find it all very difficult and are unlikely to succeed in staying away from the group if they do escape. They would be much less

likely to manage independent living and would probably be forced to return to the group unless they had a very high level of support.

The outside world and society's rules and values are so very different from what many a survivor grows up with and learns, that relearning and adjusting is extremely difficult. It can be done though as the survivors who have succeeded in escaping from the abuse and found ways of surviving can testify. It often takes a long time though before survivors feel confident and content in this world. Some never feel entirely at ease and some never feel as though they properly belong. For some it feels as they are living in a foreign country.

Survivors Accounts

Kay

"Because for most of my life I'd no childhood memory, except for a few traumatic events, I wasn't aware of a culture clash. However, I never felt I belonged in the world, and often felt like a visiting alien from space, having to learn how humans behaved things like 'hello' and 'goodbye' rituals. I act pretty well now, and 'fit in' up to a point, but then I'm mostly not there in the way I'm expected to be. So I'm always an outsider except for a few good and kind friends who know what I'm up against, and some work situations. I've always been great with six to ten year old kids because I had to look after them so much in my Ritual Abuse life.

People have such security and luxury in this culture. It astounds me the things they take for granted, and the things they can do seemingly easily. I have really no conception of what it must feel like to be able to earn your own living and do as you chose (within limits). Likewise how people can negotiate social situations happily and without terror. To be able to have and keep children seems to me an amazing miracle that was never permitted me. Yet even animals have young.

In this culture it's accepted that people have free choice. In Ritual Abuse we were controlled and if we infringed the rules, we paid. In Ritual Abuse if we loved, we lost, and everything always turned out for the worst. Mistakes were not allowed. My main aim was not to be noticed, whereas here that doesn't lead to trouble. I tried to censor everything in my head there, to avoid trouble, but here people expect you to.... is 'exist' the word? People expect you to have reactions and wants and needs and limits, but mine are out of line and no one could understand them, for instance the passion I have for security."

Nat

"Is there a difference in culture? I would have to answer yes there is. The difference between growing up the way I did, and then suddenly being free to make decisions, not only free but having to make these decisions was a hard and arduous learning curve for me.

The rules and dictates with which I grew up, disappeared physically overnight, I was left with a void, a space that I had to fill. It seemed as if the world, which I had entered had never existed before. I had been to school, university, but still didn't feel like the world that I was now in, belonged to me then. It was like I was a bystander, a peeping tom on a life that I would never have. People seemed to have a free will, a purpose that was denied to me, the freedom, which I thought most people took for granted I truly believed I would never have.

The most obvious difference to me was the different rules, the apparent lack of a structure, which I now realise was more covert than the rules I had grown up with. The definite structure and dictates of the group left little room for manoeuvre. There was no space to decide things for myself. No room I think to be me. I was defined by them, the rules and the stifling structure. To suddenly be placed in a situation where I had to make, as some would say trivial decisions, such as what to eat and what to wear, as well as having to discover who I was and where I fit in this new place was and still is an enormous hurdle for me.

I think in my opinion that the cultures are very different. It is like growing up in the same planet but only being allowed to see one country or one city even, but you can look out and see a different country passing you by. But every time you go out to try and touch it disappears. I think that people underestimate how difficult it can be to adjust to a completely new way of living. There is now choice, opportunity, and the opportunity to discover who you are without the confines of their rigid box.

Even the opportunity to feel, to think for yourself, to have expectations and to realise that there is life after them is a hard adjustment to make. Some of these I don't think I have managed to adjust to yet. It is a huge step, there is a huge difference and it takes time to adjust."

Annie

"I wouldn't really know about much of this as I've not had time to 'adjust yet'"

Lucky

"Adjusting was very hard because I didn't know how to be in a world without the group and the family. By leaving I was effectively cutting myself off from my whole life. Everything and everyone I knew was cut off from me and I was, for the first time ever in my life, completely alone. It was horrible and very scary. I didn't know what to do. I didn't know where to go. I trusted no one and couldn't cope with a life without the rules I already knew. I had trouble even believing the reality of my new life as it felt so very strange.

Living without abuse was easy but living without people, without hope and without my whole background was, to my mind impossible. I couldn't cope at all and suffered badly in trying to come to terms with it all. It was as though I had coped fine with all that I was living but when I left it, I fell to pieces. I started hearing and seeing my abusers everywhere. I soon became completely paranoid and imagined all sort of things going on around me. My thoughts and feelings were distorted. Sleep was nearly impossible, eating was difficult and I lived in a constant state of fear of being found and taken back. Several times I tried to kill myself, as life was just too hard to bear.

I found it almost impossible at first to work out the rules in society. English was not my first language and everything was very confusing to me. I knew all about the Law of the Land. That was not a problem, as my family had made sure I knew that bit. What I never knew about was the unwritten rules of social engagement. There were basic things like making eye contact with other people. My upbringing had taught me not to make or attempt to make eye contact with a 'superior' person. Yet now the rules of engagement had changed and not making eye contact made other people think that you had something to hide or that you were not trustworthy. It was all so difficult. Then there were things like hugging! People did it all the time as though it was something acceptable. Not to me! To me it was very frightening. I could not bear the thought of someone trying to hug me and quite literally dodged people who attempted it with me.

I am intelligent. I am a survivor. I knew there were huge gaps in my learning and experience and I began to actively watch people to find out what was normal and expected behaviour. I spend a very long time watching people as I tried to work it all out. Even once I had it worked out to some degree, it was not always easy to adjust my behaviour enough to fit in. I had no confidence at all and had very limited self-esteem. I also had a whole cultural learning in a particular way to overcome.

It was like being a stranger in a foreign land where though the language was similar in many ways it was not quite the same. Even some words seemed to often have different meanings from what I understood.

People also said things all the time that they did not mean. The way I grew up taught me that words have a defined and literal meaning and that people use them to communicate thoughts, feelings and ideas to others. To this day I cannot fully comprehend how it is therefore that most people consistently say one thing with their words but mean something entirely different from what they are saying."

John

"The heading of this chapter sums it up, 'world's apart'. We are humans trying to survive in a world governed by and breeding soulless apathetic animals that are conditioned to be apathetic and rewarded for being more brutal than their peers.

In a way survivors are ultimately stronger than those around us due to the fact that we see life for what it is, not the rosy picture. As far as adjusting to the culture goes, we were never given the choice. We choose ourselves instead."

FAITH AND BELIEF

behind
enemy lines

278

FAITH AND BELIEF

Some survivors who have reached the stage of trying to talk and heal from the abuse often ask if the abusers really believed in what they were doing. They wonder if they were abused because of a faith, belief or religion. Sometimes because of their feelings for some of the abusers it would be easier to lay the blame on a religion or a faith rather than on a person that they still love or care about. There is of course no answer to the question about why the abusers did what they did. The simple fact of the matter is that whether or not the abusers believe in what they are doing to someone, they also know it to be wrong and illegal in this society. They know what would happen to them if what they were doing ever got out publicly. Otherwise they would not hide behind a wall of silence and force that silence onto their 'victims'.

From the accounts of many survivors it seems clear that some, indeed most of them, are brought up in a particular faith or with particular beliefs. Those who talk about growing up with satanism for example talk about it as a real faith and religion. In the same way that Catholics and Protestants have to learn prayers, songs and the various rituals of worship, so too do children growing up with satanism. So it is also with the beliefs and trappings that go with any religion. Some of the beliefs that are taught to survivors of satanic abuse are part of what allows for the accompanying abuse.

In many of the abusive groups there is a strict hierarchy, which has all children firmly at the bottom. The hierarchy is, in some groups based on the belief in survival of the fittest and the principal that 'might is right'. The belief is that the strongest and the most intelligent will acquire the top positions of power and then do everything within their power to keep their positions. The belief is that those who rule should be those most fit to rule by virtue of their superior strength and intellect. There is no democratic process in a group and definitely no allowances made for meekness or weakness.

Often the people at the top try to favour their own children and attempt to pass their positions of power on to their children after them so that in some groups the positions of power and authority become an inherited position. Even those who inherit a position in such a group though must be able to fulfil it properly and prove themselves worthy of it. Otherwise, a more powerful person will soon topple the leader regardless of who they are. This is the basic philosophy of many groups. The strong survive and lead. They own the most wealth and dictate to those who are perceived to be weaker and thereby less worthy.

The belief in a deity, Satan or something similar often forms the basis of many of the groups' faith. From this the Laws, rules and religious rituals follow. Like most religions the belief in a deity is often just not enough for the people. There are also the associated beliefs, which go along with it, standards of acceptable behaviour and the worship or giving thanks to or appeasing the deity. Children are taught the faith, rules and rituals while still very young and impressionable as happens in any religion and there are often various stages and initiations throughout childhood, again this is similar to many religions. If the abusive side of things were removed, taking a look at the rite of passage, different initiations and the rituals which take place in more acceptable religions can provide some insight in to a ritual.

Robes of different colour for different times of year, different occasions and different 'officer bearers' are standard in many religions. Altars, candles, bibles, incense, chanting, singing and call responses are all familiar to many ordinary churchgoers. At home, small rituals such as prayers before dinner and at bedtime or on special occasions are part of normal family life. So too is this the case for many survivors of ritual abuse who have grown up with their different religion. One of the main differences for those with a secret religion is the very secrecy of it, which must be maintained at all times.

Children are taught that they must not tell because they and their families and others will be persecuted. This is probably true. They are taught as with every other religion that theirs is the one true religion and only god but that others have and will persecute them for believing in it. There are other examples available from the history books of families and whole communities having to hide their particular religion because of persecution from others including the state. Often the survival of a family has meant that the children in particular were forced into secrecy. Children do manage very successfully to keep this a secret. So too with the religion of satanism. Loyalty to the family and the faith are believed to be everything. To betray this would put all in extreme jeopardy and the children have this drilled into them long before they ever reach school age.

Rules learned young and lived on a daily basis are hard for anyone to move away from. So too is belief in the power of a faith that all people around you embrace. In an arena where from an early age children and young people learn that only the strongest will survive and the weak are beneath contempt, there is no choice but to believe this as that is indeed their only experience of life. This is their lives and their reality for many

years so of course they believe what they live. It is only when people grow older and perhaps get away from the group and the religion that they become more able to question in any way the faith and beliefs that they grew up with.

Many groups teach that weakness and stupidity are great sins. Trying to leave the group would be construed as a weakness. A person who is not up to doing what it takes to worship the deity properly and in the manner dictated is regarded as weak. Survivors talk about being pushed to the limit of endurance and pain to test their worthiness and fitness to survive. This is not uncommon in other religions either where self-sacrifice and suffering are viewed as paying homage to their deity.

It cannot be denied that satanism exists as a live religion in this country and in others. One only has to take a look at the number of books that are sold on the subject and any search on the Internet shows up numerous web sites, which promote the religion. There are churches of satan in this country and in others and some people openly declare themselves to be practicing satanists. This book is not for a second suggesting that all who believe in and worship satan will be people who will abuse children or anyone else. Neither is it saying that all who believe in God are good and honourable. Neither do all who abuse children in a ritualised manner believe in satan. What is clear though is that many survivors of ritual abuse do talk about growing up with a form of satanism in their family which permits and condones the abuse of children.

Although many survivors talk about satanic abuse, some do also talk about christian ritual abuse. They talk about the so-called normalcy of openly going to a christian church but then being abused in a side room or later in the night in the same church and by the same people in a ritualised manner following the christian rituals. Others have talked about groups of people claiming to be practicing Druids who commit ritual sacrifices and also abuse the children in a group setting. Abusers it would seem are more than prepared to use any belief system available to them which they can pick up and twist in a variety of ways to suit themselves to do what they want to do to children and vulnerable people.

Some survivors, even after they leave the group continue to believe in the religion they have grown up in. Though some people find this surprising because of the abuse, it is not really all that surprising at all. A person may not like or be able cope with the abuse they are experiencing but it is a very difficult thing indeed to turn away from all that is taught in the formative years. Some survivors even believe that it

is they who have failed, been too weak and done wrong in not being able to cope with all that was expected of them by their family. It can be very hard for survivors to turn their beliefs around and start to believe that the abusers were wrong. Even if they get to the fact of believing that the abusers were wrong, survivors may still keep their faith in the basics of the learned religion.

Beliefs and faith can be a difficult concept for many survivors and it is something that may be wrestled with for many years. Religion often haunts some survivors as having grown up in a faith they need to hold onto something. Sometime the faith and belief is all that they have left. Many survivors look to other religions to fill the gap in faith that they need. Many turn toward christianity in this country but that is most likely because it is the dominant religion in this country. Some continue to believe in Satanism as a religion but without the abuse. Some would argue that the abusers have corrupted the pure faith.

Survivors Accounts

Lee

"I believe in myself and others. I am different but on the scale of my life experience as an individual, rather than some alien who others cannot relate to. I am by no means a typical British twenty four year old. But then again, most friends I have are not typical of their societal images, and maybe this helps in some ways.

No they weren't right to do what they did. My mother had mental health problems but that does not absolve her from what she did. I have a couple of friends who have mental health problems and they don't do that stuff (oh yeah and they weren't abused as children either - do you see the psychiatrist shouting out - oh no, what happened, you should be normal?'). People who do this should be stopped. They're causing harm, and not doing anyone any good."

Sheila

"It's an individual thing to everyone. I have no faith or belief system. 'I believe it will rain when I see it'. I'm not convinced that I do trust people. Not sure that I will ever fully trust anyone again. Yes I do believe that I'm different. I believe I'm stronger than other people due to past experiences. Different because I have inside knowledge and other people don't. I live in this world and society when I was also part of another society 'Normal and Abnormal'. I have to live in both.

No they do not have the right to do what they did to me or anyone else. I didn't want it to happen and they took away all that I had rights to. I didn't question before, I didn't know how to. But now I realise they had no right to do anything to me."

Kay

"I was brought up I think, to hate God. A father God was a non-starter for me, anyway. I discovered what religion was about through Buddhism, but can't swallow their cosmology, though I love the meditation. I chant and pray to the Goddess and try to believe in her. I'm amazed by the goodness of two of my friends (incidentally, or not, Christian) and how they stand by me. I'm stunned at the support of the phone lines and feel deeply towards my therapist who saved my life and began analysis when everyone had told me not to. I've had to trust, life has been such a battle I've never had an option. I trust like a child and have got resigned and philosophical about getting so often let down.

I think the abusers were demons, completely inhuman, to do what they did. I know there was blackmail everywhere and I was used to entrap people, especially at three and five years old, but this excuses no one from gang-raping and torturing small or tiny children - or teenagers or anyone. Ritual abuse - child pornography, child rape, is demonic. I hope hell is big enough (at any rate for a while) to hold the men who smashed my life, lost me my two brothers and made my mother a stranger to all and ill all her life."

Nat

"I think there are two parts to this. One is the faith and belief I have in myself and other people. But I also think that somewhere in here has to be the faith and beliefs that I grew up with. I think that both are equally important, as I believe that one affects the other. Faith and belief in myself is not an easy task for me. I believe that to have faith and belief in yourself is an immense achievement, and one that I haven't managed to figure out yet.

I am still in a quandary about it. Is faith and belief in yourself something that can be learned? Can it be recovered if you have lost it? Where does it come from? Does it come from within, or without? I am not sure. I don't have faith in myself. I like to think I do. I like to put forward to others that I have some faith in myself and in my abilities, but the truth is that I really don't know what it is to have faith in yourself. I think to have faith in yourself requires that you know yourself, know who you are and where you fit, where you have a place.

But even then, even knowing you have a place does not preclude to your having faith in yourself. I think that you can have faith in yourself to be able to perform certain tasks. But is that faith or luck or an ability to do certain things?

I think that more of an answer will be forthcoming if I asked myself whether I trust myself. I trust myself to know right from wrong, to know that I will keep breathing and that I will keep surviving. Is that faith and belief in myself? I don't think so. I think in some ways I cheat. I use the faith and belief people have in me. Or at least I try to. It is hard for me to believe in myself. But other people have faith and believe in me, so in some ways I borrow that. I don't always believe this faith and belief, but I accept that it is there, and use it to achieve things.

I found it hard to trust other people. That came when I had some trust in myself, the trust in myself to know who to trust. I think I still get it wrong sometimes, but who doesn't. It is difficult to know how to trust, when in every sense your trust in people has been eroded. I find it difficult to let people know who I am. I am wary of strangers. But I am stubborn. A stranger is only a stranger until they become friend or foe. In my opinion it is better to know which they are.

I think that the faiths and beliefs I grew up with steadily eroded my faith and belief in myself. They certainly eroded my trust. I am not going to go into the intricate details of the faith, or the rules which govern it. Suffice to say I think that the faith and my faith in others and in myself are interconnected. I have certain views of myself that were planted by the faith I grew up with, the position and place I was in, the way I behaved and what I and others thought of me, even how I saw myself and how I presented to other people. It dictated to a certain degree my abilities and capabilities. Was that because I allowed it to?

I had no choice, no space and no opportunity to change that. These were the rules and that was the environment I grew up in, and to be honest one I believed in. I didn't believe in the hurt, and in a lot of ways I didn't accept it. I had no comparison. I believed that according to my faith I was born into a certain position. I had a place. I had rules that governed my every action and dictated how I saw myself, how I behaved.

It is hard to have faith and belief in yourself when everything around you, the very core of your existence says otherwise. The faith, their faith permeated and eroded my faith in myself, it didn't encompass, it suffocated. It moulded me into what and who I was.

Do I still believe in the faith I grew up with? Sometimes it is hard to change beliefs. You can see the faults. You can know the limitations. You can see the abuses and destruction that it causes. But to be without it! What does it leave behind? What will replace it? I think that in some ways I still believe it, for me anyway. I know that sounds hypocritical and in some respects a little naïve. I think it is difficult to completely change the things you believe in. Adjust yes, try and change yes, and challenge. But to completely disregard it would be nearly impossible to do, for me anyway.

I can disagree with a lot of things. The way they are. The way they hurt and abuse, the pain and destruction. I can try by writing this, to help other people to understand a little bit, but I can't completely disregard everything I grew up with. Change is a hard thing to do. To change so completely would have left me with nothing, no foundation, no core, and no notion of how to fill that."

Jill

"To have managed to survive ritual abuse I think that I must have had some form of faith or belief in something. Perhaps at the time it was just a kind of twisted and tormented hope. When you are being abused, tormented and tortured, survival just kind of kicks in for you and keeps on kicking in whether you want it to or not.

For those of us lucky enough to survive to some degree with our reason intact, I believe that these experiences strengthened our instincts and faith. There has to be something positive that I can find and take from this. There is no limit to this basic instinct to survive. Even on occasions when I really wished I could just lie down and die, something deep inside me refused to lie down and let me die. I would continue to struggle even against my own wish for it all to end. Survivors who get away are incredibly strong people because they have to be and they can heal from the trauma. This I do have a lot of faith in. It is truly amazing what people can survive and move on from.

I have over time found it easier to believe in a loving and compassionate God than I ever did to believe in a loving and compassionate human being. I knew from a very early age what people were capable of doing to others and all in the name of faith. My trust in people was shattered forever at an early age. When the chips are down and survival is the issue, it is generally everyone for themselves. Never mind the ideal of women and children first. Men are stronger and in any survival situation, they are the ones who survive. There is no room for compassion. That is an indulgence. But I have managed to find faith in something greater than myself. Perhaps I needed to believe in something.

Satanists have a belief in the power of Satan and that his power is everywhere in this world. God seeks for goodness. Satanists have chosen to be Evil. They are on the opposite path. They would say that survival of the fittest is the way of the world. They would say that the strongest will inherit and rule the Earth. They would say that might is right and it is right that the strongest dictate over the weakest.

No they did not have the right to do as they did but they did have the power and the choice to do as they wanted. No one could stop them from carrying out their own will. Mind control is a big part of satanic abuse and they controlled as much as they could for as long as they could do so. They would have continued if they could but my faith helped me to get away from them in the end. Perhaps there is something in faith after all."

Annie

"Faith and belief - well I believe faith is believing in something or someone without having to actually see them. I think belief is more of an idea or thought you have with regard to what you think rather than what you know. I do believe I am different to many in my group as I am a survivor rather than an abuser.

No, I would say that they didn't have the right to abuse me then nor do they have the right to abuse me now. I believe this as my body belongs to Christ and me no one else and therefore no one had or has the right to touch, use or abuse my body without my consent."

Lucky

"I believe myself to be a product of my upbringing. Though I have turned away from all that I was taught by my family, everywhere in the world, I see where their truths actually came from. Most people truly are out for themselves. Altruism is definitely not in abundance in this world. The most powerful really do take what they want and do what they please to who ever they choose.

I reject totally the beliefs and faith into which I was born and raised, but everywhere I look I see their ideals ravaging the planet in various guises. I do also see many people opposing them, but they cannot match the power that prevails. I choose to side with those people without power who stand against those in power who abuse it. Yet, I suspect that if the whole thing turned around, the powerless on attaining power would abuse it also. Perhaps I have now become way too cynical for my own good.

I try to hold onto a basic faith and belief in myself. I cannot believe in gods of any kind not just because I cannot see them but because I know I could do so much better if I were a god. I am a mere mortal therefore there can be no such thing. I like to believe that like the movies on the television there will be a good ending and the good people will win in the end. I fear this is not the case though. I think we need to consider using some of the tactics of the abusers or we shall all lose. There are many ruthless people in this world and unless we stand up to them and not back down, they will walk over us all. Until we change the beast that is within mankind, we cannot stop abuse. Most people are capable of forgetting their compassion and humanity when their own survival is at stake and most people will abuse power if they get it. We need to change ourselves before we can win.

I have no faith that we can do this."

John

"Faith is when you believe in something for no apparent reason. I believed I could heal people with my mind. Years down the line I read books on bio energy, psychosomatic illness, placebo's, faith healing, morphic resonance and I am now able to heal with my mind. Working on the 'project', 'the colourway prophecy', I had faith that what I was working on would cause the abused people of society (that wanted to stop the abuse in a constructive way) to break out and see the truth of the system and how to combat it.

I started working on colourway in 1998 and every day there is something to confirm my faith was not in vain. I have faith in myself and only myself. It's not that I don't trust people. I just go with the flow, as painful or as beautiful as it is because what doesn't kill me makes me stronger and if it does kill me then I was meant to die.

I believe I am different due to an intense experience I had when I was writing 'colourway'. It was a mixture of prophecy, spirit guidance and synchronicity all these things happened at specific times to rip me away from the grip the system had on me. Quantum physics, occult research and 'colourway' starting to come true combined with free association writing all made me realise my true purpose.

Abusers don't have the right to abuse, but I do believe that their actions and belief had been ordained. I say this due to the irony of life. Abusers feel that life is here, do what thou wilt, materialism and self-gratification being their faith and secret societies provide a system to let them practice their faith of vital existence. The irony is that the deeper they get into abuse, the more they realise there is a higher meaning. That is being provided by survivors everywhere. We are the true believers in god, spirit, humanity, unity, whatever you want to call it. If we didn't believe, we wouldn't be fighting abuse, we would simply give in. that realisation is my suicide stopper. If I give up it's only helping abuse spread. So I have a purpose. I have faith."

THE SCALES OF JUSTICE

THE SCALES OF JUSTICE

Ritual abuse is not a recognised crime as such in Scotland and the United Kingdom. This is not really surprising since the denial of its very existence is still so high in this society. The many abusive acts that survivors talk about happening such as rape, sexual and physical assault and murder are of course recognised crimes and if a survivor were to go to the police and report these particular crimes, they would most certainly be thoroughly investigated. According to the experiences of most survivors there is a better chance of an unbiased investigation if the survivor does not mention the words 'rituals' or 'groups', or 'religion', or 'organised' abuse, or 'abuse by women', but just concentrates on talking about the 'normal' crimes that have happened to them. Some survivors have successfully taken this course of action to try and stop their abusers from harming any more children.

Ritual abuse survivors seldom try and seek justice from the police and the courts. Some never try to go to the police because they believe they would never be believed by them. Most survivors grow up being told that the police will not believe them and many fear that there are abusers working within the police. For some survivors, they grew up knowing that some of their abusers worked in the police. Sometimes the police taking young people home after they have run away has reinforced the belief that the police are against them. The abusers use this to show the survivor that there is no point in talking to police as they are always on the side of the parents and family. The other thing that abusers sometimes do is tell the young people they are abusing that many of the police are involved in the abusive group. Sometimes they are.

It makes a kind of twisted sense that abusers will go to some lengths to ensure that survivors are afraid to talk to the police. Most survivors are taught to fear and distrust the police. Every opportunity is used by the group to show that the police are indeed corrupt and cannot be trusted. Survivors of ritual abuse also live with the knowledge that they too have committed many crimes and that if the police knew this, they would most likely be prosecuted by them. The fear of police as an agency runs so deep that some survivors are terrified whenever they even see a uniform. Many survivors will not report crimes committed against them simply because they fear the police so much. This fear serves the abusers' purpose well and few survivors would ever consider reporting their own abuse to the police.

Some survivors do not go to the police because they fear the backlash from the abusers. They may have already had a degree of backlash and fear that it will all become much worse. Some survivors have on occasions tentatively approached the police with a view to maybe making a complaint. The first thing they often ask is if the police will be able to offer any protection if they do talk about the abusers. The answer to this request is invariably 'no'. The police usually let the survivors know that if anything happens they can make further complaints but they cannot offer the survivor protection of any kind. This is often enough for the survivor to decide not to take the risk of stirring up the abusers by telling about what they have done or are currently doing. Survivors know better than anyone what their abusers are capable of doing and without the promise of any increased safety very few could contemplate making a complaint against persons or people who they perceive to be so much stronger and more powerful than themselves and the police.

Many survivors are afraid to make a complaint to the police because they fear that they may face prosecution also. Many of the abusive acts that occur during rituals involve children and young people of all ages. It is common for older survivors to be involved in some way, albeit reluctantly, in the abuse of others. It is also common for survivors to have been initiated into some form of criminal activity and to believe that their abusers will incriminate them. Regardless of whether the survivor was forced, coerced or tricked into doing something which is criminal, they can still be held accountable for any of their actions if they are over the age of criminal responsibility. In Scotland at the moment the age of criminal responsibility is eight years old. The survivor may also fear that the abusers have kept some evidence of the criminal activity they were involved in. Though this is unlikely, it can have the effect of stopping a survivor from reporting the crimes against them to the police.

Some survivors have such an intense loyalty to their family and to the group that they would rather die than make a complaint about them to anyone. Some feel genuine love and respect for those who abused them. Some feel as though they deserved what happened and as such would have no right to make a complaint to anyone. Some feel that they are complete failures and it is for that reason they were abused. They may feel that their family was only trying to improve them and make them more 'worthy' people. Some just cannot stand what they would regard as the shame of betraying those who gave them life. It sometimes gets down to the feelings that people have and the beliefs of the individual. Certainly the abusers will have made every effort to

ensure that the feelings survivors have will make it less likely that they will ever be able to complain against them. So too will the beliefs that survivors grow up with make it unlikely that they tell on or report the abusers to the authorities.

Other survivors, a few, do decide that they would like to try and see if they can get some justice done. Sometimes these few do attempt to talk to the police. A few is better than none. Certainly, many more survivors seem to now be talking about trying to make complaints to the police than ever before. Unfortunately, the police are not quite up to speed on ritual abuse yet. One survivor while trying to give his statement to the police became upset and angry at what he was remembering and trying to talk about and leapt up and hit at the wall. The police officer decided that his behaviour was not good enough and walked out of the room.

This happened several times in several different ways. In the end, the police officer told him that he was not ready to do this and point blank refused to work with him. Though the survivor acted aggressively in his distress, never at any point was he in any way threatening towards anyone. It did stop him from talking to the police though. Unfortunately, his brother and cousins were also waiting to tell about the abuse they had all experienced. They were not sure about the police and were waiting to see what kind of reaction he got first. The whole attempt to tell started and ended with an upset and angry male survivor. He had every right to be angry at his experiences and deserved better treatment from the police officer who was assigned to talk to him. This particular police officer, who was a nice enough person, was the one who was in reality not quite ready to deal with hearing this kind of stuff.

I have watched and tried to support quite a few survivors now in talking to the police and have to strongly suggest that the success lies in the quality and personality of the police officer who is taking the statement. Those very few who are prepared to keep an open mind, take the time to allow for trust to build and are prepared to learn more about ritual abuse, are the only ones that it seems worthwhile that survivors try and talk to about their experiences. These officers are good at their jobs and do not put down or ridicule the survivor. They do not judge and they are prepared to admit that they do not really know much at all about the subject. These officers are fair, compassionate and seem to understand how hard it might be to talk about any abuse issues. Some of these officers have even taken on training and read

up on the subject so as to try and better understand what they are dealing with in working with the survivor. Unfortunately not all police officers are of this calibre.

Others make it very clear that they do not believe in ritual abuse at all. They have already dismissed in their minds the possibility of it being a reality for anyone and have already decided that the survivor is misguided, attention seeking, mad or full of false memories. They are half hearted and appear uninterested in taking the statements from the survivors which makes it even harder for the survivor to disclose. If the survivor gets upset, which would be a normal thing to happen while trying to talk, they declare the survivor 'not ready' and constantly suggest that the survivor just stop and come back in a few years. They do not investigate the alleged crimes thoroughly and they make no attempts whatsoever to engage properly with the survivors or keep them informed. Many survivors never get past the ignorance and disbelief of the police officers they first meet.

Some survivors do manage to get their cases all the way to court. This happens most often when ritual abuse has not been mentioned. Often the supporters of the survivor know what was involved but advise the survivor that they will succeed better if it is just not mentioned. In my experience this is true. Some survivors have achieved this kind of justice through the courts though few would ever say that it was a positive experience. The court system is not designed to be supportive of abuse survivors and the whole process is regarded most often by those who have experienced it as at best, an unpleasant experience and at worst a very abusive experience. Though there are many moves afoot to improve the criminal justice system in Scotland, it is a long time coming and there is a long way to go before survivors are likely to get anything close to justice.

There are other forms of justice available. For some survivors the fact that they have managed to effectively thumb their noses at their abusers and family is justice enough for them. The getting away from the family and healing from the trauma can also be regarded as justice. For some people, getting on, raising a family and living a normal life proves the abusers were wrong in all they said and did. Some want to prove that they have been able to recover despite the abusers and all that has happened to them. Some survivors settle for this type of justice. For some this is winning the fight. Some do not want to go the way of police and courts and many believe in a more natural justice.

Other survivors hit back at their abusers by telling, teaching, raising

298

awareness and training others in how to support survivors. They shatter the silence of the abusers and by doing so regain a sense of their own power. Sometimes they even write books about ritual abuse. Some do the thing that always brought the biggest threat of retribution, they tell about it! For some this is pure justice and more than enough.

Some survivors do not want any kind of vengeance or punishment to befall their abusers. Some do not want to use the power they now have over the abusers. Some are prepared to settle for raising as much awareness as possible about abuse. Some stand up and expose the abusers in a variety of ways and see this as a more appropriate way of getting justice. For some survivors, justice is not the issue at all. Rather, the issue becomes one of finding ways of making the abusers stop what they are doing, making it more difficult for the abusers to continue and making the world awaken to the reality of ritual abuse.

Survivors Accounts

Sheila

"Anything is possible if we work hard at it. If enough people believe then it is possible. Yes it would be nice to see justice done whatever that may be. It would be good if somebody was to line them up and do something to them. But as they enjoy pain and suffering what kind of justice would that be?"

Billie

"Justice for me would mean to let the punishment really fit the crime. I would like them to suffer as I did and in the same way. There is not much chance of this happening in this country today. My recovery and continued survival are like a kind of justice though. They don't like the fact that I got away and they definitely don't like me talking. It's too bad really. I am fighting back against them by writing about my life. I am fighting back by talking about it. I am beating them every inch of the way. This is my justice.

My abusers can no longer get to me and I now no longer fear them as much as I did before. They really have lost their hold on me and also most of their power. I wish I could believe in a god that someday will make them pay for all their crimes but I may have to work on faith to achieve this.

My family used to say to me that I must never tell anyone anything about what was going on. Well, guess what I went and done? I went on and told about it. I broke their silence. I got strong. There's a type of justice in that and they never expected it.

My abusers now wish that I would die for them. Maybe I would have once but certainly not now. They could do me a real big favour and drop down dead now. I'm too busy living. I have a lot of catching up to do.

I have spoken to the Police a little bit but it was very hard. It was so clear that I was not being believed. The policeman kept asking who my doctor was and asking me if I have mental health problems. What that has to do with me making a complaint about a crime beats me. I do not expect justice from the justice system. I do not know if I will try again to talk to the police. Perhaps I will wait till they get some training. They do need it but they will not like me or anyone else telling them that. They really put me right off trying to tell.

There is not even a crime called ritual abuse. I would hate to be the first person to stand against the abusers. The media would have a field day. Then again, if the police were to listen and then investigate maybe others would come forward to back up the things I say. There are many grown up survivors who could if they were to get brave enough. Then imagine if the abusers were stood there in court facing us all. Now that would be justice. Even better than that would be that they are found guilty and sent to prison for life. Now that would definitely be justice. If it ever actually happened I would be so flabbergasted I would have to start to believe in a god of some kind or good fairies or some such thing."

Nat

"Justice is a controversial term at the best of times, when applied to abusive situations I think it becomes more so. Justice for whom, for what benefit, what would justice achieve? I think that there has to be some separation of the term, at least to understand what the term justice means.

Is it the court system where supposedly abusers get their just desserts, what and where is the crime, there is no specific crime to answer, the charges get watered down and the more palatable version of events is put forward, is this justice? Surely this harkens back to the chapter on the unbelievable, to have to water down your story so that it can go through the court system, denies the survivor their experience, however unbelievable that may be to hear.

There is also the question of whether justice can be sought through the established judicial system. Would the abusers get convicted? The conviction rates are not good. There is no guarantee and at the end of it all, all the statements to police, the medicals, and finally the court proceedings, would there be a sense of justice apparent to the survivor? Or would this just be another ordeal which had to be overcome?

This leads to the question of justice for whom, justice for the survivor? I think in some cases yes it would be for the survivor. I believe that if people want to pursue their abusers then that is a tremendous thing but that is not to say to those that can't or don't want to that they should be thought of as any less.

I think that it is up to the survivor. I know people will not agree with me, but surely the only ones that have the right to seek justice for the wrongs committed against them are survivors, in whatever form that justice may take. Is getting away from the group justice enough? I think in some cases it can be, to know you got away, to know that we managed to stay away is justice enough.

Is justice an illusion that people think that we need? That after hearing us talk think that we need the justice that only the police and the courts can provide. Is that just justice then for those people who can't handle hearing the story?

I think for me and my views on justice would be that I could tell my story and people would believe me. That by telling my story I can in a direct or indirect way help someone else. That it helps people to have a little understanding and awareness, that because of my experiences, I can use this to help other people, to uncover the lies and secrecy, in some small way and to help others."

Annie

"Yes we can get justice and there are different types of justice we can get. The most obvious although one of the hardest is to report the abusers and groups to the appropriate authorities.

I believe the best way we can have justice is to get on with our lives to break free and not let the abuse dictate any more of our lives."

Lucky

"Justice is a wonderful ideal, which we can all aspire to, aim for and hope to achieve some day. The reality is not quite the same as the ideal though. Even the legal system rarely provides real justice for anyone.

Not every survivor wants to get legal justice. I for one do not care about that kind of justice. I accept the things that happened to me were wrong and terrible and accept that it all had an impact on my early development and my life, but nothing I do now can change any of this. I choose to look forward in my life and if I were to attempt to seek legal justice, I would be forced to look backwards to some degree. I prefer not to do this.

On top of this it would be very difficult to get anyone in the police to listen to and believe the story of what actually happened. I have met and spoken to several survivors who tried to tell the police and have yet to hear a good report back from anyone about it. I don't think the police are well enough trained or aware enough to listen to a survivor of this talk about it. Most of them do not belief that the abuse happens anyway and they are just not open enough or helpful enough to the survivors. They seem to think that you just walk into their offices and make a statement at their convenience, not ours. I don't think so. There would need to be some time spent building trust. They do not want to know about it anyway I suspect.

And then it would be a very hard thing to ever prove in a court of law. All the ritual stuff would have to be removed or people would think you were just a total nut case of some type. If other witnesses would speak out then maybe some charges would stick but it would be so hard. The thought of ever having to stand up in a witness box and tell about any of this stuff makes me cringe. I personally do not think I am brave enough to be the test case on it in Scotland. I will leave others who are more inclined to want justice to go for this one. I personally just want to be able to get on with my life.

I would like to find a way of putting an end to the abuse and would love to be able to expose the abusers, but the cost to me and my family would be far too high to ever think about doing it through the criminal justice system as it currently stands. Perhaps other ways can be found that are less harmful to the survivors. I think more of the survivors would tell about the abusers if it was just a sharing information session rather than ending up in the criminal justice system and having to face abusers in a courtroom without any real protection.

I would share information with the police if there was an okay police officer and I did not have to go to court. I would only do so though if it was a real attempt by the police to stop the abusers from getting any more children. I just cannot see this happening though. The police like the other child protection agencies wait till after things have happened before they try to do something. They are not really there to protect or they would try and find out more."

John

"This is where my mind always splits into fascist dictator and faith healer. The fascist says that I am ultimately responsible for the actions of my abusers. I have broken out of their system and so I have a duty to end their lives so that they can never sexually abuse another child.

The healer says that my abusers were abused themselves and simply weren't strong enough to break out and so deserve even more love and compassion. Needless to say the fascist always wins by saying, 'If they were abused and broken, why do they want to break innocent children knowing the pain it caused in them.' And so the only justice I can see is castration and branding and death to those who actually groom children or are part of the larger satanic picture.

Justice is the responsibility of the individual consciousness. But I can safely say I would pull the trigger if it didn't involve the risk of further buggery in jail or destruction of spirit in me. Knowing that they ultimately win by making me something I am not, a murderer."

POWER

POWER

It is all too easy for ritual abuse survivors to think and believe that the abusers have and hold tremendous power over everyone. Many survivors believe that their abusers can even tap into supernatural power. Some survivors believe that their abusers can raise demons, talk to the devil, read minds and do a variety of other equally incredible and seemingly impossible feats. Most survivors are extremely afraid of the power of their abusers and most have very good reason for what they believe and for what they fear.

As children, growing up with the abuse on a daily basis, the power and control of the abusers over them is absolute. For the child concerned there is absolutely no question about who are the most powerful people in the relationship. The abusers do of course know this as they have set this up to their advantage and they build on it at every available opportunity. Abusers of this type quite literally hold the power of life or death over the child in their hands. The child will have experienced examples of this power many times. From the perspective of the child, at any time, the leader of the group can decide to hurt, maim or even kill someone within or even out with the group. The survivor will have experienced the effects of the immense power of the abusers repeatedly.

The abusers try to ensure that their power remains absolute, and of course it usually does with a helpless child. Using everything at their disposal including love and loyalty, force and threats and tricks and deceit, they continue to control the child completely even as they become adults. They use their power and control to ensure silence, a silence so complete that it sometimes lasts for a lifetime. They demand total obedience from the child and such is their power, they most usually get it. They teach the child from an early age that resistance is useless and indeed as a child, it would be both futile and foolish to resist such power. From the perspective of a child trapped in this, there is no question that the abusers have and hold all the power.

It is only when the child begins to grow older that some may seek to begin to question and even test the absolute power of the abusers. Some survivors do begin to resist and try to seek their own power in the only way they can. The most usual way they resist is in carrying out acts of defiance at home, in school and in the community. Some children begin to behave anti-socially, exhibit a variety of criminal behaviour in particular arson attacks and vandalism, and some become very violent. In some cases, particularly if the survivor is in some way destined for a position of power, such rebellion is encouraged providing the authority of the group is not directly challenged. It usually is

not. Few would be mad enough or brave enough to challenge power and authority while still in its clutches.

Some survivors also try to escape from the group, not because they think the abusers have lost any of their power, but because they are so afraid and desperate that they are driven to try and run away. They run while believing that the power of the group will be able to reach out and grasp them at any point. They run believing that they may be caught by the group and killed at any time. They run mainly because they really cannot cope with their lives anymore. Some would rather face the uncertainty and fear than remain any longer with the group and their family. Most survivors run away and escape from the group through such fear and desperation.

It would be a very rare concept for a survivor to decide that they must leave the group because they think that they deserve any better in their life. Most survivors would find this hard to believe particularly while they are still involved in the group. Few would have the confidence or good enough self-esteem to believe that they ought to have a better life. Few who are still living with the group would dare to question the beliefs and few would dare question their family or their fate. Indeed, in running away from the group, many survivors would judge themselves to be weak and inferior to those who stay behind. They, and the group, would judge those who leave as traitors to the group and to their faith.

For many years after survivors get away from the group most live with the fear that they will be found by the group. These fears are not without foundations. Time and time again survivors are tracked down by group members and repeatedly threatened and attacked. Some survivors have moved many times, changed their names and identity and done everything they can think of to disappear from the sight of their abusers. Despite all precautions, many survivors are found again and again. For some, this leads to reinforcing of the belief that the abusers are all powerful or are able to use supernatural powers to find those who try and escape. This is not always the case.

It is in fact very easy to find people in this country. Debt collection agencies are particularly good at it and track people down all the time. People's National Insurance numbers cannot ever be changed except with extreme difficulty. Medical numbers and notes travel with the individual as they move about the country and anyone claiming social security benefits will be given numbers, which will also remain with them for life. People can be tracked through schools, Universities, Electoral Registers, Social Security Departments, Housing Benefits Departments, Disability Living Allowance, Medical Numbers, Tax offices, National Insurance, Banks, housing, etc. Unless an individual is prepared to go to great and extreme lengths to assume a completely new

identity, they can usually be tracked by a determined person. It is not all that hard at all to trace someone particularly if you have the money to help with this. No supernatural powers are needed at all to find a person in this country.

When survivors get away, stay away and begin to heal from their trauma and move on in their lives, the power dynamic slowly begins to change. Some survivors reach a stage in their lives when they finally realise that in many ways they have become far more powerful than the abusers. The abusers begin to fear the free survivors because they know too much and can ultimately expose the abusers to society. Some survivors get to a place of realising that if they talk publicly, or even go to the police, they will become much safer from the abusers.

Some survivors realise that if they go public and speak out the abusers will not dare to go near them in case this proves some of what the survivor is saying. The abusers power comes from maintaining the silence and secrecy. Some survivors get to the stage where they realise that they do want justice. Some survivors finally reach a stage where they realise that the abusers have no more power over them at all. Not everyone gets to this place, but for all survivors the potential is always there to do so.

In many ways, this book is an example of survivors finding their own power. When survivors begin to expose the abuse it strikes fear into the hearts of the abusers. When this happens the shoe is on the other foot so to speak and it is the survivors who begin to hold the power. As survivors begin to find their voices more and more of the abusers will be exposed. Some may even end up in court and ultimately some may be convicted for some of their crimes. None will be prosecuted for the crime of ritual abuse as it does not exist as such in this country, but some survivors are making complaints against their abusers for other serious crimes. This is beginning to happen now and is gathering momentum as survivors find their power at last and as other survivors begin to see the results of speaking out.

Some survivors are using their reclaimed power to rebuild their lives, get a career for themselves, have relationships and raise their own families. Some survivors decide to raise society's awareness of ritual abuse to try and stop the abusers from continuing what they are doing. Some are raising awareness by speaking at conferences. Some are providing training for agencies. Some have set up support help lines and web sites and many are even writing their own books or contributing to others such as this one. These survivors no longer hold their abusers in awe and have begun to see them for what they are. They have finally broken the power that the abusers once held over them. Though some may still have fears from time to time, once survivors have found their own power, they will not easily let it go again.

Survivors Accounts

Lee

"Abusers aren't more powerful than others, but others are scared of them and with society hiding its face, this only adds to their power. Survivors have power and are able to use this power to rebuild their lives if they are able to break away."

Sheila

"I don't know that the abusers are more powerful, but they're certainly more cunning.

Yes survivors do have power. The fact that they've survived is power. At the time you assume that they are powerful, certainly more physically powerful than a child. The only power a child has is to tell, but they can only tell if somebody is willing to listen."

Kay

"I'm only just emerging from a lifetime of powerlessness. As children, my father held all the power and we were like his puppets, and even when grown I never really argued with him.

He held psychic control probably in calculated ways and was also very cunning and I can be naive. Also, you don't expect your father to be you and your mother's cruel jailor. It was so hard to get free of the feeling of duty to father's that runs through this patriarchy like sap through trees.

Through secret societies the abusers hold hidden, possibly massive, power, like octopuses. In Belgium a demonstration of 300,000 failed to get justice in that paedophiles kidnap case.

But justice and truth, anger and life and love are on our side. And when Ritual Abuse survivors heal they are very dedicated to ending the suffering of children and adults. I think when we get together, together with our supporters, we will be a power to be reckoned with, and these profoundly sick men will lose their sway."

Jill

"Survivors do have power. They grow into it in time and as long as the abusers have not completely overwhelmed or damaged them too completely then they can reclaim their power.

When you are a child you are totally powerless because you are small and completely dependent on the adults in your life. There is nothing that you can do about this at the time. The abusers hold all the power while children are small. Though there is no power for a child what there usually is inside is a drive to survive at all costs. Perhaps this is a power of a kind? Even the power of speaking freely is denied to us while we are children. Then we grow up. One day we realise that we are as big as them, or nearly.

Most survivors are quite intelligent. I don't know if that's because it takes some degree of intelligence to get away and stay away from the group. Perhaps the less intelligent do not get away. That sounds really awful but I do wonder about it sometimes. Perhaps it really is survival of the fittest in a group setting. It certainly has felt like that often enough so I think it must be.

It is a hard thing for survivors to realise that they have any power in the world. When you have been powerless for a long time it is hard to know what to do to even begin to try and get in touch with your own power. They held the child captive and silent so one of the most important things for a survivor to realise is that freedom and free speech is everything. Beginning to realise and then to utilise the freedom and the words. Now that is power. Survivors can begin to realise through time and healing that we actually have more power than the abusers. We can point the finger at them if we ever choose to. We can expose them if we ever want to. We can even tell on them if we decide to do so.

It might seem as though sometimes they had power over us but as we resist and break free we do retake our own power. Sometimes I feel less strong and at those times I waver a bit and wobble. Then I remember that I am now a grown up person with my own power. They do not own me any more. I am mine and mine alone. I hold my own power.

Abusers are total cowards. Only total cowards would behave the way that they do. Only a person who feels that they have no power of their own would seek to take power away from children and helpless people. Only cowards work in gangs or packs as they do. Unfortunately it is one thing to know this when you are nearing your fifties and another thing to live it as a child.

Abusers are cowards but nasty cowards. They tried to make me be the same as they were. They tried to force me to like the things that were happening. They tried to make me accept all that they did. They wanted me to become just like them but I refused. I choose freedom and speech. I will continue to fight back against them. Fighting back is my personal power. I choose to work against them and always do the opposite from them. If I am ever in any doubt about what to do in any given situation I think about what they would do and I just do the opposite. Makes decisions so much easier to make"

Nat

"Who has the power? Isn't this the eternal question, which has the subsequent question of what is power and if we don't have any power can we get it?

Do the abusers have power? I would have to answer yes to that question although I can now qualify that with they used to. To be honest to some extent I think that they still hold some power over me, in the sense that they are my family. And in that sense I feel their power, that in some weird way I still do and think I will always have a sense of obligation and duty towards them, although I do not know if that constitutes power.

I also believe, to a point that survivors hold the power, and I think that the abusers are all too aware of the power that they hold. Survivors hold the key, if people are willing to listen; survivors are willing to talk, to uncover the secrets and to exert their power over the abusers. This is regardless of whether they believe they have power or not. Power comes in many forms and I believe that the most important facet of power that anyone can possess is information, the information to uncover the lies and the secrets, the power to uncover the abusers, to make the world sit up and pay attention.

The problem is very few people want to listen, to truly listen and to believe. There is also the fear that surrounds it all. I was scared, am scared. I was scared to talk, to tell, to let out the precious secrets that I had been keeping for so long. But I knew that the power was mine that I held all the cards. I am not saying that overnight I suddenly became aware of the power that I possessed but it was more of a gradual process. The fact is that if I talked about some things, they couldn't touch me, I had the secrets, and I held the power.

So who has more power? Now I believe that I have more power. I have the power to talk, to tell, the power to decide if I want to talk. They can't stop me, and would they try I can unmask them, would they really want to risk that. I doubt it. Survivors have the power and other people have the power to decide whether they want to listen, not just listen but to believe."

Annie

"Survivors do have power, and each one of us holds that power. No the abusers aren't more powerful than any others. They are weaker. They think they have power because they can hurt people. But they can only do that through fear. Exerting fear in order to get something to do some thing is a sign of weakness and shows a lack of power."

Lucky

"We have the power of speech when we get to a certain place in our healing, but few of us use this power to try and bring the abusers down. By the time we are able to get to a place of healing enough to tell, the things that we are able to tell are often worthless. We cannot save the children we left behind because too much time has passed. We cannot tell much about abusers who are still a risk to children as we have no proof. In some ways, the power is worth very little unless survivors get together and combine it.

At the moment the abusers are still the ones with the most power. They are still able to carry out their acts of abuse. They still command silence from those they have abused. And they are still getting away with crimes both past and present. The fact that society as a whole is still tending not to believe those few survivors who escape and then try to speak is also indicative of the power that they hold.

Every time there is any indication that ritual abuse might be happening, even to a young child, there is a huge media outcry. The trial by media that then unfolds prevents the truth getting out. The huge backlash of 'there is no such thing as ritual abuse' drives whoever is attempting to get to the truth into hiding. Workers have lost jobs and positions and agencies have been forced to write policies that do not allow for any mention of ritual abuse. Now that is power!

If we all keep on writing and talking about it maybe we can use our experiences to get people to listen to us. Maybe in time if the world becomes more aware things will change. The power of our experiences and our knowledge could be shared and maybe other survivors could be helped. Maybe, if we all work together we can even get some agencies to be pro-active and get them to seek out the abusers. Now that would be power."

John

"This is another difficult one. I always say we are at our most powerful in weakness. By that I mean if you can accept there is no way of changing something, but instead adapt it as all survivors have to, then ultimately the power is yours. You are evolving whereas abusers are devolving, becoming more animal and less spiritual. For example if you took away the material things needed by an abuser to groom a child, then the abuser is useless, relying on a trust. Put a survivor on the street and he or she will adapt. It's two completely different types of power but the abusers type of power is reliant, ours is self-reliant and so much more powerful in a spiritual sense."

BETRAYAL

321

BETRAYAL

Many survivors commonly talk about their feelings of betrayal. Some, as they continue to talk about the abuse and find ways to heal from their experiences, begin to talk about feeling betrayed by their family. Many survivors feel strongly that they were let down by the people in their lives who should have protected them from harm. As survivors begin to look at how other families nurture and protect their children, they begin to realise just how badly they have been let down by their own families. They quickly realise that most parents choose to have children and ought to protect them from harm. Instead of protection from harm and basic love and nurture, the survivors were used and abused within the family and more widely in abusive groups. Some survivors reach a stage of becoming very angry about the betrayal by their immediate family.

Even survivors who were not abused by one or both parents can feel betrayed and let down by their parents. Often there is the belief that the non-abusive parents should have noticed that something extreme was happening to their child and the belief that the parent or carer ought to have done something more to protect the child and put an end to what was going on. Most survivors insist that good parents would have noticed something. Certainly, it is hard to believe that good parents would not question their child being absent from home for a number of days and returning on occasions with trauma and injuries. Most survivors suffer extreme treatment at the hands of abusive groups during the rituals and it is hard to accept that parents would not notice that there was something wrong with or troubling their child after being involved in such events. Some survivors do talk about a non-abusive parent trying to rescue them.

Then there is the betrayal felt by survivors who feel that there were people around them when they were children who ought to have noticed that there was something wrong and helped them. Some survivors talk about non-abusive people such as teachers, social workers, police officers and health workers who were involved to some degree with them and who ought to have noticed and intervened on their behalf. Some survivors even talk about telling a statutory worker about the abuse that was happening yet still nothing being done to change things for the better. For those survivors who had expected the professionals in their lives to take some action on their behalf, yet to no avail, there is a huge sense of betrayal and even a wondering if the person might have even been a part of keeping the secrets.

Survivors of ritualised and organised abuse sometimes talk about occasions when an adult who they thought was not associated with the group, got to know them and over time built trust with them. Survivors tell of how the adult would go to great pains to gain their trust and then deliberately betrayed them to the group or family. This is a common theme for survivors and is probably deliberately staged by the abusers. To have begun to trust in someone and perhaps even thought there was a chance of getting some help and then being let down has a tremendous impact on a survivor. In most of these cases, at the point when the child or young person begins to tell about the abuse, the family is swiftly informed. The survivor is then severely punished for talking out of turn. The person who has worked to gain the child's trust has been as it usually turns out, part of the whole set up. From this, survivors learn another important lesson. They learn at a very early age that they can trust absolutely no one. This makes it harder throughout their whole lives to ever completely be sure about who they can trust.

Betrayal for many survivors means more that having been betrayed by family, friends or people that were trusted, but also frequently includes the betrayal they themselves feel they are committing in regards to exposing the family or group. For many survivors they find it hard to talk about what has happened to them as they have a high degree of loyalty to their family. When they try and talk, they feel that they are actually betraying their families by telling. Many people find it hard to understand how loyal survivors can be to their families and they seem to think that blood ties and loyalty no longer matter if someone has been abused but it is not all that simple.

Most people feel some love towards their families and those who brought them up. Even if the parents or carers were not all that good, most people still have positive feelings towards them. This is very normal. On top of this, religion and family values play an important part in what people believe. For those who grow up with ritual abuse, there will have been a huge focus on not betraying the family and staying loyal to them. The belief that it is the family's business and not anyone else's business can stay with a survivor all their lives. Even for those survivors who do manage to find a way of talking, they often have to struggle against their own feelings of betraying their family to outsiders. For those few who go on and talk to the police, it is even harder as they are totally going against the family.

Some survivors after escaping from the group try to get help from agencies. Most usually in the beginning because there is no trust the survivor only reveals a few small details of the problems that they are experiencing. It is common for agencies to say that they can help the survivor when they are first approached for help. Unfortunately, it is even more common for most

agencies to then begin to withdraw their services as it becomes clearer what they are actually dealing with.

As the survivor begins to trust more, they begin to tell more and it becomes more apparent that there are many complex issues involved. Very few agencies feel knowledgeable enough or equipped enough to deal with this. Before long, the agency withdraws its services leaving the survivor feeling let down and betrayed yet again. From the agency perspective they often feel unqualified to help and often think that more specialised help is needed. They are often wrong in this as what many survivors actually need is someone to go the distance with them. It is common for survivors to report that support agencies and others have often let them down by withdrawing their services.

Many survivors feel betrayed by the denial of society to recognise their experiences. To live in a society that does not legally recognise and name the crime that has been committed against them feels like a betrayal. On top of that, there is no acceptance of the experiences of survivors. People prefer to deny survivors' experiences rather than take on that this type of abuse happens. People prefer to believe in such things as false memories rather than accept that abuse might be an issue. People prefer to believe that survivors are mentally ill or deluded or attention seeking rather than accept that there just might be some truth in what they are saying. It is little wonder that survivors often feel betrayed by society.

Survivors Accounts

Sheila

"Betrayal? Yes, I have been betrayed. By adults, by abusers, by people who were meant to protect me. It's no longer an issue for me because I no longer trust or expect anything from anyone, so I can't be betrayed."

Kay

"I don't know much of the past yet. All the same, I feel that in my uncle's gang at least, the deepest addiction, besides profit, was to the destruction of the human spirit and the enjoyment of mortal terror, the pain of gang-rape, mutilation, etc. To this end they made us betray each other to destroy our spirit, our faith in ourselves and our trust in others. Or perhaps the main thing with these betrayals was that it stopped us organising any active resistance, and perhaps in the end this was the main point. Because as teenage mums losing on our babies, we sure aimed to resist.

I feel awful about betrayal. For, after my baby brother was killed or died of the epilepsy brought on by the electric shocks of our torture, I feel I was a bit safe. Two dead children from an upper middle-class family of three would have attracted attention. So I think I was used to create or access resistance and then betray it. I would be saved and others would die, be tortured, etc. These betrayals silenced powerful inner teenagers and were a large contribution to my thirty five years of chronic depression.

They were also constantly betraying and probably blackmailing each other in their ruthless jockeying for power. The man I saw shoved into sulphuric acid had a look of horrified surprise on his face. He didn't expect this sudden awful death from his co-conspirators.

I was also betrayed all my life by my father and other relatives."

Jill

"I have been betrayed thousands of times by many people. At least that is how I feel. When I was young I expected it to happen all the time. After I escaped I somehow thought it might be different. It wasn't. Each time I am betrayed it hurts to the very core of my being and beyond. One would think that you would get used to it. When someone betrays me these days I go deep into myself and pray and meditate. I try to work out why. I never succeed. Each time I am betrayed by someone that I love; I fight back in whatever way I can. Usually I use words to their best advantage. I have a right to protect myself and try to do so as best I can.

The abusers think that we who have survived have betrayed them. I guess we have. We told on them. We left the group and you are not meant to do that. It is betrayal of the family and the faith. So I suppose the backlash is that we get betrayed in return. That's how it feels sometimes anyway. Someday I will learn to rise above it all but not today. Today I will continue to feel very aggrieved at being betrayed. Perhaps in time I will work out how this affects me as it does. Perhaps in time I will work out why it happens. Perhaps in time I will not care as much about it."

Nat

"Betrayal: Another word with a myriad of meanings, betrayal of whom, betrayal by whom and do I think that I have betrayed all spring to mind here. Do I think I was betrayed, the answer is an unequivocal yes. I feel that I was betrayed by a lot of people, not only my family and others, but I feel that in a lot of ways the entire system let me down.

I went right through school, even had experience with the social work department and I was probably the quietest person I know. Do I blame them, no, I don't blame anyone, that was my life and I was living it the best I could. Keeping out of the way, keeping their secrets because I had to.

There is no-one to blame. I was doing what was expected of me. Could I expect people to notice? I did all I could so that people wouldn't notice me. So in that sense can I really feel betrayed by anyone? Should I have been noticed? Maybe I can look back and feel some sort of remorse for not talking before, but I cannot blame people or feel any bitterness for not being noticed. I feel let down by systems that are meant to be there to protect children, but being let down, is in no way comparable to being betrayed. The latter shows and requires some notion of intent. People didn't notice because I didn't want them to notice. I couldn't let them notice.

To have gone from speaking about the difficulty people have in believing that abuses like mine occur, how are people supposed to know, to notice, to be aware? I do not feel betrayed by anyone other than my family, and others. They betrayed the power and the position they had over me.

In another sense I feel that I betrayed both my family and my group. I know that that may be somewhat controversial, but I escaped. I got away. I broke the ties with my family and my group, because I had to, but in a sense I betrayed them and their teachings. Now this may have been an issue of safety and something that should have been achieved long before now. But that in no way lessens the betrayal I felt, about leaving them. It is hard to describe the nature of this feeling and be able to justify it to others.

To sit here and logically think of an argument as to why I feel that in some ways I betrayed my family, other than saying I was taught from an early age, my family was everything, they controlled my every move. These teachings are hard to get away from, to disobey, to leave, to turn your back on them was and is seen as a massive betrayal, and in some respects my feelings echo those teachings.

Feelings are not logical as I have found out, and trying to understand and justify why I feel the way I do is like moving in ever decreasing circles with the answers always achingly out of reach. No matter what I try and say my family are my family. I feel betrayed by them but similarly I feel that in a way I betrayed them too. I disobeyed them. I turned my back on them and although I would and will never regret leaving and getting away the feelings remain."

Annie

"Yes I have been betrayed. I've had friends leave me when they have found out what's going on, and more recently I've had a friend turn out to be a group member. Betrayal will always be an issue for me but I am aware that not everyone will betray me and I have to remember that."

Lucky

"Betrayal means different things to different people but for me, ultimately, it means what I had to do in order to survive.

Betrayal of my family, my way of life, and my sense of who I was, all of it was a betrayal and I have struggled with this all of my life. Though I believe that I had to betray all of these things and all of these people, it does not make it any easier to live with the sense that I turned against my family. I would have preferred for there to be any other way of achieving my own survival but there was none that I could find at that time or even now.

I do believe that my family completely betrayed me and feel it more about my mother who I felt made more active choices in what was happening. But I get tied up in knots about that bit where they would always say that everything they were doing was for my own good. I have watched so called normal families do things with their children in the name of the child's own good, yet have difficulty sometimes in agreeing that it truly is. It is hard to see the differences except in degrees.

Friends have on occasions betrayed me and I have to confess that betrayal of one kind or another, is something that I have come to expect from people, though perhaps not always accept. I always think with the people I get close to, just give it time and they too will turn against me. It takes me a very long time to make friends but it doesn't take a second for a friendship to end if I feel that I have been betrayed. Real trust is very difficult if not down right impossible when you build a relationship within which you expect some day to be betrayed. When your experience is to have faced betrayal it is easier to think that a betrayal will happen again rather than to trust that it might not.

Whenever I say anything about my past life I feel as though I am betraying my family by talking about it. I was taught to remain silent about our religion in order to safeguard it and the believers of it. I was also taught that any betrayal would be the worst possible thing I could ever do. I went and talked to the police once and the feelings of betrayal almost completely overwhelmed me. Even although I know in my mind that my family were so very wrong, the early messages still sit there and eat at me whenever I try to talk. Though this does not stop me from talking, it feels very painful and extremely confusing on occasions."

John

"I have been betrayed by almost everyone I have come into contact with including family, friends, lovers, religion, society, police, social work, council, doctors and therapists. All because they want to tell you how it is and what is best or simply just for some power trip.

I can honestly say the only people I have met who haven't fully betrayed me are survivors and people I talk to for ten minutes or so in every day life. But even then they sometimes betray you because they don't know you all that well. Betrayal, detachment and relationships in general are all issues for me."

Helen

"Betrayal - for me this is the biggest issue. I was born with a right to be loved, protected, fed, kept warm, given safety to grow into the person I was, not what someone else wanted or needed me to be. I believe that every child has this right and I got none of the above. I was betrayed on every level. I feel betrayed by my parents who abused me, the cult who nearly killed me, by society for not protecting children, and as a child I was taught to believe in god and Satan and felt betrayed by god as well. I now have my own belief system but I still feel that betrayal is the issue I have felt most.

I support a lot of human rights issues and ritual abuse is in defiance of all human rights. I am still angry with a society which spends so much time coming up with excuses and elaborate ideas as to why this abuse does not happen or can not happen. Every adult in this society, including me, has a part to play. We are all responsible for the society we live in and for changing it. Every day another child is betrayed as I was. By talking freely, being aware of children who are unhappy or behaving strangely, doing some thing when we see a child or an adult being treated badly, we can all, and do all, have the power to change a society that betrays its children daily.

My dream is to live in a world where all children have all they need and then they will grow into healthy adults who will in turn be able to give their children all they need, and then abuse will be a thing of the past. I will do all I can to make this happen, starting with myself and my son. Some people may think my dream unrealistic, but I have lived with betrayal all my childhood and I believe that changing that is worth working towards."

A SENSE OF BELONGING

A SENSE OF BELONGING

Some survivors say that they have never, ever felt any sense of belonging anywhere or to anyone. They have always felt completely alone and apart from everyone else in society. Even within the family as children they have not felt as though they belonged and some talk about how they always felt different, odd and unable to fit in with anyone. Those who talk like this tend to have had this feeling of not belonging grow as they matured. For some this sense of not belonging has come about because they were never able to accept on any level the religion or beliefs of their family. Some have never managed to conform in any way and were more harshly treated and judged by their families because they did not even manage to fit into 'normal' family life. In some cases the family has deliberately set this up so as to totally isolate the survivor. Other survivors talk more about only belonging to the family or to the group.

Children do not choose their families of origin. When a survivor grows up within a family, like any other child, they usually have a sense of belonging to, and loyalty for, that family. There is little choice in this as this is, for the child, all that they know. Any child needs to feel some sense of belonging to something regardless of the kind of family it is. Children are totally dependant on their family and the younger the child is, the more dependent they are on the adults in their lives. Even as children grow up, their family and the people they love are everything to them. Belonging to a family is vitally important to people as people are social creatures by nature.

When a family is part of a group, which practices a particular religion, even a religion that others would regard as abusive or wrong, all the members of the family belong to the group. While young and dependent, there is no question of any choice in this matter. As in any family, the adults are the ones who dictate the rules and bring their children up as they believe and in the manner that they think is right and proper. As people grow older and develop their own thoughts and opinions, though they may have greater choices than before, the choice to leave an abusive group is not an easy one to make or, on making it, to actually achieve. The abusive group has a huge investment in keeping group members both actively involved in the group and totally silent. They do not allow people to just choose to leave. In fact, they employ every means at their disposal to stop people from leaving the group.

Even when survivors do manage to get away from the group and often the accompanying family, they can feel very isolated and lonely. The world they

knew best and felt they belonged in is gone to them. They often feel as though they do not belong anywhere at all in the world except with what they grew up in. This does not necessarily mean that they want to go back to the group; rather, it can mean that the outside world is so different to their own experiences of life that they find it very hard to feel any sense of belonging within it. Everything is different in the outside world including culture, beliefs, language and values. It is also very hard to live without any family connections at all.

Some survivors feel as though the group they grew up in actually owned them. This is what they were always taught and has always been their own experience. Every thing they ever knew as they grew up taught them that they not only owed allegiance to the group but they were owned by it and that the group could do with them as it willed. They had no free will, or so they were taught. They had no right to make any decisions for themselves and would not be allowed to even try. In fact they had no rights at all. It is like a modern day system of slavery hidden within a family. It is also all that they ever had or knew. What many survivors say though is that at least they had a real sense of belonging to somewhere and someone and that was very important to them.

When survivors get away from the group they often feel as though they belong no where and that nothing is familiar to them at all. These survivors often struggle to accept that no one owns them and to accept that they belong only to themselves, not to the group. People often feel the need to feel as though they belong to something or someone. It is the nature of people to feel this. Many people feel very frightened when they feel disconnected from everything. When survivors leave they most often lose their whole family, friends they knew and everything that meant anything to them including possessions and pets. The very nature of having to run away, escape and hide from the group means that all has usually to be given up, including the things that were good or that mattered in any way to them. This is a tremendous loss for anyone to bear and there is generally little or no understanding within society about the impact upon the survivor who has lost everything.

Even as survivors stay away from the group and begin to build lives for themselves they often feel very different from the rest of society. Most people have family connections and are able to talk about their family. It is part of normal life for most people. But this is not the case for many survivors of ritual abuse. These survivors cannot join in the conversations about family at work and when socialising. They can feel quite left out of things when people are talking about such things as the family barbecue or the latest

birth, wedding or even funeral. Most people do not even notice how common it is to be talking about family but survivors cannot help but notice what it is that they are missing. It is not usually the case that someone has no family at all.

Even when survivors have children of their own they can experience problems due to having no family. Survivors are more likely to worry in case their children meet any of their birth family. They are more likely to resist any contact between their children and their birth family as they will fear that their children might be abused by them. In addition to this, as the children grow up there is no extended family to help and support the new parents. Most people rely to some extent on brothers, sisters, parents, grandparents or aunts and uncles to occasionally baby-sit or even chat to about the problems and dilemmas of being a parent. Survivors who have had to give up their family do not have this kind of luxury.

Even the children of survivors suffer and can feel very isolated as they begin to realise that they are different from their friends in that they have no aunts, uncles, cousins or even grandparents on one side of the family. They will discover that for most people there are many relatives and even at the level of not getting the same amount of birthday presents as others, they will often feel different. Often the children will begin to ask some of the very difficult questions and some will even go in search of relatives. This can raise many difficult issues for all concerned and might even lead to the abusive family finding out where the survivor is now living. Survivors have to explain at some point, to some degree, why it is that there is no contact with the abusive relatives. This raises further difficulties for the survivor and indeed for the children.

People prefer to belong and fit in with everyone else but for survivors of ritual abuse it is always a very difficult issue. There is no getting away from the fact that it is hard to fit in and belong when it is clearly the case that you are very different from other people. In addition to not having relatives, having to learn how to live in what seems like a different culture, cope with threats and even attacks from the abusers, survivors may also have other problems in trying to belong and fit in to society.

If people know that the person is a survivor of abuse and particularly of ritual abuse, they may well pass judgement on the survivor. There are many myths abounding about survivors and most of these myths are derogatory. The survivor may also be suffering from trauma as a result of their abuse, in fact, it is unlikely that they will not be suffering from trauma. This can manifest in many ways such as mental health problems, panic attacks or flashbacks. Again this sets the survivor aside as being different from those

around her or him. Then there is the very high possibility that the survivor may have developed many different personalities as a response to coping with the abuse they have experienced throughout their childhood. Generally people will not be able to understand this type of coping mechanism and the survivor may feel completely out of step with everyone else. Survivors often struggle for many years to come to terms with all of this and it is little wonder that they often feel that they belong nowhere.

Survivors Accounts

Sheila

"I don't ever feel that I belonged to anyone, anywhere or to anything."

Kay

"I don't recall if I felt I belonged to the Ritual Abuse group, but I guess I did. Belonging then meant I was property, a child prostitute slave, but it might also have felt exciting. By contrast my daytime life was centred on trying to help people. When I was eight I started a club called the 'Happy Helpers', then another for refugees and the hungry in my teens.

I belong to a few things such as a class and my kid's classes, a couple of groups, a few close friends. But I still feel an outsider because I can't talk about what's most important to me. Maybe I belong to this book, as here I express myself freely, and then the phone lines are a bit like a good family.

It seems to me you can belong to things, places, people, in different ways. A shared purpose is a great way to belong, and a shared belief is nice. Good neighbours are nice. It seems to me you have to look hard, sometimes, at what is there, not what you'd like or feel you have to have to be happy or whatever. To be needed may make you belong. It's totally important to belong - without connections you can't live."

Nat

"Can one have a sense of belonging yet feel like they don't belong? I had that feeling when I was growing up. I belonged in all senses of the word to my parents and to the group. Yet I did feel that I was somehow alien, different from them. It set me aside from my family and the group. In one sense I believed I belonged there, that this was my lot. I knew my place. I knew my station and I knew what was expected of me.

But is that the sole definition of belonging, to know where you are in the world, to know what is expected? I have to think that a sense of belonging is more than that, more than merely having a place within a group or structure. I think that you have to feel comfortable in belonging, need to know the rules but also need to feel a common bond, an interest in common, a place to fit into.

I found this extremely difficult, both when I was part of the group and when I left. I had a very limited sense of belonging when I was with my family. They were/are my flesh and blood, but I didn't particularly like them. I didn't like what they did. But in a sense I knew I belonged to them, that my place was with them.

When I left I was lost, tossed around on the sea of confusion. Where was my place? Where was my sense of belonging? I had left behind the unsafe but solid structures of the group. I had to discover where I belonged, to find a sense of belonging within myself, because the world had been passing me by. I had never really had the opportunity to be part of this culture, this world. I needed to make a place for me, to understand where I belonged, and more importantly that I belonged to me. That I didn't belong to the group that I had the capacity to belong to only me.

I think to realise that I didn't belong to the group, to my parents, that I belonged to me, is a struggle. One that is hard to realise, to be responsible for knowing who, and where you are in the world, after the rigidity of the group structure was and still to some extent hard to adjust to.

Sense of belonging I think comes from within and without. I believe it is created within by learning that belonging has to start with realising that you belong to you, and is shaped and moulded by your interactions with others. The roles that you take on throughout your life, the associations that are made all contribute to a sense of belonging."

Annie

"Belonging is something I struggle with. I have a negative idea of what belonging is and I see it as a control or restraint to a group or person. Living without connections is hard. I don't feel as I belong to the normal world. I am a member of a group, which I don't want to belong to but feel I am."

Lucky

"I don't feel that I ever belonged anywhere. In my childhood I knew that I didn't belong because I felt so at odds with things and with people. Everyone else seemed to be more able to accept everything and I could not seem to be able to accept anything. I always believed throughout my childhood that there was something seriously wrong with me that I could not belong in the right way to the group, the family and the religion. I rebelled relentlessly even in the face of punishment. I could not seem to find a way to fit in. I tried so hard sometimes but never ever made it. I even tried to pretend for a while but I never was any good at pretending.

On getting away from the group, I always felt lonely, out of step and at odds with everyone else. I never fitted anywhere. Work was okay I suppose as I got by. I would do my best in the various jobs I had but never really felt connected to anything or anyone. I always felt as though I was heading in the opposite direction from everyone else. I was always swimming frantically upstream while the rest of the world was floating downstream. I was always against the flow and completely out of step.

I had relationships with others because I knew that was what normal people did in life. Don't get me wrong, I would feel some feelings for people, but there was never anything like a real connection. I could not understand it and I always though that there was something fundamental lacking in me. It was like I could go so far and then I would stop short of any real connection with the people in my life. I think I always felt a bit superficial or even unreal.

It was only when I had family of my own that I had a sense of belonging for the first time. At last and for the first time ever I felt that I had achieved something worthwhile in life. My kids became the most important people in the world and they belonged to me and with me. At the same time I belonged to them and with them. It was only then that I began to realise what was missing from my life and had been missing all these years.

Everyone needs to feel a sense of belonging to someone, somewhere or something. No wonder I had always had the sense of something being missing. I had thought that it was me and it wasn't at all. It was them! All my life I had been missing out on part of what makes us human and social creatures. I had never been loved and had never felt love. I had never been able to belong anywhere or with anyone. I had been denied basic love and had been kept apart from belonging. What is worse is that I never knew what I had been missing all these years until I found it through my children. It was like wakening up after a long sleep."

John

"I belong to me. I never belonged to the churchy people. They were fakes. I am real. I don't feel like I belong to anything, even to survivors, because there is so much suspicion, which is needed, but I want to trust and have no doubts. But until I can talk openly to all survivors and we all agree what has to be done (i.e. the big picture). I don't think I can belong wholeheartedly to the movement. It's simply because I think it goes deeper than child abuse.

It's to do with the masons, the illuminati, whole world consciousness, sacrifice and mental imprisonment. If we can't agree on what we are fighting, how can we fight it? Music is probably the only thing I could say makes me feel like I belong. I can put on a song and disappear."

THE INVISIBLE PEOPLE

THE INVISIBLE PEOPLE

Most survivors of abuse are invisible while they are children and while still enduring the abuse. The children experiencing abuse are taught by their abusers not to let anyone know about what is happening and most do not tell. Abusers take a lot of trouble trying to ensure that the children remain invisible. Even as adults some survivors of abuse maintain their silence and remain completely invisible in society. They do not wish anyone to know what happened to them and that is of course their right.

For others it is only when they grow up or somehow the abuse comes to light, or the survivor finds their voice that other people find out. Only then can the abuse survivor be seen and details of the abuse suffered by them can come to light. There are only two sets of people who can reveal what is actually going on and that is the abusers or the survivors. The abusers cannot and will not tell about what they are doing therefore the only way that the world will ever know the truth is if survivors find their voice and break silence. This is never an easy thing to do.

Up until about forty years ago, adult and child survivors of abuse were for the most part totally invisible to society. Abuses of different kinds were not spoken about and although survivors of physical abuse, sexual abuse and domestic abuse were everywhere, few people in society knew anything about the survivors or the effects of the abuses upon them. With all kinds of abuse, there was the general view that it was part of life and had to be tolerated and just not spoken about. Abuse was not thought to be very widespread and was thought to be confined to poorer working class type families. And, if it was thought about at all, the victims of the abuse would be regarded as being in some way to blame or responsible for the abuse that had happened to them. There were many myths and very few facts available about abuse of any kind.

Over time, there has been a shift in awareness and attitudes in society, and there is now a bit more attention being paid to abuse survivors and their problems. This shift has not come about easily though. Feminists have campaigned for many years to raise awareness of men's violence against women and children. In the 1960's women survivors and their supporters began to organise and form support groups to help other women and children. Over the years many survivors have repeatedly broken silence in order to raise awareness of abuse. All of this, and more, has made it much more possible for survivors to get support and break their silence about their experiences. This has helped to educate the general public and although there is still a long way to go before the true extent of all kinds of abuse is realised, at least more abuse survivors are now listened to and believed than previously.

With ritual abuse, we are still very much at the beginning of the journey and we have a very long way to go. Even at the beginning of this journey, there are already set backs and obstacles in the path to awareness. Survivors of ritual abuse are still very much invisible because society is not yet aware enough of the existence of such abuse to acknowledge its existence. Though some of the awareness work is now happening across the country in terms of some types of abuse and there are organisations in existence to help many abuse survivors, there is still a major problem with society taking on the more extreme ritualised and organised types of abuse.

Ritual abuse is often regarded as so extreme that many people find it very difficult to come to terms with the idea that it may happen in their own society or community. Some elements of ritual abuse are so hard for people to accept and believe that it is far easier not to believe in any of it. Ritual abuse survivors often find it easier to not mention the ritual aspect of their abuse and are much more likely to remain invisible than any other type of abuse survivor. In addition to this, there is a huge media campaign every time ritual abuse gets mentioned anywhere, which usually focuses on the absolute denial of its very existence. Coupled with that is the often vehement denial from agencies and individuals that accompanies attempts to ever suggest that ritual abuse exists in their part of the country. For some, if it exists at all, then it must be in another part of the country and not 'here' where ever 'here' happens to be for an individual.

Though some survivors of ritual abuse are beginning to speak out, it is extremely hard for them. They are very easily silenced. Many of them find it particularly hard to get together in groups for obvious reasons and many find trust an almost impossible concept to manage. Because of the extreme nature of the abuse, many suffer from mental health problems or from trauma related conditions and many have physical, emotional and psychological disabilities. While it is exceedingly difficult for any abuse survivor to speak out publicly, for ritual abuse survivors it becomes an almost impossible task.

Yet, the only way the world will ever know about this type of abuse will be if the survivors manage to break their imposed silence. They are the only people who can say what happens in this kind of abuse as they are the only ones who know and might be prepared to tell if the climate for telling was right. Even without the right climate for telling some survivors have tried

and do keep trying. Some survivors have stood up at conferences and on training days to share personal experiences in order to raise awareness.

To admit to being a survivor of ritual abuse frequently invites ridicule, disbelief and judgement from other people. Those who totally deny the existence of such abuse will certainly never believe that a survivor is telling the truth. Such a person would demand absolute proof. The survivor would be instantly judged a liar or at best, mentally ill. Many of those who do believe that ritual abuse happens also swallow the many myths which surround it such as the myth that survivors are dangerous to others and will always return to the group and report back to the abusers about people who are helping survivors. Any way you look at it, it could be regarded as foolish to admit to being a survivor of this type of abuse. One of the quickest ways to lose all credibility in this society would be to admit to such an unbelievable thing.

Survivors are usually extremely cautious about telling anyone that they are a survivor of such abuse for many of the reasons already stated. Another reason they are cautious though is that, from the perspective of the survivor, the abusers could be anyone, and be anywhere. Ritual abuse is highly organised and involves many people on many different levels of society. Survivors will more usually know their immediate abusers, but they cannot ever know all who are involved in this type of abuse. The facelessness of most of the abusers means that, from the survivor's point of view, it could quite literally be anyone who is involved with the group or even with associated groups. This does not lend to readily trusting strangers or even people known to them. Most survivors take quite a long time to get to know someone before they ever try to tentatively disclose anything about their past.

In time, some survivors do become angry enough, or heal enough, to become more public about their experiences. Some do also reach a stage of just not caring any more about what other people think or say. To quote one survivor, "I lived it. I survived it. They did not help me then. They had an excuse as they did not know. I have spoken now. If they do not want to listen or believe me now nor want to help then nothing has changed and I should not be surprised. I know what happened, not them. I was there, not them. Why should I care about what they think about me now when clearly they do not care about people like me?"

Some survivors in this country feel very strongly that ritual abuse ought to be recognised as a crime in its own right. They would regard this as some sort of validation of their experiences and a recognition of what actually happened to them. Those who have gone forward to the police to report the crimes against them are often dismayed to discover that the focus is very

much upon the sexual and physical abuse. For many survivors of this, these are not the most important aspects of the abuse that they experienced. For many there is a greater importance on other things that happened to them.

Many people talk about such things as their experiences of extremes of neglect, degradation, brainwashing and mental torture that has deeply affected them. Some talk of being forced to witness abuse, forced to make impossible choices and being forced to abuse others in the group. For many the enforced belief system that validates and excuses the actions of the abusers is one of the worst features in the abuse as it is what many are taught from the day they are born. Many struggle for the rest of their lives with the belief that they have betrayed their faith and their family. Very few survivors regard the sexual abuse or the physical abuse as the worst aspect of their experiences in childhood, yet this tends to be the things that society views with the greatest horror. Perhaps this is because people can only imagine what would be the worst thing for them or perhaps they just do not know all that goes on.

Survivors are becoming much more visible and part of the proof of this is this book. Many survivors have contributed to this publication and some have gone off to become much more openly visible as a result of being involved with this project. Increasingly survivors are standing up and finding their voices. This type of abuse is no longer totally invisible and that is because the survivors are beginning to make more demands on services and to take action to make the world more aware of some of the things that do happen even in a so-called civilised society such as this.

Survivors Accounts

Lee

"Survival of a crime that isn't recognised - yes this is an issue. I want to change things for people coming through the system so that it is recognised. I cannot let certain people, generally official types know I'm a survivor of Ritual Abuse as they would only want to flag up the mental health card, but I had all the tests already and really would find it rather pointless to go through them all again just so they can stick labels on me. I can let my friends know in fact they do know and my credibility's fine with them but outsiders? No way."

Sheila

"No we are not seen as credible, no one believes it happens. But for me it's not an issue, it doesn't matter because we know it happens.

The only people that are experts are the survivors, but it could also be the abusers. I trust very few people.

Labels are not helpful for anyone other than therapists, doctors or those working in mental health. But for survivors they have been of no consequence at all.

Some are willing to help. My therapist does not profess to be an expert, but she has been willing to learn, listen, support and has tried to understand. She has been non-judgemental."

Kay

"Isolation is one of the most awful things about Ritual Abuse and therefore one of the weapons with which the abusers try to destroy us once we've passed our usefulness to them. It must be broken. The growing number of people prepared to believe and help Ritual Abuse survivors is lovely. My closest friend finds it hard to believe what I say. What slowly opens her eyes is that she sees me grow and change with the therapy that surfaces the atrocities. (She now notices different people looking out of my eyes.)

I recently spent two years looking for a good therapist, writing over twenty letters, interviewing about ten people, trying with three and getting nowhere until I wrote to someone famous for help and she kindly did. I recommended it. I found many had the attitude I was "escapist" when I said I couldn't do analysis or "inner" work. Most of my life I felt most therapy was for people, children who hadn't really been very badly hurt, and that there was nothing for people like me. It has been amazing that, away from father, going into the past is possible. I have been incredibly lucky, I now realise, in having a Ritual Abuse trained therapist.

I think that many "Experts" are stuck in the past. The revolution in psychology, that has been taking place in America since the 1970s, seems only slowly to be trickling down to the United Kindom. The essence of this revolution is this. The founder of psychology, Freud, had at first said incest and sex abuse was the cause of much "mental illness", but fury at this idea (familiar??) made him recant. He then came up with the complete opposite and poisonous theory that little girls long for sex with Dad and have incest fantasies. This total lie sat at the centre of psychiatric and psycho-analytic theory for most of the last century.

A combination of two areas of study exploded this lie. Firstly, in the study of trauma from shell-shock survivors of World War I to the disturbed veterans of the unjust Vietnam war, they discovered that it wasn't innate character that caused the breakdowns, but rather the sheer amount of trauma endured that would make anyone crack. Next, from the 1970s on, the womens movement discovered that 1 in 4 girls and 1 in 7 boys are sexually abused by the age of eighteen. Applying the theory from the study of war trauma, that there is an outside cause for trauma, women in the area fought for the acceptance that sex abuse was the origin of much "mental illness". Suddenly women and some men weren't mad because of mysterious innate causes, but rather were survivors of childhood sexual trauma.

But almost all the people now working in the area were trained on the old textbooks, based on Freud's lie and developments of it, that said we were "mad" in various ways and degrees. For people to shift from seeing incest and sex abuse survivors as feckless nutcases to seeing us as courageous survivors takes an effort. And then for Ritual Abuse survivors the effort is immense, because none of the models of childhood they study would seem remotely applicable to us. In addition it is apparently traumatic in itself to work with us. I certainly think they can see us as manipulating when we are just plain desperate and fighting for our lives.

It seems possible that we are both far more damaged and far more courageous than any expert yet realises. And I do think everyone should listen more to us who have been through it."

Nat

"I think that you are only as invisible as you want to be. There is much said about the invisibility and isolation of survivors, but it makes me wonder, especially about the invisibility, how many survivors does it take for them to be visible. Is it a question of survivors being invisible or perhaps more apt to say that it is others who do not see, for whatever reason.

But is it that they don't see, or the fact that they don't listen. There is such a movement of survivors. There are numerous support groups. Survivors, sadly, are everywhere, so perhaps it is more apposite to say that people see but don't hear.

Why don't they want to listen? Maybe we have to go back to the incapacity of people to believe what they deem to be the unbelievable, but there are conferences, seminars on the subject now, they manage to listen at those. Is it survivors that they have a problem listening to?

I think there is the age old myth that survivors are not credible, and as astounding as that thought may be, I can think of no other explanation. The long-term damaged individuals, who have gone through so much, are to be listened to on a superficial level, but the experts know, the ones with the bits of paper, the ones who had to listen to survivors to know, now abandon them in favour of recognition as experts in the field. Am I being too harsh, possibly, maybe not?

Who are the experts? We are. We alone know all the intricacies, the rules, the hurt and the destruction. We know what it felt like. We were there. There are too many people waving bits of paper around saying that 'we' know best. I for one have had a lifetime of people telling me that they know best. I know my experiences. I know what I went through, and if I tell someone my experience that does not suddenly propel them to the lofty position of being an expert on me, or on the subject.

I want to be listened to. I want to let people know that this abuse exists, that if they want the truth then they are going to have to listen to me. I want to raise awareness of this issue, of what it was like. Does that mean that I have to get a bit of paper before they take me seriously, before they can truly take on board what I have to say?

Being a survivor does not seem to equal being credible, it doesn't mean that people will actually listen, but in all honesty who else are they going to learn from, who do they learn from, it is the survivors that tell them the truth, the way it was, but suddenly we are being too subjective, and lack credibility.

If I require a piece of paper, a qualification that gets people to sit up and listen to what I have to say, then that's what I will get, seeing as being a survivor and being aware of my experiences is clearly not enough."

Annie

"We have a right to be allowed to say we are survivors and at the end of the day what others think or say should not matter. I know that many times I have felt isolated, caught in a type of abuse where there is little help openly offered. No one these days doubts women who to go to police after domestic violence but if we go to the police about Satanic Ritual Abuse they freak and don't believe us. This is not fair and this is not right.

I believe that even if we ourselves are the only people who believe what has happened we have to hold on to that belief. We can't let other people's doubts in our credibility put doubts in out minds. It is difficult to be a survivor of any crime but even more so when the crime you have survived is not even recognised as such."

Lucky

"I am a professional person. These days I have a well paid job. I am regarded quite highly I think in the job I work in. I am fairly credible and think that no-one would easily doubt the things I say. If I was to ever let my colleagues know that I am a survivor and furthermore, a survivor of this stuff, I firmly believe that I would lose all credibility. I like to think that people who have known me for a long time would listen to me, believe me and would not see me as any different but I do not really believe that is what would happen.

I feel that I owe it in some ways to survivors of ritual abuse to stand up and be counted in a public way but when it comes to the crunch I just cannot do it. I do feel that being a professional would carry some weight in the world and I might stand a better chance of being believed than many folk. But then I get to a personal and possibly selfish place and fear that I will just lose all my hard earned credibility if I ever let anyone know about my background. I have to say here that I have seen what has happened to other survivors in this. I would very much like to help and would like to make a difference but I am not willing to sacrifice myself just yet. Maybe I'll do it in a year or two when I am getting past it.

I would prefer to be invisible though I often feel guilty about the continuation of the abuse. I am trying to fight it where and when I can. Sometimes I wish that someone could look and see me and understand that I am a survivor of this stuff. It would be a surprise to many of my workmates to realise, as they think I am so normal. Well, I am normal as it just so happens. I have no mental health problems. I never have had. I talk to no therapists. I never have done and probably never will. The only thing that makes me not so normal would be saying that I am a survivor of ritual abuse. I think no one would believe me if I were to say, partly because I am so normal. It is not what people expect. They do not ever see what is going on inside me. I hide the problems that I have from time to time. Though everyone knows that I have no family, no-one ever asks me anything about it. Some people I work with are a bit closer to me and perhaps they suspect that I am a survivor of something or other. I wonder sometimes because there are often bits in the newspapers about abuse and they tend not to talk about it in front of me. Sometimes I think that they do know or suspect something. They never ask me about it though. I am not sure what I would ever say if anyone ever asked me. I would probably just say. After all if someone were to take the trouble to think and ask me about something then it shows that they do care to some extent.

I have been away from my abusers for a very long time. I have had to heal myself and move on in my life. I have found a way of surviving in this world and no-one bothers me anymore. This is enough for me and I can ask for no more. I do still dwell on the past from time to time but it no longer affects me in the ways that it used to. Every now and then, I see in the newspapers that one of my abusers has died. It is good because no matter how powerful they were in life, at the end of the day they all come to the same end as the rest of us. Death is a great equaliser."

John

"This is a big issue for me. It's why I bought a guitar when I was sixteen. The way I see it is like this. Nine to five people are thick as fuck. They follow because it's just too much effort not to fit in with the crowd. Sexual abuse spoils their pint. Sexual abuse means they have to use their brains. They just want an easy life and they can't have it coz it's them that fuck life up. So I decided at a young age that I was going to make it as difficult for them as possible to ignore the truth.

As for letting people know. I see it as a quick way of weeding out the good from the bad. People who treat me with contempt and the predatory abusers and people who don't want to know are the covert abusers. And people who ask or support are the good guys.

I know that the abusers will be planning a way how to get me to shut up spreading the truth. But they have always planned things and the good guys always win."

Helen

"The cult taught me that no one would believe me, that I was wicked like them, so if I did tell, I would be despised. That if I told, people around me would die. I would die. They set me up to not tell. They set me up not to be believed. The first time I told, I was eight and I was not believed.

The next time I told I was thirty six, in counselling, and had built up a bond of six years with my counsellor. The brain washing all came back and I went through hell inside my head because I had told. It got easier after that.

All my friends and the people around me know that I have been ritually abused. I have found that my attitude toward my past makes a lot of difference to how other people respond. If I am full of shame and not wanting to believe it myself, other people may respond to that rather than the facts about the abuse. The only people who have not believed me since I have been an adult are family members who need to protect their own wounds.

Three years ago I went to a rally in London to help raise awareness of child abuse. I stood up on the base of Nelson's Column at Trafalgar Square and said that I was a survivor of satanic ritual abuse, and I talked about my experiences and my beliefs. I broke the fear that day of telling, and of not being believed. I broke the hold of the brain washing. I took all my courage and determination and I won that day.

I go to the rally every year and speak out because I have a voice and I know that so many others who were and are being ritually abused have no voice. Doing it for others as well as myself gives me the courage. I use my anger at what happened to me to help raise awareness. I turn the anger into courage. Some of the children in the cult were murdered. I was made to witness their murder. I refuse to be invisible. I will stand and speak until people listen.

In their memory, and for all those people still being abused, I will stand up until I am seen. I will not let my abusers still have a hold over me. I set myself free by challenging everything I was taught by them.

I reclaim my power."

FIGHTING BACK!

FIGHTING BACK!

Not everyone thinks in terms of fighting back against ritual and organised abuse and the abusers who are involved in it. Some would not consider any value in fighting back against something that they do not believe exists in the first place. They just dismiss the whole thing out of hand as imagination, mental illness or scare-mongering. These people consider there to be no problem in the first place therefore see no point in looking at it or discussing it. This is fine for them providing they do not then turn their attentions on trying to silence the survivors who are trying to do their best to raise awareness about the issues, which are important to them. Unfortunately some people who claim that they do not believe that this kind of abuse happens begin to actively campaign and fight against the survivors who are beginning to become vocal. Surprisingly, some people who claim not to believe it then work extremely hard at trying to silence anyone who even mentions ritual abuse.

Others, particularly survivors who are struggling to stay alive, do not have enough energy to fight back against it. Surviving is on occasions a struggle in itself and sometimes just breathing takes up all their available energy. Staying alive can, for the survivor who is in a particularly vulnerable place, be regarded as fighting back. It would on occasions be so much easier to give up and commit suicide. The abusers would prefer that survivors take this course of action. Some survivors are so vulnerable at times that there is no way that they can fight back against anyone. They may be doing all they can to stay out of the sight of abusers. This usually means staying out of sight of everyone.

Some survivors may have fought back in their own way for a while and have suffered from a severe backlash because of it. Some may even have been attacked. Many are often threatened and all are usually frightened of the power of the abusers. Survivors have few illusions and they will all know that to fight back against the abusers is to invite trouble. Every now and then they too might understandably decide to lie low for a little while and let others do the fighting back for a short time. Fighting, in whatever form the fight may take, is a very tiring thing to do. Survivors can become very weary of it all and may decide to stay out of things for a while. If there has been a backlash against the survivor they may have many new fears or may even suffer a set back in their healing. Sometimes the backlash rekindles memories and causes the survivor to experience further trauma.

There are many different ways that people fight back against abuse but all have one important aim, to stop the abusers and finally end the abuse for everyone. People may have different ideas about what the best method of fighting back might be but nothing is more certain than if we do not fight back at all, we cannot ever come close to winning. The main thing is to engage with the enemy. Once survivors have escaped and managed to heal a bit, they are the people who are most likely to want to fight back in as safe a way as possible with the enemy they have managed to escape from. This fight is rarely for themselves. Rather the fight back is because the survivors know the reality for the remaining 'victims' who are still at the mercy of the abusers and they cannot bear the thought of the abuse continuing for another generation and for other children.

Some people believe that what is really needed is for the survivors of ritual abuse to simply step forward, go to the police, make complaints, provide statements and reveal all to the powers that be. The thinking behind this is that the police would investigate the matter and prove or disprove the alleged abuse. This would, it is believed, provide the world with the ultimate proof. And it has to be said that in an ideal world where there was understanding, awareness and properly trained police officers plus quality support and safety for survivors, this might to some degree. Unfortunately, we are not in an ideal world.

Survivors are very clear about the many reasons they might have for not simply going to the police but one of the main reasons is that the police do not as a rule respond well to the survivors. The Criminal Justice System in this country rarely provides a good service to any abuse survivor, rarely convicts sex offenders and is often extremely damaging to the survivors. It would be hard to suggest to any survivor of abuse that it might be a simple or a good idea to approach the police.

It takes a very long time for survivors to get away from this type of abuse and a long time to heal from the effects of the abuse. As a priority survivors have to find a safe place to live. This is rarely easy. They have to find a means of survival and they need to be able to feel safe. Few survivors of any abuse, let alone ritual abuse would ever be able to simply walk out of an abusive group and go directly to the police. Fewer still would regard the police as a safe option. Even if they did, they would be very lucky to get any help or understanding from the police if the experiences of other survivors who have already tried are anything to go by. This does not mean to say that survivors ought not to keep trying to demand justice.

At the end of the day, to more effectively fight back, the more survivors who do manage to go forward to the police, the better it will become. If survivors keep going forward, in time, there will be prosecutions and in time there will be absolutely no choice but to believe the survivors. Though survivors may have to fight against the ignorance of some of the police officers and then the justice system, the more who do so, the better it will become for others. Unfortunately, as with everything, it is not always good to be in the vanguard.

Hopefully too, in time, the police will improve the service that they offer survivors of all kinds of abuse. Some survivors, only a few at present, have had better experiences of the police than previously was the case. Some can relate positive experiences of talking to the police. Perhaps, in time, the voices of survivors will become so many and so persistent that the police will listen and take positive action. The system as it currently exists is not particularly helpful to the survivors but it can be improved. The police and other agencies need to be able to become more pro-active if they are to gain the trust of survivors and eventually get the survivors to tell of what goes on in this society. If all the agencies were to look at really working together, there would be great steps forward.

Some people believe that the best way to fight back against ritual abuse is to carry out research into the subject. Some research has already been carried out but this is fairly small and the subject matter has not attracted enough interest and funding to make it possible. There would need to be some clarity about just what the aims of any research was to be. So much always seems to get back to proving or disproving the existence of the abuse in the first place. Even research would not change the minds of those who categorically will not believe what survivors say. Research into the needs of survivors would perhaps help survivors and those who support them. Research into many different aspects of any kind of abuse would probably be a useful resource.

Ways of fighting back include constantly trying to raise awareness of the issues of ritual abuse. Through providing such things as awareness raising, training and talks, particularly with input from survivors, more people do become more aware of the many complex issues surrounding this subject. Perhaps if more people have a greater awareness of the issues they will become more able to provide support for survivors and help more survivors escape from the abuse. Awareness will also help workers in the various organisations know how to deal with the abuse survivors effectively. Awareness about what really goes on in the world is not a bad thing. No one can know what they do not know so it is good when people try to find out what they do not know.

Some survivors write articles or books and some have written for this book and can see it, quite rightly, as a form of fighting back. Some even go on to write their own story of their abuse. Some survivors name the abusers publicly and some do become brave enough to go to the police and make a statement in an attempt to exposing the abusers. Some survivors fight back by supporting and helping other abuse survivors either directly by offering a service to them or indirectly by encouraging the setting up of support services for survivors.

Perhaps the real truth about the fight back against ritual abuse is that it does not really matter what form the fight back takes. What matters most of all is that the enemy is engaged in every way possible. It is important that for the fight back we employ every possible weapon at our disposal. It is important that we fight on all fronts and expose the abuse that is still going on. It is important that we keep on trying to find ways of protecting the children in this society from abuse of any kind. It is surely everyone's job to ensure that all children, young people and vulnerable people are safeguarded from any harm. This cannot ever happen if people do not know and accept what can actually happen in this society.

Survivors Accounts

Sheila

"This is everyone's responsibility. People need to lose the blinkers and stand up and be counted I suppose. Give people the opportunity to learn. Lose the labels and not see us as a threat but as people."

Kay

"Christianity, at best, brought a respect for every single male human being after eras of tribalism and slavery. It's now time "human beings" included all women and girls - not just Fathers, Sons and Mothers.

Participating in this book feels like fighting back - it's been a good journey. I try to accept that getting through each day is part of the fight back, and that some day I'll be able to do more. I think survivors and supporters are the ones who'll do most to stop it at first - though I don't understand why an investigative journalist does not research the abusers. Is it more dangerous than war journalism, are there no Pilger-type journalists around, or is it that sex crimes are not sexy news?

Protecting people, especially children, from crime, should be the responsibility of the state via the police. But when it comes to sex crimes men and the state (are they the same?) don't want to know. Battered wives who flee for they and their children's lives have a tough time. I think getting more women into positions of power would help.

I guess we survivors and supporters will do the rest, an anthropologist, Margaret Meade said, "Never doubt that a small group of determined people can change the world. It is the only thing that ever has." We are as determined as the Jewish people who survived the holocaust to found a new country. We can refuse to be silenced and speak out in every art form, location, state of mind and means of communication until the perpetrators of these atrocities are exposed and their secret societies laid open to the sky."

Nat

"Fighting back is a hard concept for me. I think that by breathing, managing day by day to live is fighting back. I think that in this section I am going to be rather hypocritical, because I know the answers, for me, I know that if I stop breathing, stop getting up each day then in a lot of ways I am continuing to let them have power over me and win.

Life is a battle. There are hurdles and obstacles to overcome. There are fights to be fought. Sometimes I lose these fights, have periods where I can't seem to function, times of year, where I can be so paralysed by fear that, it takes all my willpower to just keep breathing. Yet I know I have to. What other option is there?

I have let them take so much of my life already, and here I am sometimes giving them more. Logically I can understand this. But then again logic never managed to get rid of memories or fear. I know that I need to live my life, not just exist in it. The getting out and participating, not being a bystander anymore. I try to, but sometimes this is too difficult so you go back to basics, breathing, getting up each day, and in this sense I believe that they aren't winning.

Do I need to have a sense of anger or injustice in order to be able to fight back? Sometimes I think that I do, and that in some ways I am incapable of it. I do get angry but more at myself. I haven't managed to transfer that anger on to those who deserve it. Will I ever get this anger or feeling of injustice? I can't answer that. It seems that sometimes anger is all I feel. My problem is that I never seem to direct it in the right place. Maybe it is just too difficult to do that?

I want to win. I want to have a life that I can live, not merely exist in, to reach out and touch all of life, to experience all that life has to offer, do I manage to do that all the time, not yet, but I think that I am more able to do that now, and the major component in all this is that I am alive to do it, I am still breathing and although sometimes I struggle, nothing can change the fact that I am alive and capable of living. I have the chance and the opportunity that has been denied to so many people.

I think that in this sense I have fought and in some respects I have beaten them, and I will continue to fight."

Annie

"We can stop it by stopping giving our abusers the power we let them have. Too many of us as survivors help our abusers continue their evil work by not telling. We can fight back by taking a stand and when somebody says they don't believe us remind ourselves that we were the ones that were there. We saw and we felt it all happen. It is our responsibility as survivors to help others survive and work together. So that it will {someday} get to the point where people don't need to be taught how to survive because none of them will ever be victims in the first place."

Lucky

"This kind of abusive activity has been going on for centuries and it will not be easy to root out and stop. But the same is true for all forms of abuse. So much of our society condones abuse and we must remember that as long as there are imbalances in power between people there will be those individuals who will abuse their power over others. To end abuse, will not be a simple act. There are no quick fix solutions available. Our society is complex and the structures that maintain and permit abuse to flourish are complex and rooted very deep within this.

To end ritual abuse we need first of all to get it recognised for what it is. We need to get people talking. After all if it is not even regarded as a problem or even something that is real, then how can we even begin to tackle the problem? There is a very long way to go with this, but the first steps are being taken. Survivors are increasingly finding the courage to stand up and talk. People are beginning to listen. Though it is slow, it is completely unstoppable. Survivors as individuals may hit a rocky path from time to time and stop talking but so many now have started that there is a steady trickle. Books and articles are being written. Not just by academics but also by the survivors, which is much more important. More importantly these books are being read.

It is everyone's job to protect the children in society and it is therefore everyone's job to root out and end all abuse within society. The only way this can be achieved is through people increasing their own awareness of the issues and taking steps to identify survivors, particularly children and young people. A lot could be learned from adult survivors if we could just listen to them. Through this we might be able to identify the younger people and help them earlier.

Though we have a long way to go on this journey we need not to get disheartened at the apparent length of the journey. Every journey has to begin with one small step before it can ever achieve the possibility of reaching an end. If each of us just take one small step and then another. Then we just keep right on going. Then we will get there in the end. That will be part of fighting back."

John

"The only way that ritual abuse will stop is if people start taking responsibility for their actions and also see the signs. Books are a good way. Music is a good way. Anything that is universal and mass produced aimed at the fifteen to twenty five age group, the age of rebellion and also a thirst for knowledge and truth. It is ultimately the abusers responsibility. But they don't give a fuck. So we take the responsibility because we have a soul."

CONCLUSION

CONCLUSION

All things have to have an ending and that obviously includes this book. However, having now stated the obvious, I would prefer the ending of the writing of this book to also become a beginning of something good and useful for survivors. I hope that this book inspires others to put pen to paper (or even start typing on the computer) and perhaps join with others to write their own truths. Only through getting our narrative out there into the public arena, can we ever peel the onion and begin to reveal more of the truth about ritual abuse. As we reveal our narratives, so too will other people find the courage to write, talk, draw, whatever it takes to add to the jigsaw so that someday, when all the pieces have come together, the whole truth will unfold itself to the world. That is the day we will have really turned the tables on the abusers and begun to win the fight back against them.

This book began as an idea, initially a vague idea that I floated by a few people to see what they thought about it as a vague idea. The idea was to get the survivors of ritual abuse to contribute in some way to a book. The response I got at first indicated that the people I had talked to clearly thought I had a screw loose. Now while they were possibly accurate about my mental capacity, I still figured I was onto a winner of an idea. I saw no reason at all why lots of survivors could not be afforded the opportunity to say their own bit. For this negative response I had received, I reasoned that I had floated my idea past the wrong people. Never for a moment did I consider that this book might not become a reality because I already had the picture of the finished product stuck firmly in my head.

I turned to the people who really mattered in this and began to ask them what they thought about the idea for this book. The survivors I spoke to came back with a very clear and very positive response. All thought that it was a good idea. Many wanted to get involved on some level and some began to write even before the chapters were outlined. Clearly the idea was sound and was approved by those survivors I spoke to at the time.

This book was not an easy book to write. It was not easy for any of the survivors who contributed to it to share their thoughts, feelings and experiences. It was not easy to put it all together and it was not easy to edit. In other words, this was a very, very hard book to bring to life. Yet, for many who contributed to this book, they have reported it to be a positive experience for them. Two of the survivors involved have now written their own books based on the chapter headings provided for them. Others have reported

that thinking about some of the issues raised by the questions became a positive and healing experience for them. Though there have been for some, worries and concerns about telling and revealing a bit about their abuse, no one involved in this project has reported any negative impact. I do hope this means that there has been none.

Survivors of all kinds of abuse find ways of getting out of it, healing and moving on with their lives. For most it is a long and hard struggle but eventually many are able to live a good and fulfilled life. Most survivors find a way of creating or finding a family of their own. Most learn how to trust enough to form positive relationships and friendships. Many go on and get a career, hobbies and find ways of enjoying their life. Though some may carry scars relating to the abuse all their lives, they can and do live life to the full.

Many will never forget what happened and some do not ever want to forget but this does not mean that they dwell on it daily. Many survivors use their past experiences to help other people in many different ways. Some raise awareness about abuse issues in the hope of helping to get it stopped. Some work in child protection, care services and support organisations in order to help care for those who are most in need of care. Some help bring up the next generation in a loving and non-abusive environment.

For many of the survivors who contributed to this section of the book there is a strong message that they would feel closer to conclusion if the world would only accept the truth of what has happened to them. The non-belief in the existence of ritual abuse coupled with the constant need to raise awareness of the issues before survivors can get help makes it very hard for survivors to move on with their lives. Effectively when people declare that ritual abuse is not a reality, it denies many people their own reality. Many survivors feel that they live in a world that will not acknowledge their suffering and that will not take any responsibility for protecting the children of the next generation or helping survivors get justice.

This book is part of the actual evidence that ritual abuse is a bitter reality in this country. The survivors are sometimes the only evidence of a disaster or a calamity. Why is it that more evidence than the presence of the survivors is constantly demanded? Now is the time that we need others to acknowledge our reality and get off of their cosy seats and out of their comfy offices and do something to put an end to this wrongness in our society. We cannot do it all ourselves and so far the survivors are the ones who have done all the work. In conclusion it is down to the rest of you to do something about all of this.

Survivors Accounts

Lee

"Yes conclusion is possible. There was a time when I thought it never was. I want to say that once you make that break away, that first step is taken. That building block may be a little unstable but the more bricks you add to it, the more your life becomes shaped to what you want it to be, the more stable it becomes. Add as many as you want to. Remember, that you're a survivor. Your life is now your own to do with what you want. Those around you who provide you with support when you want it and equally leave you alone when you don't want to talk, be they family or friends doesn't matter. What does is that they allow you to keep on adding those bricks to your life and don't ever get in the way. That they support what you decide.

To the World: We're survivors for a reason. We've survived. If you'd really like to help then listen with out prejudgement when we ask you to, recognise ritual abuse and don't treat us like an alien species (something to be feared medicated and caged)."

Sheila

"No, it's not all over.

It is possible to survive and move on, but it's not possible to forget. We cannot wake up and it all is gone but it can become less painful. It would be nice if people could see and really believe what goes on behind closed doors. If that will ever happen in my lifetime, I don't know."

Kay

"What people are being asked to believe is equivelent to Auschwitz and the concentration camps. That tiny and older children live like tortured slave-prostitutes, watching or taking part in atrocities, etc. Gang-rape of an adult is bad enough. We had that regularly while growing up. The scale of the evil beggars the imagination. As a marvellous help-line woman told me, "It's like Hitler, make the truth so awful then no one could believe it, so they go for the huge lie." That's what they've done.

Moreover we live in a society that not only sanctions, but almost deifies what one might call Prick Power. "Being a real man" is seen as having sexual power over women, and our streets, subways, magazines and TV are littered with women's humiliated bodies used to sell any and everything. All this benefits big business especially the booming pornography industry, which sends its tentacles far into our lives. Individual good men do not subscribe to this prick power culture. But youths and men with inadequate socialising (which includes many "public" schoolboys) drift into the "anything goes" nets and nests of pornography and paedophilia behind which lurk the huge ritual abuse societies.

The only opposition to this, the publicly scorned "post-feminist" womens movement, is in disarray, staggering under the immense backlash of the last fifteen years, which has lost us much of the gains of the 1970s and 1980s.

I think the fight against ritual abuse could be one of the keys that unlock a better future. I think that when society actually accepts that these things happen, that men (90% ritual abuse is male) actually do these things to children (mostly girls, I believe) for the sake of lust or power, a huge change will happen to consciousness. Men will no longer be able to hold their heads up without realising how incredibly destructive and uncivilised their unharnessed sex drive can be. They will then have to begin to see girls and women as people first, not just as sex objects.

Steve Bike said, "The most powerful weapon in the hands of the oppressor is the mind of the oppressed." And now we, who were raised in hell, are being helped to reclaim our own minds.

"If I am not for myself, who is for me?
If I am for myself alone, what am I?
If not now, when?"
Rabbi Hillel (after Primo Levi)"

Nat

"Can there ever be a conclusion, I think that no matter how much time passes the memories will be there, what I think can change is the way that I deal with those memories, and the way that my past affects me.

I can not go back and eradicate my past, I cannot change what happened, but in essence would I want to? I don't mean that I would not have liked to have had a perfect childhood, because I would have, just that I never. I find that there is little point in sitting here thinking if only, because it wasn't if only it just was, and in various ways it has helped shape me into the person I am.

There are negative and positive connotations to be taken from every situation, and although generally I am an extremely negative person, I can see that somewhere they gave me the strength, or the stubbornness to get on with it. I know the things I don't want to be and strive to be the complete opposite of them, and I have succeeded.

I am the way I am in some part thanks to them, all I have to do is build on that, learn who I am and where I want to be in this world, what I want to achieve, and in a lot of ways, I have achieved the hardest of these things already, I survived and I am still alive.

So then isn't this more of a beginning rather than a conclusion, an introduction into a life that I can dictate, a life free of them. I believe so, I believe that in a lot of ways my life has just begun, that I have the power and the stubbornness and essentially the opportunity to make what I want of my life, go where I want and be what I want to be.

So maybe this section should have been called the beginning, not the end, because life is just beginning, and I can make that whatever I want it to be."

Annie

"Don't treat us like we are 'something' different. We are normal humans at the end of the day that have been treated in a way no human should. Respect us and respect the ways we cope with our abuse, and most importantly if you don't understand something we say ask us. Don't make up your own ideas as to what we meant.

John

"If conclusion is possible then I can only see two forms of it for me.

My death or

Acceptance that sexual abuse is part of nature and must go on in everyday life

And so I conclude that I can top myself or wait for death to take this pain away. Most people have picked choice 2. But as I said, I have a deep fear of sexual abuse being part of everyday life. Mainly because it relies on the total absence of hope that something can be done to save this corrupt world, and the total selling of the individual freethinking soul.

What I conclude about ritual abuse is that it is meticulously planned by evil people who have a purpose. Is carried out by evil people who wish to be part of that purpose and is denied by weak people who actually help fulfil that purpose and complete it by turning a blind eye. It's all grades leading towards manifest power. The higher the grade, the lower you stoop. Something I have noticed however is that due to increased desensitisation and zero tolerance, the ritual abuse is now accepted and laughed at. i.e. white trash America incest, Cambridge and Oxford buggery, prison sodomy, the list goes on from altar boy abuse to barely age 18 schoolgirl porn and pop stars selling their own abuse for ratings.

The conclusion is that the everyday Joe has accepted abuse as part of life and chooses to say, 'just deal with it.' This allows the purpose of the evil people to expand and employ. We had covert abuse in Victorian times, overt abuse in times of war. What I now foresee is a culture like the film 'invasion of the body snatchers' where those not on the side of the abusers are weeded out.

To those trying to dispose of the true survivors I say, 'come and weed me out, you're too weak and my roots are too strong.' To those who are made abusive so easily because it's just 'too hard' not to give up and side with the apathy and repetition, I say, 'You don't know the meaning of the word hard'. Survivors have had to endure every second of their existence, suicide so easy, but only causing more despair for the survivor left living. You gave up your soul for an easy life. Our lives were taken because we wanted to create a life where misery was not the normal state of emotion.'

In conclusion to my rant, I would say this: you die and go somewhere or you die and cease to exist. If you go to some other dimension then life is only a test, the real life beginning when we die. If we cease to exist then life is all we have. So either we were abused so as to be tested for a higher plane, a strength of spirit test if you will. The test is being passed if we did not give up trying to stop the abuse of the world or we were abused simply as a random act of violence. No meaning, no purpose, no escape. And when we die, it's all over for good. I don't know about you but that makes death seem like the climax of life whichever way it goes. But also it says to me that I've found my purpose in life either way. For if its part of a test, I want to be opposed to abuse to pass. And if it's not a test, but simply just a random event then I want to oppose abuse just to piss the abusers off while I'm still here, because I can.

In conclusion, life is beautiful and death will be beautiful also. All we have to do is keep fighting the abuse."

Lucky

"I wish that I could believe that conclusion is possible. I would love to waken and find that my memories were all mistaken, not real and distorted. Waken to find that I have a family that loves me and respects me for myself. Waken to find that there is no abuse anywhere in the world. That would be totally brilliant. I wish I could engage with this 'false memory syndrome' and pick up a few good memories of my childhood. If I thought that might be possible, I might consider looking for a therapist who would provide this service for me. One of the better services that I have heard about I think.

All joking aside, there cannot be a conclusion in this subject until people are prepared to listen to survivors and at the very least try to keep an open mind on the subject. There can be no conclusion until such time as the lid is well and truly lifted off the can of worms and all abuse including organised and ritualised abuse is recognised. If we really want to be regarded as civilised human beings who are way above the animal kingdom then we must get to grips with this. We must grasp even the most difficult of nettles. Things are changing but the changes are slow and meantime theabusers are able to continue. More survivors are now coming forward and speaking out about their experiences. These days we can even find a little but growing awareness in some statutory organisations. All of this is to the good. In addition to this, more people are providing support for survivors and more survivors are being listened to and believed. Let's face it; even ten years ago a book like this would have been impossible. We are though still a very long way from a conclusion of any kind. Perhaps we need to set some objectives then we will be more able to see the progress that we are making in this war against abuse."

Helen

In Conclusion

"I was abused by members of my family and their acquaintances, by many adults. I was one small child and they tried to break me, they couldn't. One small child with no help, no outside resources, and they couldn't break me.

I am amazed by that child that was/is me. I survived against all the odds, whether people believe what happened to me or not is really about them, not me. I know and I survived. If I managed then as a child, how can I say to myself that I cannot manage now? Now as an adult when I can ask for help, read books and question. How much more powerful am I now than I was as a child?

So much more, I will not let that child down. I am alive and I will do everything I can to honour my life and my survival.

To other survivors I would like to say 'we have already survived the worst part', I know it does not feel like it sometimes but we have.

To everyone I would like to say that we are all responsible for our society and what happens in it, abusers depend on you turning away from child sexual abuse in all its forms. You can all help by getting informed.

Together we can make a safer world for our children.

I will continue to do what I can until this happens.

You can too."

APPENDIX ONE

Appendix One

This is the basic outline of chapter headings which was originally sent out to survivors of ritualised and organised abuse. Survivors were invited to comment or write under any or even all of the chapter headings with as little or as much as they chose to say about the subject. The outline was kept deliberately loose so as to allow survivors to write in their own way about their own thoughts and experiences. The outline provided was merely intended to provide a loose framework for survivors to follow and also to make it easier to know which chapter to place each survivor's contribution in. Survivors were left to interpret the headings, chapters and questions for themselves so their contributions are entirely their own interpretation of the subject matter.

This is what the survivors were sent.....

Behind Enemy Lines

The Idea: A Book written by RA survivors and aimed @ helping other survivors and supporters of survivors.

Chapters to be on:

Behind Closed Doors: How did you become involved in RA? Was it a family affair? Any brief background you want to share here?

A key to the Door: Failure of society/individuals to recognise? What do you think could have/should have been picked up on by those who might have been in a position to help particularly in childhood? Did you want someone to help? What can/should people do now? What can society do about it?

Chain Reactions: What were/are people's reactions to you as a survivor? What were/are people's expectations of you? What are your expectations of other people?

The Great Escape: How did you get away from the family/group? What's more important to you, you or the group? Did you try more than once to get away?

Seeking Sanctuary: Where was sanctuary in the end? Did you find it? Was it easy? What is it? Does it exist anywhere except in the dictionary?

Seeking Safety:
What were the safety issues for you? Have the safety issues changed? What are the dangers for you? How did you get safe? What is meant by safety? Is it a feeling, a state of mind, people, a place? Do we care about it? Should we hide? Do/did we hide?

Help and Support:
Who provides it? Do you need it? Is it any good? What more is needed? Should we (survivors) be the ones to teach others how to help us? What was/is it like dealing with agencies? Is there a conspiracy do you think?

Damaged Beyond Repair?:
What are the effects of such abuse on you? Are we (survivors) damaged? Do we need pills? Will we ever be okay? Sleeping, eating, trust, fear – emotional and physical effects?

The Backlash:
Have you experienced any backlash since getting away? Do you expect a backlash? What do you expect to happen if/when they find you?

Survivor Issues:
What are/were the important issues for you? What problems have you experienced? What problems do you still experience? Have the issues changed over time? If so, in what way?

Insiders:
mpd, d.i.d. and all that kind of stuff. How do we use creativity to survive? Do you have inside people? What do you think about them? Why are they there? Is it normal do you think?

Worlds Apart:
What is life like in this culture? How easy is it adjusting to this culture? Is there a difference? What's the difference?

The Unbelievable: What about such things as magick, rituals, betrayal past and present, colours, astral stuff? Anything to say on any of the above?

Faith and Belief:
What is it? What about faith and belief in self and others? Without faith can you ever really trust anyone? Do you believe you are different? Why? Do you believe that they had the right to do what they did? Why do you believe as you do?

The Scale of Justice?

Is it possible? Do we want it? Can we ever get it? Are there different types of justice? What are they?

Power:

Do survivors have power? Who holds the power? Are the abusers more powerful than others?

Betrayal:

Have you been betrayed? In what way? By whom? Is betrayal an issue for you?

A Sense of Belonging:

What does it mean to belong to a place, a person or a group? To whom? To what? Living without connections – how easy is this? What is normal? Do you feel as though you belong? Explain? Did you feel that you belonged to the group? Explain?

Family Matters:

What is it? What should it be? Do we need one? How did/do we create family? Are families important?

The Invisible People:

The isolation of survivorship –What about it? Are we seen as credible? Who's credibility matters? Can you let other people find out that you are a survivor of this? Survival of a crime that is not recognised? Is this an issue?

What Experts? Health? Therapists? Police? Who?

Can they be trusted? Can they help? Are labels needed for us? Will they ever listen to us? Do they just pay their mortgages off the back of our suffering?

Fighting Back!

How can we ever stop it? What can we do to make people aware and get them on our side? Is any of this our responsibility? Whose responsibility is it?

Changing Lives: What do you want to change in legislation, society, agencies, and other people? What do you want to change in your own life? Is change possible or desirable? If you had 3 wishes what would they be?

In Conclusion:

Is conclusion possible? When we waken will it all be over? What do survivors conclude about RA? What last words would you like to say to the world?

Biography

"Behind Enemy Lines" is the author's 4th book on the subject of ritual and organised abuse and the fourth (she claims) in a trilogy covering this subject, the others being "Who Dares Wins", "Where Angels Fear" and "Fight! Rabbit! Fight!.

Laurie Matthew has been working with survivors of ritual and organised abuse for over 3 decades. She was supporting survivors of this type of abuse during the 1970s and 1980s when many professionals were debating the existence of ritual and organised abuse. She was instrumental in organising the first national conference on ritual and organised abuse in Scotland. Throughout the past 3 decades, she has been tireless in her support of survivors of this type of abuse and workers from a plethora of agencies, both voluntary and statutory who were working with survivors of ritual and organised abuse including mental health professionals. Identifying that there was clearly a gap in information about ritual and organised abuse she designed and ran training days and began to write resource packs. And it is from the latter that the first book was born.

Laurie works full time as the co-ordinator of Eighteen And Under, which is an agency supporting young people who have suffered any type of abuse. Despite this, she continues to support survivors of ritual and organised abuse in her spare time, in between looking after her 5½ children and menagerie of pets, including one large intellectually challenged dog. She is regularly requested to speak at conferences, both national and international.

behind
enemy lines

Other Titles by
Vip Publications

Subject	Title	Price	Postage
■ **Abuse**	**Teen Vip Training Pack:**	£60.00	plus £5.00 p&p
Prevention	**The Tweenees Resource Pack:**	£55.00	plus £5.00 p&p
	Jenny's Story	£6.50	plus £0.50 p&p
	Wee Vip Pack: Game, Story, Video.	£100.00	plus £5.00 p&p
	Jonny Cool: Storybook	£10.00	plus £1.50 p&p
	Jonny Cool: Workbook	£5.00	plus £1.50 p&p
	Jonny Cool: Workbook & Storybook	£15.00	plus £5.00 p&p
	The Cool: Workbook	£6.00	plus £2.00 p&p
■ **Games**	**Truth! Dare! Scare!:** Safety Game	£60.00	plus £5.00 p&p
■ **Poetry Books**	**Hear We are again**	£4.00	plus £0.50 p&p
	Listen! Hear!	£4.00	plus £0.50 p&p
	Hear! We are!	£4.00	plus £0.50 p&p
	Hear! Us!	£4.00	plus £0.50 p&p
■ **Music**	**After the Storm** CD	£10.00	plus £5.00 p&p
	After the Storm T-shirt	£6.50	plus £1.50 p&p
■ **Information**	**Postcards** (8)	£3.50	plus £0.50 p&p
	Information Booklets	Free	plus £0.50 p&p
■ **Books**	**Who Dares Wins!**	£15.00	plus £5.00 p&p
	Ritual Abuse book		
	Where Angels Fear	£15.00	plus £5.00 p&p
	Ritual Abuse in Scotland		
	BeAware	£15.00	plus £5.00 p&p
	How to support Young Survivors of Abuse		
	Fight!Rabbit!Fight!	£15.00	plus £5.00 p&p
	Short Stories about Ritual Abuse		

All these publications are available from:
Young Women's Centre (Trading) Ltd,
1 Victoria Road, Dundee, DD1 1EL
Telephone: 01382 206 222
Web sites: www.18u.org.uk   www.rans.org.uk